The Emotions of Nonviolence

OXFORD NEW HISTORIES OF PHILOSOPHY

Series Editors
Christia Mercer, Melvin Rogers, and Eileen O'Neill (1953–2017)

*

Advisory Board
Lawrie Balfour, Jacqueline Broad, Marguerite Deslauriers, Karen Detlefsen, Bachir Diagne, Don Garrett, Robert Gooding-Williams, Andrew Janiak, Marcy Lascano, Lisa Shapiro, Tommie Shelby

*

Oxford New Histories of Philosophy provides essential resources for those aiming to diversify the content of their philosophy courses, revisit traditional narratives about the history of philosophy, or better understand the richness of philosophy's past. Examining previously neglected or understudied philosophical figures, movements, and traditions, the series includes both innovative new scholarship and new primary sources.

*

Published in the series

Mexican Philosophy in the 20th Century: Essential Readings
Edited by Carlos Alberto Sánchez and Robert Eli Sanchez, Jr.

Sophie de Grouchy's Letters on Sympathy: *A Critical Engagement with Adam Smith's* The Theory of Moral Sentiments
Edited by Sandrine Bergès and Eric Schliesser.
Translated by Sandrine Bergès.

Margaret Cavendish: Essential Writings
Edited by David Cunning

Women Philosophers of Seventeenth-Century England: Selected Correspondence
Edited by Jacqueline Broad

The Correspondence of Catharine Macaulay
Edited by Karen Green

Mary Shepherd's Essays on the Perception of an External Universe
Edited by Antonia Lolordo

Women Philosophers of Eighteenth-Century England: Selected Correspondence
Edited by Jacqueline Broad

Frances Power Cobbe: Essential Writings of a Nineteenth-Century Feminist Philosopher
Edited by Alison Stone

Korean Women Philosophers and the Ideal of a Female Sage: Essential Writings of Im Yungjidang and Gang Jeongildang
Edited and Translated by Philip J. Ivanhoe and Hwa Yeong Wang

Louise Dupin's Work on Women: Selections
Edited and Translated by Angela Hunter and Rebecca Wilkin

Edith Landmann-Kalischer: Essays on Art, Aesthetics, and Value
Edited by Samantha Matherne. Translated by Daniel O. Dahlstrom

Mary Ann Shadd Cary: Essential Writings of a Nineteenth-Century Black Radical Feminist
Edited by Nneka D. Dennie

Slavery and Race: Philosophical Debates in the Eighteenth-Century
Julia Jorati

Maria W. Stewart: Essential Writings of a Nineteenth-Century Black Abolitionist
Edited by Douglas A. Jones Jr.

Slavery and Race: Philosophical Debates in the Sixteenth and Seventeenth Centuries
Julia Jorati

The Emotions of Nonviolence: Revisiting Martin Luther King Jr.'s "Letter from Birmingham Jail"
Meena Krishnamurthy

The Emotions of Nonviolence

Revisiting Martin Luther King Jr.'s "Letter from Birmingham Jail"

MEENA KRISHNAMURTHY

OXFORD
UNIVERSITY PRESS

Oxford University Press is a department of the University of Oxford.
It furthers the University's objective of excellence in research, scholarship,
and education by publishing worldwide. Oxford is a registered trade mark of
Oxford University Press in the UK and in certain other countries.

Published in the United States of America by Oxford University Press
198 Madison Avenue, New York, NY 10016, United States of America.

© Oxford University Press 2025

All rights reserved. No part of this publication may be reproduced, stored in a retrieval system, transmitted, used for text and data mining, or used for training artificial intelligence, in any form or by any means, without the prior permission in writing of Oxford University Press, or as expressly permitted by law, by license or under terms agreed with the appropriate reprographics rights organization. Inquiries concerning reproduction outside the scope of the above should be sent to the Rights Department, Oxford University Press, at the address above.

You must not circulate this work in any other form
and you must impose this same condition on any acquirer

Library of Congress Control Number: 2024061394

ISBN 9780197697238 (pbk.)
ISBN 9780197697221 (hbk.)

DOI: 10.1093/9780197697269.001.0001

Paperback printed by Integrated Books International, United States of America
Hardback printed by Bridgeport National Bindery, Inc., United States of America

*For my parents, MV and Seetha Krishnamurthy,
who gave me everything.*

Contents

Series Editors' Foreword	xi
Acknowledgments	xiii
Author's Note	xix
Introduction: The Letter and Its Motivation	1

PART 1. BACKGROUND

1. Desegregation	29
2. Self-Reliance	46
3. Sensible Sermon	69

PART 2. EMOTIONS

4. Fear and Fearlessness	93
5. Dignity and Indignation	121
6. Love	150

PART 3. NONVIOLENCE

7. Nonviolence	177
8. Transformation	205
Postscript	227
Bibliography	243
Index	261

Series Editors' Foreword

Oxford New Histories of Philosophy (ONHP) speaks to a new climate in philosophy.

There is a growing awareness that philosophy's past is richer and more diverse than previously understood. It has become clear that canonical figures are best studied in a broad context. More exciting still is the recognition that our philosophical heritage contains long-forgotten innovative ideas, movements, and thinkers. Sometimes these thinkers warrant serious study in their own right; sometimes their importance resides in the conversations they helped reframe or problems they devised; often their philosophical proposals force us to rethink long-held assumptions about a period or genre; and frequently they cast well-known philosophical discussions in a fresh light.

There is also a mounting sense among philosophers that our discipline benefits from a diversity of perspectives and a commitment to inclusiveness. In a time when questions about justice, inequality, dignity, education, discrimination, and climate (to name a few) are especially vivid, it is appropriate to mine historical texts for insights that can shift conversations and reframe solutions. Given that philosophy's very long history contains astute discussions of a vast array of topics, the time is right to cast a broad historical net.

Lastly, there is increasing interest among philosophy instructors in speaking to the diversity and concerns of their students. Although historical discussions and texts can serve as a powerful means of doing so, finding the necessary time and tools to excavate long-buried historical materials is challenging.

Oxford New Histories of Philosophy is designed to address all these needs. It contains new editions and translations of significant historical texts. These primary materials make available, often for the first time, ideas and works by women, people of colour, and movements in philosophy's past that were groundbreaking in their day but left out of traditional accounts. Informative introductions help instructors and students navigate the new material. Alongside its primary texts, ONHP also publishes monographs and collections of essays that offer philosophically subtle analyses of understudied topics, movements, and figures. In combining primary materials and astute philosophical analyses, ONHP makes it easier for philosophers, historians, and instructors to include in their courses and research exciting new materials drawn from philosophy's past.

ONHP's range is wide, both historically and culturally. The series includes, for example, the writings of African American philosophers, twentieth-century Mexican philosophers, early modern and late medieval women, Islamic and Jewish authors, and non-western thinkers. It excavates and analyses problems and ideas that were prominent in their day but forgotten by later historians. And it serves as a significant aid to philosophers in teaching and researching this material.

As we expand the range of philosophical voices, it is important to acknowledge one voice responsible for this series. Eileen O'Neill was a series editor until her death, December 1, 2017. She was instrumental in motivating and conceptualizing ONHP. Her brilliant scholarship, advocacy, and generosity made all the difference to the efforts that this series is meant to represent. She will be deeply missed, as a scholar and a friend.

We are proud to contribute to philosophy's present and to a richer understanding of its past.

Christia Mercer and Melvin Rogers
Series Editors

Acknowledgments

This book was written in conversation with many people—my students, my colleagues, my friends, family—and many books.

It began as a series of lectures for my graduate seminars at the University of Michigan and at Queen's University. These classes provided an invaluable collective space of development for my ideas. I am and have been continually inspired by the imagination and intellect of my students and the vigor with which they approached King's philosophy of nonviolence and the emotions. I hope that my work here will contribute to their ongoing exploration of the emotions and tactics of nonviolence and the possibility and power of political transformation.

As I began to turn these lectures into draft chapters, I had the privilege of presenting them at conferences, workshops, and talks, where I received invaluable feedback. I am very grateful to Alison McQueen for organizing a workshop at Stanford, where I received thoughtful comments from Christopher Lewis. I am deeply indebted to Joshua Cohen at Berkeley, who hosted a three-hour seminar on my work that led to discussion after class, over dinner, and throughout the evening, and which then continued over email for weeks. I am grateful to Christia Mercer for organizing a panel at the Eastern APA with comments from Justin Rose and Vanessa Wills, which helped me clarify my own views regarding the relationship between King's humanism and his theology. I was lucky to be able to share an early draft of the chapter on dignity with Chike Jeffers and Peter Adamson on the amazing *History of Philosophy Without Any Gaps* podcast. I also developed some of my ideas about dignity and indignation in conversation with Myisha Cherry during a panel on her wonderful book, *The Case for Rage*, at the Pacific APA. One of the most memorable talks that I gave in this early period of work was organized by Mike Doan at Eastern Michigan University. The room was packed, and I talked late into the night with students about the meaning and possibilities of King's message of nonviolence. These conversations shaped the trajectory of my work for the coming years.

As the years passed and I developed the chapters further, I benefited from presenting them to many active audiences at universities and colleges across Canada, the United States, and the United Kingdom: Concordia University; University of Calgary; McMaster University; University of Montreal; University of Ottawa; University of Toronto; Western University; University of Boulder, Colorado; UC, Berkeley; UC, Davis; Cal State; Cornell University; University of Chicago; Fullerton; Eastern Michigan University; George Washington University; University of Illinois, Chicago; University of Michigan; New York University; Oberlin; Ohio State University; University of Pennsylvania; SUNY, Buffalo; Sienna Heights; St. Louis University; Stanford University; Syracuse University; Virginia Tech; University of Antwerp; University of Sheffield; University of York Frankfurt; Ashoka University (India). I am grateful to all the organizers and audience members at all of these talks.

In the middle of writing this book, the pandemic arrived, and I was no longer able to travel and to discuss my writing with live audiences. Luckily, I found a group of people who were as excited about King as I am, and they joined me in a virtual Martin Luther King Working Group. Thank you, Brandon Terry, Corey Brettschneider, Alexander Livingston, and Erin Pineda—I learned so much about King's work and ideas from our concentrated monthly conversations.

Over the years, I have remained in intellectual conversation with many other scholars. I am grateful to Michele Moody-Adams, whose mentorship (since graduate school) and seminal work on self-respect and moral progress have long had an influence on my thinking. I am grateful to Robert Gooding-Williams for conversations about the emotions and for his own work on Du Bois, which continues to be a guiding light for those of us working in Black and white moral psychology.

I am continuously inspired by Tommie Shelby and Brandon Terry's edited collection of essays, *To Shape a New World*, which contains some of the most important recent philosophical scholarship on King. It is hard to articulate the influence of this book on mine; it is always there in the background of my thought—as are other important works on King: Robert Birt's edited collection, *The Liberatory Thought of Martin Luther King, Jr.*, Andrew Douglas and Jared Loggin's *The Prophet of Discontent*, Justin Roses's book *The Drum Major Instinct*, and Alexander Livingston's thoughtful work on King's theory of civil disobedience. Classics in King scholarship such as Rev. James Cone's *Martin and Malcolm & America* and Rufus Borrow's work in *God and Human Dignity* also shaped my thinking, and the musings of June Jordan, Nina Simone, and Nikki Giovanni on the enduring significance of King's thought and work stayed with me as I wrote.

I began this book in earnest when a colleague at the University of Michigan, Derrick Darby, suggested I collect into a book some of the papers and lectures I was writing on King's political philosophy. I wanted to write a book, but I wasn't sure that it was the most practical path toward tenure or the most palatable form for mainstream political philosophers. Derrick told me to put those worries aside and to follow my gut, which told me to keep digging more deeply into King. I am especially grateful to Angela Dillard and Kristie Dotson for echoing these sentiments and for encouraging me to keep doing what I was doing. I am grateful to Sarah Buss and Ishani Maitra for thinking with me about how to start the work of creating this book. I am also grateful to Richard W. Miller, Janum Sethi, Kira Thurman, Kisha Simmons, Laura Ruetsche, and Sukaina Hirji for their staunch support and encouragement during this time.

I'd like to thank my colleagues at Queen's, who are generous, thoughtful, and open-minded about what philosophy is and what it could be. As soon as I moved to Queen's, I felt free to write the kind of book that I wanted to write. I am also grateful to my Canadian colleague Patti Lenard for publishing (as a guest editor) my first piece on King in the *Monist*. Her warmth and enthusiasm helped me see that there was a broad audience for my work on King.

I am especially and eternally grateful to Melvin Rogers, one of the editors of the series *Oxford New Histories Philosophy Series*. Melvin has worked with me from the start, even when I wasn't sure that what I had would make a coherent project, or even that I should be the person to do this work. He helped me generate ideas and connected me with others who generously gave feedback on early drafts that determined the shape and structure of this book. I am especially grateful to him for graciously organizing and funding a manuscript workshop at Brown University, where I received feedback from some of the King scholars I respect most: Alexander Livingston, Jared Loggins, and Erin Pineda. I am grateful to each of them for their detailed and reflective feedback. They helped me make the draft that I had into something much better, encouraging me to dig deeper into King's philosophical and practical methods and the historical context surrounding them. I am also indebted to two anonymous reviewers who gave thoughtful feedback and helped me fine-tune the argumentative arc of this book.

I am grateful to the editorial teams at Oxford and NewGen: Peter Ohlin, thank you for believing in this project. Christia Mercer, thank you for your constant support, encouragement, and time. Meredith Taylor, Leslie Johnson, Sruthi Manogarane, Dorothy Bauhoff, thank you for carefully editing this manuscript and smoothly helping it reach publication. I am very grateful to my amazing editor Heath Sledge, who has read and given me detailed and encouraging feedback on almost everything I have written since 2016.

This book is the result of the support, encouragement, and conversations of many others who are part of my broader support system. I am eternally grateful to my best friend and platonic soul mate Colette Botosan, who talked with me about this work in so many different ways and who has always kept me grounded and moving forward—both through the writing process and through life in general. I have learned so much about myself and the world from talking with you, and I know I will continue to do so. I am also grateful to my other forever friends, "the girls"—especially Natalie Buziak, Keri-Anne Mizzi, and Sarah Jones, as well as Angie Campbell, Christa Hammond, Celina Isen, April Kemick, and Tash Saunders—who have been with me from the beginning and will be with me until the end. Sarah, I miss you every day. Ana Sabau, my dear friend, I am grateful to you for just being you, and for gently accompanying me as I made my way through the writing of this book.

I am grateful to my newer friends in Kingston and at Queen's—Kerah Gordon-Solomon, Lisa Guenther, Rahul Kumar, Margaret Moore, Melissa Noventa, and Elliot Paul—who have helped me build not just an academic community of support but a group of friends whom I can depend on. I am deeply grateful to my long-time partner in life and in parenting, Patrick McEneany, for supporting and prioritizing my career and my life's work. Without him, this book would not have been possible. I would like to express my immense gratitude to my daughter, Sage, who rather tellingly was born with one gray hair, and who continues in her wisdom to teach and challenge me daily. I am who I am because of you. And I am thrilled to see who you are becoming. I am grateful to the smallest members of my family, my dogs—Charlie, the late and gentle-souled bulldog, and Georgie, the energetic mastiff who still doesn't know how big she is. Thank you for keeping me company and for always keeping things fun. I am grateful to my grandma, Elizabeth (Boukje) Wiegman, who taught me that love is action. I continue to be inspired by everything you accomplished throughout your life and compassionate work. I would like, finally, to thank my parents, to whom this book is dedicated, who made many sacrifices to give me everything I needed—materially, emotionally, and intellectually—to have a good life filled with family, friends, work, and passion. I will always be grateful to you for your love, encouragement, and support.

In the end, I am thankful to Martin Luther King Jr., whose inspired dream of what we and the world can be continues to both challenge and move me.

Author's Note

In 2014, I was recovering from a traumatic brain injury. For almost eight months, I wasn't teaching, reading, or writing, but lying in bed in a dark room. I had to start somewhere. I decided to start by learning more about politics and political thought in India. This was something I had always wanted to do but had somehow never found the time for. I was interested in these things because my family migrated to Canada from India, and my parents often talked about British colonialism and Indian independence. They also talked about how the dialogues between Gandhi and Nehru that took place during the formation of modern India had shaped their own thoughts and experiences in India during the time. Essentially, I wanted to learn more about where my people were from and what had shaped their history and thinking about political life. At the time, I took my reading about these things to be largely recreational.

I began with *Hind Swaraj*, Gandhi's treatise on the immorality of British colonialism and the moral importance of Indian self-rule. To get a better understanding of some of Gandhi's views about nonviolence and its importance in political resistance, I turned to Martin Luther King Jr. as a contemporary American interpreter of Gandhi. I thought this would be a small detour. I began with *Why We Can't Wait*. I was immediately completely enraptured, especially with the "Letter from Birmingham Jail." Because my working memory and vision were still recovering, I had to re-read every paragraph multiple times before I could fully understand its content. This process of re-reading became the basis of the next decade of my work. As my working memory and vision improved, I moved on to King's other books, including *Strength to Love*, *Stride Toward*

Freedom, and *Where Do We Go from Here*. To understand King better, I read Malcolm X. Then I slowly started reading the Black political thinkers who had preceded both King and Malcolm X and shaped their thinking: W. E. B. Du Bois, Marcus Garvey, and Booker T. Washington—thinkers who I would later come to realize had greatly influenced Gandhi and some of his Indian critics. I then returned to King, reading his less well-known sermons, speeches, and letters.

Through my very close reading (and re-reading) of his work, I was confronted with a version of King that I hadn't known before. Yes, he was warm and fuzzy, as his popular image suggested. Yet there was also something darker and more realistic. King was both dignified and indignant. He was courageous, but also fearful. He was faithful and loving, but he was also sometimes despairing and disappointed. These complex emotions, King says, are the ones that drove him to join the Civil Rights Movement. I came to see that the Letter was an attempt to stimulate these same emotions in his readers, as he sought to move others to act in the way that he himself had been moved.

This book is my attempt to share my novel reading of King with a broader audience. I began it at the University of Michigan and continued to develop it at Queen's University (Canada), as a series of lectures for my annual graduate seminar on the political philosophy of Dr. Martin Luther King Jr. Because the book derives from an extended and close reading of King, much of it is inward-looking, devoted to uncovering King's thoughts, in his own voice, about the emotions.

Following my own trajectory, the book uses the Letter as an entry point into King's theorizing about the emotions of nonviolence, how they hang together, and how to use them to move people—especially the racially oppressed—to participate in the nonviolent direct-action campaigns that are needed for deep structural transformation. King's views on these matters emerge across a vast set of writings, which are sometimes disjointed (in time or place), and they are sometimes difficult to put together into a coherent package. This is perhaps why some commentators have thought that King's view is not systematic and that he therefore ought not be considered a philosopher. This book guides the reader through King's work and puts the pieces together to show that King in fact has a developed theory of emotions. He is indeed a philosopher, worthy of philosophical study.

The first chapters (1–3) set the background for King's account of the emotions of nonviolence, explaining the historical and social context for the Letter. The following chapters (4–6) are devoted to understanding specific emotions—fear, fearlessness, faith, dignity, indignation, and love—and how King hoped to arouse these emotions in readers and inspire them to action. The final chapter (7 and 8) concerns King's view of nonviolence—what it is and why it is worthwhile. We find here a novel argument for the value of nonviolence: nonviolence is the proper expression of the emotions, and it is a way to foster the kind of personal transformation that is needed to sustain these emotions, as well as the action that is needed for structural transformation. The book closes (Postscript) by situating King's views of emotions and motivation among those of other central Black political thinkers. This chapter is written especially for my students, who often come to King through their understanding of the broader history of Black political thought.

This book is my attempt to share what I have learned about King's views on the emotions, not only through my deep reading and re-reading, but also through discussion with my peers and, especially, with my students. I have tried to include as many online resources as possible, so that readers can work through King's opus along with me, making their own judgments about his views on the nature of the emotions and how to use them to stimulate nonviolent direct action.

We might wonder why it is important to explore King's theory of the emotions now. It is because we live in times that require the same moral courage and emotional commitment to justice that

King sought to inspire. Activists know that more people on the streets mean more pressure being exerted and a greater opportunity for structural transformation. Activists will therefore always be concerned with the question of how to draw people into the streets. This is precisely the question that King is most concerned with. He offers both concrete strategies that activists can evaluate and consider and an underlying theory for why these strategies do and have worked. Today, "injustice is here" in the United States: there is growing anti-immigrant sentiment, mass voter suppression, rampant economic inequality for Black and Brown Americans, denial of women's rights to abortion and trans rights to access healthcare. It is worth revisiting, clarifying, and evaluating King's views and considering whether they provide a plausible road map for today.

Introduction

The Letter and Its Motivation

As Martin Luther King Jr. tells it, in 1963, Birmingham, Alabama, was one of the most segregated cities in the United States. Black children played in the streets, while white children played in parks. Black families could not shop or eat at the same places as white ones. At work, Black and white Americans used separate drinking facilities and restrooms. Black families attended Black-only churches. Schools were segregated, and although in 1954, the Supreme Court of the United States had issued a decree calling for desegregation of schools with "all deliberate speed," defiant segregationists found ways to evade integration; as King says, the Court's decree was "heeded with all deliberate delay."[1] At the beginning of 1963, only 9% of Southern schools were integrated,[2] and those Black activists who worked to hasten school integration were subject to extreme violence. Reverend Charles Billups—a Black pastor at New Pilgrim Baptist Church in Birmingham, Alabama, and one the founders of the Alabama Christian Movement for Human Rights (ACMHR)—was kidnapped, beaten with chains, and branded on the stomach with "KKK."[3] This was intended as a message to Black people to stop sending their children to white schools. In Birmingham, this type of violence against Black Americans was common. The bombing of Black homes was so commonplace that certain neighborhoods

---

[1] Martin Luther King Jr, *Why We Can't Wait* (New York: Signet, 1963), 5; hereafter "WWCW."
[2] Ibid., 5.
[3] Ibid., 13.

had nicknames like "Dynamite Hill," and the city itself was often referred to as "Bombingham."[4] There was little organized support for the individual activists who were targeted: in Alabama, there was no local branch of the National Association for the Advancement of Colored People (NAACP) to advocate for equality for Black Americans. Alabama segregationists had classified the NAACP as a "foreign corporation" and declared its activities illegal.

This social prejudice was close kin to another evil, that of economic injustice.[5] National unemployment among Black individuals was high: in 1963, there were two and one-half times as many jobless Black Americans as white Americans. The median income of Black Americans was half that of whites.[6] Black Americans occupied the most contingent and lowest-paid jobs, often doing menial work where promotions and raises were unlikely—a problem compounded by the fact that wages in the South, where a high percentage of Black Americans lived, were overall much lower than those in the North. The economic conditions of Black Americans were worsened by the emergence and growth of automation, which spread mostly in the low-wage jobs that many Black Americans held;[7] Black workers were more likely to be displaced, and they had few opportunities for retraining. Unionization was suppressed across Birmingham in steel and other industries.

In Birmingham, Bull Connor—an American politician who served as Commissioner of Public Safety for the city of Birmingham, Alabama, and had authority over both the police and fire departments—would come to stand for the deep and violent injustice being done to Black residents. Connor was a committed segregationist who saw himself as the last safeguard against desegregation and integration. He believed in keeping Black Americans in their place. He was contemptuous of Black civil

[4] Jonathan Reider, *Gospel of Freedom* (New York: Bloomsbury, 2013), 13.
[5] Ibid., 13.
[6] WWCW, 13.
[7] Ibid., 14.

rights and resisted the authority of the federal government. Connor was a Southern Democrat who strongly opposed the Civil Rights Movement and supported the presidential run of Dixiecrat Senator Strom Thurmond.[8] His police force was full of Klansmen and segregationists, and Connor himself encouraged and supported the KKK in an attack against Freedom Riders in Birmingham who were seeking to desegregate buses. As the riders arrived at the Birmingham bus station, Connor reportedly said to the Klansmen, "By God, if you are going to do this thing, do it right."[9] He promised them—and gave them—fifteen minutes to attack the Freedom Riders with no police intervention, and during that dark jubilee, the KKK brutally beat the activists with pipes, wooden slats, and key rings.[10]

Connor's opposite, and working on the side of racial justice, was Reverend Frederick "Freddie" Lee Shuttlesworth. For years, he had been working against the segregationist tactics of racist Southerners such as Connor. Shuttlesworth was known for his courage: although he had been beaten by Klansmen with pipes and his homes set on fire, he had not been deterred in his fight against segregation. He and his supporters began their fight against the state when it banned the NAACP, and they went on to found several partner organizations for racial justice that operated in the South. For example, Shuttlesworth partnered with Martin Luther King Jr. to cofound the Southern Christian Leadership Conference (SCLC) in 1957. This organization differed from others such as the Student Nonviolent Coordinating Committee (SNCC) and the NAACP; it focused on coordinating the action of local protest groups throughout the South to work against segregation, desegregating buses and schools and eliminating police brutality to redeem "the soul of America" through nonviolent resistance. Shuttlesworth was

---

[8] A Dixiecrat is a member of a right-wing Democratic splinter group organized by Southerners who objected to the civil rights program of the Democratic Party.
[9] Reider, *Gospel of Freedom*, 15.
[10] Ibid., 15.

also the head of the SCLC's largest affiliate, the Alabama Christian Movement for Human Rights (ACMHR).

In 1963, Shuttlesworth invited the SCLC and King to come to Birmingham to lead a campaign to desegregate Birmingham through mass demonstrations. Shuttlesworth called the campaign "Project C": the "C" stood for "Birmingham's Confrontation with the fight for justice and morality in race relations."[11] After a three-day retreat and planning session with SCLC staff and board members at a training center near Savannah, Georgia, King went to Birmingham. He brought with him his executive assistant and chief strategist, the Reverend Wyatt Tee Walker, and his friend and fellow campaigner from the days of Montgomery, the Reverend Ralph Abernathy, SCLC's treasurer.[12] During the retreat, King and his team met with members of Shuttlesworth's ACMHR in Birmingham's Gaston hotel, which became the headquarters for all campaign strategy sessions and planning.

According to King, the first major decision they faced together was setting the date for the launch of "Project C." Their plan was to begin by putting public pressure on merchants who placed racist "No Blacks" signs on their doors and prevented Black residents from eating at their counters and shopping in their stores. They initially decided to begin mobilizing the community in the first week of March, six weeks before Easter (on April 14 that year), since this holiday was the second biggest shopping period of the year. However, they delayed it somewhat, because they did not want their campaign to be used as a "political football" during election season. They decided to start demonstrations two weeks after the local elections, which would take place on March 5.

The leading candidates in the mayoral elections were Albert Boutwell, Bull Connor, and Tom King. All of them were segregationists, but Connor was by far the worst; next to him,

---

[11] WWCW, 54.
[12] Ibid., 55.

the others seemed like moderates. Dr. King hoped, of course, that Connor would be defeated, but it was a slim hope, for Connor had already served as Commissioner of Public Safety for the city of Birmingham for more than two decades. Connor sought to retain his power by running for mayor, for Birmingham had voted to convert from a city commission system to a mayor/council system in 1962.[13]

While King and Abernathy stayed at the Gaston, engaging in strategy sessions and meeting with Black community members, Walker worked on the mechanics of the campaign, organizing a transportation corps, and laying the groundwork for an intensive economic boycott. Walker scheduled workshops on nonviolence and direct-action techniques for new recruits. By March 1, King reports, "the project was in high gear and the loose ends of organizational structure were being pulled together. Some 250 people had volunteered to participate in the initial demonstrations and had pledged to remain in jail at least five days."[14]

However, the campaign faced several difficulties. First, no candidate in the March 5th election won a clear victory, and a run-off vote was scheduled to be held the first week in April. This uncertainty made it more difficult to anticipate the response to the campaign. King had hoped that the run-off would be between Boutwell and Tom King, but, unfortunately, the competing candidates were Boutwell and Connor. Reluctantly, King and his team of strategists decided to postpone the demonstrations until the day after the run-off. King worried that with this delay, the momentum created by the groundwork they were doing in Birmingham's Black community might peter out.[15] King was right to worry. Although on April 2,

---

[13] "Connor, Theophilus Eugene 'Bull,'" in Clayborne Carson, Tenisha Armstrong, Susan Carson, Erin Cook, Susan Englander (eds.), *The Martin Luther King, Jr. Encyclopedia*. Available at: https://kinginstitute.stanford.edu/encyclopedia/connor-theophilus-eugene-bull.
[14] WWCW, 57.
[15] Ibid., 57.

6   THE EMOTIONS OF NONVIOLENCE

Boutwell defeated Connor (a small relief), the campaign's opening on April 3, "B day," was disappointing: only 65 people showed up to fulfill their pledge to participate in the demonstrations and sit-ins.[16]

Why was the support from the Black community so meager? First, the local media seemed unsupportive. The local Black biweekly newspaper failed to cover the campaign, giving little to no coverage of the demonstrations that did take place. In an editorial, it criticized direct action "as wasteful and worthless," instead looking optimistically to Boutwell to create progress.[17] The campaign didn't fare much better in other mainstream media in Birmingham. Boutwell advised "everyone, white and Negro, [to] calmly . . . ignore what is now being attempted in Birmingham," and the media followed his direction, largely ignoring King and his campaign.[18] This media shut-out made it difficult for King to rally the Black middle class.

Second, as King had discovered, there was "tremendous resistance" to his direct-action tactics among some Black Birmingham activists, ministers, businessmen, and professionals.[19] Upon arriving in Birmingham, on April 3, King had expected to be welcomed warmly by key members of the Black religious community. Instead, as his aide Abernathy told it, when King met Reverend J. L. Ware, the head of Birmingham's alliance of Black Baptist ministers, at an alliance meeting, there "was no burst of applause and no ripple of friendly smiles. Most of the faces were grave and enigmatic."[20] Later, on April 8, the Monday of Holy Week, King accused the Black ministers of subscribing to a "dry as dust" religion "that extoll[ed] the glories of Heaven while ignoring the social conditions that cause men an earthly hell."[21] He accused them of

[16] Taylor Branch, *Parting the Waters* (New York: Simon and Schuster, 1988), 708.
[17] Ibid., 710.
[18] Ibid., 711.
[19] WWCW, 70.
[20] Ralph Abernathy, *And the Walls Came Tumbling Down: An Autobiography* (New York: Harper & Row, 1990), 238–239; quoted in Rieder, *Gospel of Freedom*, 29.
[21] Rieder, *Gospel of Freedom*, 32. See also WWCW, 73.

being "preachers riding around in big cars, living in fine homes, but not willing to take their part in the fight," concluding, "if you can't stand up with your own people, you are not fit to be a leader."[22]

He faced a similar resistance from local Black businessmen. Six days after "B-day," on April 9, King met with more than one hundred skeptical Black businessmen. The atmosphere, according to King, was "tense and chilly," and the men hurled criticisms at him.[23] Some said they didn't need outsiders to solve their problems. Others said King needed to give Boutwell more time and a fair chance. Most said they preferred cooperation over demonstrations, which only resulted in jail time and skirmishes with the police. After the meeting, A. G. Gaston—a Black American businessman who owned a number of businesses in Birmingham, including the Gaston motel—published a statement calling on "all the citizens of Birmingham to work harmoniously together in a spirit of brotherly love to solve the problems of our city, giving due recognition to the local colored leadership among us."[24] It was clear that the meeting with King, whom the businessmen saw as an external agitator, had not shifted their position.

A day later, King shifted his focus to the hesitant masses, who had so far been reluctant to participate: on April 9, eight days into the campaign, less than 150 people had been jailed.[25] On the morning of April 10, as they had predicted, the city government, led by Connor (who had refused to vacate his office and still held control of the city's police and fire departments), was granted a state circuit court injunction. The injunction, which banned protests and demonstrations, personally named King and 133 other people, decreeing that they were not to engage in or encourage specific activities: "parading, demonstrating, boycotting, trespassing and

---

[22] Rieder, *Gospel of Freedom*, 32.
[23] Branch, *Parting the Waters*, 726.
[24] Ibid., 726.
[25] Branch, *Parting the Waters*, 727.

picketing," and the "conduct customarily known as 'kneel-ins' in [white] churches."[26]

At this point, King was ready to drop a bombshell to bring the people on board. He and his advisors had known that the city was requesting an injunction against their activities, and they had spent the last several days deciding what to do if the court decided to rule against them. After serious debate, campaign leaders had decided that some among them would disobey the court order, sacrificing themselves to bring attention to the moral justice of the cause and to inspire the regular Birmingham citizens to make sacrifices of their own. The decision was not taken lightly by any of the organizers. As King later wrote, "as we talked . . . a sense of doom began to pervade the room, our most dedicated leaders were overwhelmed by a feeling of hopelessness."[27]

King was now ready to go—ready to tell the Black residents at the meeting later that day that he had decided to make this sacrifice for them, and to ask them to make sacrifices of their own in return. At the mass meeting on Wednesday, April 10, he asked "[e]very freedom-loving Negro of self-respect in Birmingham, Alabama, to refuse to shop in the stores downtown," saying, "we are asking everybody to live a sacrificial life during this Easter season and even after the Easter season."[28] Rather than his usual natty suit and tie, King wore blue jeans and a gray work shirt, saying that he was "not wearing these things merely to engage in some theatrical gesture . . . [but] to symbolize our determination to sacrifice during this period. . . . We are not going to buy suits or shirts or shoes or socks or anything in the downtown area of Birmingham, Alabama, until the walls of segregation in these stores will crumble. And we intend to keep on keepin' on until that job is done."[29] He then announced that "Ralph Abernathy and I have decided that we would like to

---

[26] Ibid., 727.
[27] WWCW, 79.
[28] Rieder, *Gospel of Freedom*, 32.
[29] Ibid., 33.

feel that we are suffering with Christ in the days he suffered on the cross. And we are going to make our move on Good Friday [two days later, April 12]. And we ask you and solicit your support as we do this."[30]

On Thursday, April 11, at the mass meeting, King declared: "We cannot in all good conscience obey such an injunction which is an unjust, undemocratic and unconstitutional misuse of the legal process."[31] At this meeting, Abernathy courageously announced, "I'm feeling better tonight because tomorrow I'm going to jail.... Tell Bull Connor to get the cell ready."[32] Abernathy was ready to act. But despite his stated intention to go to jail, King continued to waver on Thursday and in the early hours on Friday—his own Gethsemane. His mind raced as he struggled with indecision and a sense of bleakness. Was this the right course? Money for bail was running out, and without bail, there was no guarantee that those submitting themselves to being jailed would be released before trial, which could take months or even years.

King had been waiting for the right moment to go to jail. Early on Good Friday morning, April 12, he finally decided that this was it. He realized he had to "make a faith act."[33] In the Gaston motel, King announced that he would offer himself as a sacrifice to the principles of the movement. He turned to Ralph Abernathy and said, "I am asking you to go with me." Abernathy stood up without hesitation. Everyone in the room linked hands and sang, "We Shall Overcome."[34]

---

[30] Ibid., 34.
[31] "Birmingham Campaign," in Clayborne Carson, Tenisha Armstrong, Susan Carson, Erin Cook, Susan Englander (eds.), *The Martin Luther King, Jr. Encyclopedia*. Available at: https://kinginstitute.stanford.edu/encyclopedia/birmingham-campaign.
[32] Rieder, *Gospel of Freedom*, 36.
[33] WWCW, 81.
[34] Ibid., 81. The song "We Shall Overcome" had a long history that predates its use in the Civil Rights Movement. For more, see Noah Adams, "The Inspiring Force of 'We Shall Overcome,'" *All Things Considered*, NPR, August 28, 2013. Available at: https://www.npr.org/2013/08/28/216482943/the-inspiring-force-of-we-shall-overcome.

On Friday afternoon, King, Abernathy, Shuttlesworth, and fewer than 50 others drove from the Gaston motel to the Zion Hill Church, where the march began. They left the church and made their way to the downtown sector. Hundreds of Black citizens had turned out to see them. It seemed that almost every Birmingham police officer had also been sent to the area. After the marchers walked seven or eight blocks, Bull Connor ordered his men to arrest them. Abernathy and King were hauled off by two muscular policemen. All the others were immediately arrested. In jail, King and Abernathy were separated from the others, and eventually from each other.

King was held for more than twenty-four hours in solitary confinement, placed in a dark cell with no mattress and denied a phone call. No one was allowed to visit, not even King's lawyers. Left on his own, King was filled with worry and despair, reporting that these "were the longest, most frustrating and bewildering hours" he had lived.[35] He elaborated: "You will never know the meaning of utter darkness until you have lain in such a dungeon, knowing that sunlight is streaming overhead and still seeing only darkness below. You might have thought I was in the grip of a fantasy brought on by worry. I did worry. But there was more to the blackness than a phenomenon conjured up by a worried mind. Whatever the cause, the fact remained that I could not see the light."[36]

The next morning, after his night in solitary confinement, someone slipped King a copy of *Birmingham News*. He turned it over and found a column titled "A Call for Unity," by eight of Alabama's most prominent white clergymen.[37] The column

---

[35] WWCW, 82.

[36] Ibid., 82–83.

[37] It was originally published under the headline "White clergymen urge local Negroes to withdraw from demonstrations" in *The Birmingham News*, April 13, 1963, p. 2. It was written by the same clergymen who had also signed an earlier public statement, "An Appeal for Law and Order and Common Sense," demanding that the city and state leadership obey the court decisions ordering desegregation. These clergy believed that simple appeals to conscience and law would end segregation in due time—the opposite position to King's.

explicitly referred to the "demonstrations" organized by King, claiming they were the "unwise and untimely" actions of an "outsider"—actions that would "incite to hatred and violence, however technically peaceful those actions may be." They claimed to "agree rather with certain local Negro leadership which has called for honest and open negotiation of racial issues in our area." They expressed optimism about the new administration and advised patience, arguing that "racial matters could properly be pursued in the courts, but [. . .] that decisions of those courts should in the meantime be peacefully obeyed."[38] They closed the statement by "strongly" urging the Black community "to withdraw support from these demonstrations, and to unite locally in working peacefully for a better Birmingham," arguing that "when rights are consistently denied, a cause should be pressed in the courts and in negotiations among local leaders, and not in the streets."

"The Letter"

Still sitting in his solitary cell, King was roused out of his despondency by this column: in his words, "when I read it, I became so concerned and even upset and at points so righteously indignant that I decided to answer the letter."[39] King began to sketch his response—which would later be published as "The Letter from 'Birmingham Jail'"—on the margins of the newspaper in which the "Call for Unity" had appeared.[40] It was continued on scraps of paper, sneaked in by a generous Black jail attendant, and the complete version of the first draft was written on a pad that King's

---

[38] "White Clergymen Urge Local Negroes to Withdraw from Demonstrations," *The Birmingham News*, April 13, 1963, p. 2

[39] Clayborne Carson (ed.), *The Autobiography of Martin Luther King, Jr.* (New York: Grand Central Publishing, 1998), 187.

[40] Martin Luther King Jr., "Letter from Birmingham Jail," in his *Why We Can't Wait* (London: Signet, 2000), 85–112.

lawyers were eventually able to take with them when they left the jail. King and his staff—especially Walker—continued writing, editing, and revising drafts of the letter for several days after the date written on the initial manuscript, April 16, 1963.[41]

King was finally released early in May, right before the movement organizers reached an agreement with the white business leaders: within ninety days, public facilities at downtown stores (including lunch counters) would be desegregated; within sixty days, the businesses would offer better employment opportunities for Black citizens; and within two weeks, the jailed demonstrators would be released on bond and a biracial committee organized to monitor these efforts and to ensure that the agreement was followed.[42]

This agreement was a start, but it fell short of the movement's objectives. The movement needed money to take the battle farther in Birmingham and move it deeper into the South. The SCLC, under Walker's direction, decided to release the Letter as part of its fund-raising campaign.[43] The Letter was initially circulated in Birmingham and through Black churches as a mimeographed copy. As it gained attention, it was published in a variety of formats: first, in May, as a pamphlet distributed by the American Friends Service Committee, a Quaker group who shared King's emphasis on nonviolence;[44] by June, as an article in magazines such as *Liberation* and *Christian Century*; and as the summer went on, more widely, in places like *Christianity and Crisis*, *Birmingham News*, the *New York Post*, the *New York Times*, *The Atlantic Monthly*, and

---

[41] For a detailed discussion of the writing process and how it continued over time, see Jonathan Bass, *Blessed Are the Peacemakers* (Baton Rouge: Louisiana State University Press, 2001), especially Chapter 7.

[42] Ibid., 134.

[43] Ibid., 134.

[44] In 1917, a group of Quakers formed the AFSC to give conscientious objectors a non-military public service alternative during World War I. King's values were similar to those of the AFSC, and the two organizations worked together throughout the Civil Rights Movement.

Ebony magazine. Later in 1963, during the Congressional debates on the Civil Rights Act, the first half of the letter was introduced into testimony before Congress by Representative William Fitts Ryan (D–NY) and published in the Congressional Record.[45] Months later, King revised the Letter and included it as a central chapter in his 1963 memoir of the Birmingham Campaign, *Why We Can't Wait*.

Since its publication, the Letter has typically been interpreted as a justification of civil disobedience, and it has played a formative role in American and global thinking about this tactic. It has also become a key document in the philosophical canon on civil disobedience: teachers of literature and the philosophy of civil disobedience use it in high school and college classrooms across the United States,[46] it has been reprinted in anthologies alongside the writings of other core thinkers such as Plato, Thomas Jefferson, and Henry David Thoreau, and the famous political philosopher John Rawls cites King's Letter as an inspiration for his own work on the topic.[47]

The Letter responds to the "Call for Unity" calmly, with "patience and reasonable terms."[48] King begins by dismissing the claim that he was an "outsider" who should not be in Birmingham. For one thing, he pointed out, he was not an outsider; as the leader of the SCLC, King had organizational ties in Birmingham, and these organizations had invited him to come. More fundamentally, though, King asserted that he had a mandate and a mission

---

[45] "Letter from Birmingham Jail," in Clayborne Carson, Tenisha Armstrong, Susan Carson, Erin Cook, Susan Englander (eds.), *Martin Luther King, Jr. Encyclopedia*. Available at: https://kinginstitute.stanford.edu/encyclopedia/letter-birmingham-jail.

[46] Bass, *Blessed Are the Peacemakers*, 147.

[47] John Rawls, *A Theory of Justice* (Cambridge, MA: Harvard University Press, 1999), 388–391. For a detailed discussion of the role that King's Letter plays in philosophical discussions of civil disobedience, both in John Rawls's interpretation of the Letter and more generally, see Alexander Livingston, "Power for the Powerlessness: Martin Luther King, Jr.'s Late Theory of Civil Disobedience," *Journal of Politics*, 82.2 (2020): 700–713 at 702–704.

[48] WWCW, 86.

to be in the city because "injustice is here" and "injustice anywhere is a threat to justice everywhere."[49] King likens himself to the Apostle Paul, who had a duty to heed the Macedonian call for aid, saying that he was not an outsider anywhere that injustice was present. As Justin Rose argues, King believed that we have a stringent moral duty to serve others,[50] and his arrival in Birmingham was an expression of his commitment to enacting this duty. King argues that, at times, this moral duty can only be fulfilled by disobedience—the refusal to follow unjust laws and thereby perpetuate injustice. He argues that "there are two types of laws: just and unjust. I would be the first to advocate obeying just laws. One has not only a legal but a moral responsibility to obey just laws. Conversely, one has a moral responsibility to disobey unjust laws. I would agree with St. Augustine that 'an unjust law is no law at all.'"[51]

Next, King tackles the clergymen's repudiation of his campaign tactics. He says, "you deplore the demonstrations taking place in Birmingham,"[52] but he points out that the demonstrations are not reckless agitations leading to violent responses, as the clergymen had characterized them. King explains that, like any nonviolent campaign, the sit-ins and marches in Birmingham were the result of a careful process based on both rational decision-making and moral self-examination: a process of "collect[ing] the facts to determine whether injustices exist; negotiation; self-purification; and direct action."[53] King then questions the clergymen's attribution of blame to the demonstrators, pointing out that, in fact, it was Connor

---

[49] Ibid., 86.
[50] In his book *The Drum Major Instinct: Martin Luther King Jr.'s Theory of Political Service* (Atlanta: University of Georgia Press, 2019), Justin Rose argues that King believed that all members of society have a responsibility to engage in political service, and that collective forms of resistance are a kind of public service. For King, this means that even the oppressed are obligated to engage in nonviolent resistance.
[51] WWCW, 93.
[52] Ibid., 87.
[53] Ibid., 87.

and the police who acted violently: "Isn't this like condemning a robbed man because his possession of money precipitated the evil act of robbery? Isn't this like condemning Socrates because his unswerving commitment to truth and his philosophical inquiries precipitated the act by the misguided populace in which they made him drink hemlock?"[54]

He also responds to the clergymen's assertion that the political action taken was "untimely." The clergymen argued that currently, there was not much to be done about racial segregation and injustice, and that things would only improve with time. King staunchly rejects this idea, arguing that it results from a "tragic misconception of time, from the strangely irrational notion that there is something in the very flow of time that will inevitably cure all ills."[55] He argues, "human progress never rolls in on wheels of inevitability; it comes through the tireless efforts of men."[56]

Next, he addresses the clergymen's optimism about the new administration and their assertion that the new administration needed time to act—the same injunction to "wait" in another form. King explained why he was ready to protest just after a new city administration was elected, before it had much time to act: he said that while Boutwell, the newly elected mayor, may be a gentler person than Bull Connor was, King doubted that he would push for progress. Like Connor, Boutwell was committed to the status quo and to maintaining white supremacy, and as part of the Birmingham administration, he was simply the face of a political entity expressing the same nationally institutionalized racism that pervaded the United States. This is why King believed that direct action was required: it would "pressure" Boutwell and the nation into doing what they ought to do but would not do on their own: desegregating the city and the country.

---

[54] Ibid., 98.
[55] Ibid., 99.
[56] Ibid., 99.

Who was King really speaking to in the Letter, with its exhortation to immediate, direct political action? People typically remember the Letter as being addressed only to the eight white clergymen who had written the "Call for Unity." While it is true that King addressed the Letter to these men, none of them ever received a personalized, delivered, or signed copy of the letter from King. This suggests that the letter was intended for a broader audience—the American public that it quickly reached.[57]

When King wrote the Letter, he was righteously indignant: at the white clergymen, at the Kennedys, at the mainstream press, all of whom were broadcasting calls for "patience" and "peace" and "compromise."[58] This is why the Letter is so often understood first and foremost as a critical response to all "the White Moderates" of America. What is often forgotten is that King was also frustrated with the Black residents of Birmingham, especially the ministers and businessmen who had criticized the direct-action campaign, implicitly supported the clergymen's statement, and refused to act in service of justice themselves. As Andrew Young—a pastor and member of the SCLC who worked closely with King—recalled, King's Letter was addressed to *everyone* who was not actively working toward racial justice, white or Black, in Birmingham or elsewhere: "Martin was providing a comprehensive, far-ranging answer to *all* the objections to our campaign" (emphasis added).[59] King used the Letter, explicitly addressed to the eight clergymen, to respond to all his critics, especially his Black critics; the clergymen were just a convenient rhetorical target.[60]

---

[57] Bass, *Blessed Are the Peacemakers*, 137.
[58] *Time* deemed the Birmingham demonstrations "poorly timed" ("Poorly Timed Protest," *Time Magazine*, April 19, 1963, Vol. LXXXI, No. 16). The *New York Times* editorialized, "We do not expect that there will be overnight rejection of the policies that caused so much distress to the Negro community... and Dr. King... ought not expect it either" (Editorial, *New York Times*, April 17, 1963, A40).
[59] Bass, *Blessed Are the Peacemakers*, 148.
[60] Ibid., 148.

Although King always had numerous audiences in mind, the Letter ultimately represents King's decision to shift his focus from the Black middle class to the masses. His urgent call for direct action to replace patience and harmony was indicative of this shift. As he said at a student conference at Shaw University in 1960, the sit-in movement "is a revolt against those Negroes in the middle class who have indulged themselves in big cars and ranch-style homes rather than in joining a movement for freedom."[61] This, he said, ought to be the "era of offensive on the part of oppressed people. All peoples deprived of dignity and freedom are on the march."[62][63] King was speaking to the Black masses, who he believed were already supportive of the movement and were taking real action toward racial justice—action that the clergymen had failed to acknowledge in their haste to paint King himself as an instigator, an outsider who was deliberately roiling the hitherto calm racial seas of Birmingham. King said:

> I wish you had commended the Negro sit-inners and demonstrators of Birmingham for their sublime courage, their willingness to suffer and their amazing discipline in the midst of great provocation. One day the South will recognize its real heroes. They will be the James Merediths, with the noble sense of purpose that enables them to face jeering and hostile mobs, and with the agonizing loneliness that characterizes the life of the pioneer. They will be old, oppressed, battered Negro women,

---

[61] Claude Sitton, "Negro Criticizes N.A.A.C.P. Tactics," *New York Times*, April 17, 1960. Available at: https://timesmachine.nytimes.com/timesmachine/1960/04/17/99732190.html?pageNumber = 32.

[62] Ibid.

[63] See also Martin Luther King, Jr., "Statement to the Press at the Beginning of the Youth Leadership Conference," in Clayborne Carson, Tenisha Armstrong, Susan Carson, Adrienne Clay, Kieran Taylor (eds.), *The Papers of Martin Luther King, Jr.*, Volume V: *Threshold for a New Decade, January 1959–December 1960* (Berkeley and Los Angeles: University of California Press, 2005), 426–427. Available at: https://kinginstitute.stanford.edu/king-papers/documents/statement-press-beginning-youth-leadership-conference#fn4.

symbolized in a seventy-two-year-old woman in Montgomery, Alabama, who rose up with a sense of dignity and with her people decided not to ride segregated buses, and who responded with ungrammatical profundity to one who inquired about her weariness: "My feets is tired, but my soul is at rest." They will be the young high school and college students, the young ministers of the gospel and a host of their elders, courageously and nonviolently sitting in at lunch counters and willingly going to jail for conscience's sake. One day the South will know that when these disinherited children of God sat down at lunch counters, they were in reality standing up for what is best in the American dream and for the most sacred values in our Judeo-Christian heritage, thereby bringing our nation back to those great wells of democracy which were dug deep by the founding fathers in their formulation of the Constitution and the Declaration of Independence.

The Letter was thus more than just a rebuttal of his critics or an attempt to encourage the white moderates to action. It was also a commendation to the demonstrators doing the political work and an exhortation—an attempt to bring new Black people into the movement and spur them to action. Much of the Letter was based on earlier speeches and sermons that were given to largely Black audiences,[64] and he preached the Letter at an all-Black church just days after writing it.[65] In many ways, King's primary audience was

---

[64] For example, the Letter borrows from King's sermon, "Transformed Nonconformist," which he preached in Montgomery, Alabama, at Dexter Church in 1954, and later published as a lecture in *Strength to Love* (Minneapolis: Fortress Press, 2010). Some of the arguments that King makes were also anticipated in an earlier letter he wrote from Albany. See Martin Luther King, Jr., "Letter from Albany Jail," in Christopher C. Meyers (ed.), *The Empire State of the South: Georgia History in Documents and Essays* (Macon, GA: Mercer University Press, 2008), 307–308. The original letter from Albany was published in the *New York Amsterdam News*—one of New York City's oldest Black newspapers offering the "New Black View" on July 21, 1962. He also uses some of what he wrote in his "Challenge to the Churches and Synagogues" (MLKPP, Martin Luther King, Jr. Papers Project, Stanford University, Stanford, CA), which was addressed to an interracial audience.

[65] There is an audio version of this post-jail sermon in the Reverend C. Herbert Oliver collection at the Birmingham Civil Rights Institute.

his Black community, both in Birmingham and across the United States.

Why did King shift his focus from the Black elite and middle class to the Black masses? He did so for at least two reasons. The first reason is pragmatic. It was clear to him that the Black middle class, especially the Black clergy and businessmen among them, were unlikely to be moved by King's appeals. The second reason explains why he thought this was the case: unlike the masses, Black elites simply didn't share in King's democratic view of racial progress.

As Kevin Gaines powerfully articulates in his book *Uplifting the Race*, Black elites responded to the assault on their civil and political rights in the U.S. South by subscribing to what Gaines refers to as "racial uplift ideology"—a set of beliefs about how to overcome marginality and achieve security, protection, respectability, and recognition in the economic, political, and social institutions of the time.[66] These Black elites believed that rights and freedoms came to those who achieved the respectability of the middle class, marked by things like marital status, home ownership, and education. According to Gaines, elite status and racial progress were attached to cultural markers of assimilation—being "white in appearance and behaviour" according to regional norms.[67] In this way, Gaines says, through racial uplift ideology, Black elites devised a "*moral economy* of class privilege, distinction and even domination *within the race*."[68] Gaines argues that by encouraging respectability and assimilation, elites confirmed the common and inaccurate view that the impoverished state of working-class Black Americans was a matter of moral and cultural deficiency, not of coercion or exploitation. Black elites thus countered anti-Black stereotypes only as they applied to themselves, emphasizing class differences among Black Americans and their role as race leaders. Gaines aptly writes,

---

[66] Kevin Gaines, *Uplifting the Race* (Chapel Hill: University of North Carolina Press, 1996), 14.
[67] Ibid., 17.
[68] Ibid., 1717.

"by affirming their respectability through the moralistic rhetoric of 'uplifting the race,' and advocating the moral guidance of the Black masses, African American middle-class leaders and spokespersons were marginalizing the idea of uplift in its more democratic and inclusive sense of collective social advancement and demands for equal rights."[69] This is why King turned his focus away from the Black elites and middle classes and toward the Black masses.

King had come to Birmingham because he believed that, like Albany before it, Birmingham—particularly its Black religious and social elites—was falling into a state of "moral degeneracy."[70] As an advocate of the social gospel, King's ministry was concerned "with the whole man, not only his soul but his body, not only his spiritual well-being, but his material well-being."[71] He believed that any religion "that professes to be concerned about the souls of men and not concerned about the city government that damns the soul (*Yeah*), the economic conditions that corrupt the soul, the slum conditions, the social evils that cripple the soul, is a dry, dead, do-nothing religion (*Amen*) in need of new blood." The Black elites—the preachers riding in their big cars and the businessmen who focused on profit—lacked the social consciousness that King felt was morally necessary. He believed there were moral principles that are absolute and eternal: All of God's children should have the basic necessities of life—a decent home, three square meals a day, and the opportunity for an education, among other things—all of which required desegregation.[72] King articulated a different and

---

[69] Ibid.

[70] Martin Luther King, Jr., "Address at Albany," in Clayborne Carson and Tenisha Armstrong (eds.), *The Papers of Martin Luther King, Jr.*, Volume VII: *To Save The Soul of America, January 1961–August 1962* (Oakland: University of California Press, 2014), 591–599. Available at: https://kinginstitute.stanford.edu/king-papers/documents/address-delivered-albany-movement-mass-meeting-shiloh-baptist-church.

[71] Martin Luther King, Jr., "Preaching Ministry," Clayborne Carson, Susan Carson, Susan Englander, Troy Jackson, and Gerald L. Smith (eds.), *The Papers of Martin Luther King, Jr.*, Volume VI: *Advocate of the Social Gospel, September 1948–March 1963* (Berkeley and Los Angeles: University of California Press, 2007), 69–77. Available at: https://kinginstitute.stanford.edu/king-papers/documents/preaching-ministry.

[72] Ibid., 69–77.

democratic vision of racial uplift: he emphasized the material side of uplift, not merely the social, and he believed that the needs of the most marginalized—especially the poor—ought to be prioritized in the move toward racial justice.

King thus came to see that the Black elite were not likely to be convinced by his radical message of racial progress. He shifted his focus to the Black masses because he knew the masses did not need to be convinced of the truth of his democratic principles. As Cedrick Robinson argues, King

> clarioned a call to action that was heard wherever Afro-Christians could be found.... In this performance, he was less a person than a signature of a social and historical identity. King articulated a Salvationist vision of a future but accessible utopia, a golden place whose every ethical and moral stone was familiar to this widely dispersed congregation.... In King they saw their own reflection, not their master, their own ambitions, not his dictates.[73]

The Black masses were primed by their religious beliefs and practices to take King's vision seriously. King framed his arguments in the language and oral traditions of his ancestors, and especially his preacher father. As Hortense Spillers describes, "though he was trained in universities and academics, his sermons were infused and enlightened by the gospel message as heard while young and growing in the southern hill-soil of America."[74] He told stories of Moses and Paul because he believed that they would resonate with the masses. But it was not just his appeal to a shared religious framework that he believed would move the masses.

King knew that the masses understood and accepted the substance of his moral principles and goals because they were already

---

[73] Cedric J. Robinson, *Black Movements in America* (New York: Routledge, 1997), 144.
[74] Hortense Spillers, "Martin Luther King Jr and the Style of the Black Sermon," *The Black Scholar*, 3.1 (1971): 14–27.

experiencing their negative inversion. The Black elite's advocation for the "be patient" approach to racial progress had only furthered the immiseration and vulnerability to racial violence and economic precarity that the masses experienced in their daily lives. King believed that the masses understood and shared in his moral-political analysis of the elite and in his elaboration of a vision of a just future and how to achieve it. When King and Ralph Abernathy were arrested in Birmingham, they were wearing matching denim work pants and work shirts, although they were normally impeccably attired in suits and ties. In putting on denim—the uniform of workers—King became a living example of the grievances of the Black masses. He expressed their shared beliefs for the future: that, through sacrifice—as foretold through their religious legends and stories—they would build an alternative moral order.

King hoped that the inspired masses would join hands with one another and work toward a common goal: desegregation and, eventually, true integration. In the face of violence, precarity, and poverty it is hard to maintain the motivation to do this work, even when one shares its principles and goals. This is why King hoped to activate the emotions of his listeners and readers. As Frederick Douglass suggested in his famous Fourth of July speech, what was needed was not the light of understanding but the fire of the passions, "not the gentle shower, but thunder . . . the storm, the whirlwind, and the earthquake." King hoped that through his words he could light a fire in the minds and hearts of the Black masses by rousing in them a sense of fear, courage, faith, dignity, indignation, and love. He believed that together, the masses would force the rest of America and its institutions to change.

The Letter is worth returning to today simply for its historical significance. There is no piece by Martin Luther King Jr. that is more widely read or more beloved than the "Letter from Birmingham Jail." Countless articles and books have been written about its generation and meaning. But there are other reasons for revisiting the Letter: its broader philosophical significance has for the large part been missed. While the Letter has exerted particular influence over philosophical debates about civil disobedience, it has scarcely been considered outside of this context. Political philosophers and theorists have not yet managed to fully appreciate and elucidate all that is going on in the Letter and to recognize its full import for political philosophy.

As we can already see, the Letter is not merely a discussion of civil disobedience but is also—perhaps even primarily—an essay on political motivation. We revisit the Letter, then, not merely to mine yet another argument for, or about, civil disobedience, but to uncover King's answer to a central problem in democratic theory: namely, how can and ought we motivate the racially oppressed masses to engage in civil disobedience—what King called nonviolent direct action? King's answer is that we must appeal to the political emotions, both positive and negative: fear, courage, faith, dignity, indignation, and love together can play a role in motivating and sustaining nonviolent action.

When we read the Letter in this light, we restore its inherent complexity. The Letter becomes a ladder that leads us to engage with King's other works—especially the sermons, texts, and personal letters he wrote alongside the Letter—that develop his account of the emotions of nonviolence. Across these works, we see a consistency that is not often recognized in King, who is too often thought of as lacking the systematicity or coherence needed to be a true philosopher. We see him developing a nuanced account of what emotions are, and a reciprocal account of how emotions motivate nonviolent action and how nonviolent action channels the emotions. In turn, we come to a novel understanding of his preference for nonviolence: because of its capacity to continuously foster the emotions, nonviolence is the only method that has the power to continuously and positively transform individuals, society, and political structures.

When we recognize that the Letter's true addressees are not the eight clergymen to whom King was explicitly responding, but rather the Black masses (and, to a lesser extent, white moderates, Black clergymen, and Black middle-class moderates), we also see what else the Letter is doing: detailing the impediments to action under conditions of injustice; calling various audiences to account for their hypocritical, self-serving, or fearful inaction; propagandizing (or working on both intellect and emotion) to motivate a change; and commending and bolstering the efforts of thousands of ordinary Black people already in motion to pursue democracy, freedom, and justice. Read in conversation with King's other works, we see how fear, courage, indignation, faith, and love operate in King's view—as emotions he himself experiences, as emotions that he identifies as either impediments or motivations for action, and as emotional responses he seeks to arouse in his audiences. The Letter, as Jonathan Reider has noted, is worth revisiting because "it reveals much about its often elusive author. It is a supremely personal work from someone moved, and sometimes riven, by rival impulses.... An expressive man, Martin Luther King often hid his passion behind a mask of dignity."[75] In addition to a sense of dignity, fear of white violence and retaliation, and indignation at the persistence of racial injustice, we can also see the courage to fight for something different, and the love for his people that animated the Letter and King himself.

As we journey into King's theory of the emotions of nonviolence, we see another layer of complexity in the Letter's form, intent, and effect: It is an *account*, a *testimony*, and a *political action* unto itself. As an *account*—the aspect of the Letter that has heretofore received the most attention—King establishes the injustice of segregation and the problem of unjust laws, and gives an analysis of what someone who is truly committed to justice ought to do in the face of it, as well as delivering a scathing rebuke of political inaction. As a *testimony*, it is an account of King's own shared experiences of fear, fearlessness, faith, indignation, and love—the emotions that

---

[75] Reider, *Gospel of Freedom*, xvii.

have led him to action. Finally, as a *political action*, the Letter is also a "sensible sermon," a sermon that is intended to elicit a moral and emotional reaction in King's audience that will lead to action.

King's account of the emotions of nonviolence is just as relevant today as it was in the 1960s. Almost a century later, Black Americans still face mass voter suppression, police brutality, and deepening impoverishment. The very concerns that animated King in 1963 still exist and require urgent address, but change is slow to come, and the economically and politically elite remain passive. This is why King's reminder that we ought to focus our efforts on rallying the masses rings just as true today. The masses already know how unjust today's world is, and in many instances, they are already taking action to create a better world. But, as King knew, the fight for justice is long and hard, and the masses require both more fighters and emotional sustenance.

The Letter, in particular, is worth revisiting today because it is King's recipe for recruiting and motivating the masses. This book is an attempt to identify its core ingredients. It focuses on the emotions most relevant to motivating the masses. Less attention goes to disappointment, distrust, and shame, which are core to King's appeal to Black and white moderates.[76] The emotions King gives the most attention to are fear, courage, dignity, indignation, faith, and love. As we will see, the Letter, then, is not just a piece of philosophy that presents us with King's theory of the emotions and motivation. It also offers us a democratic method—something that we can *use* to bring about a democratic and just society through nonviolent action.

---

[76] I have addressed these emotions in other works: Meena Krishnamurthy, "Martin Luther King Jr., on Democratic Propaganda, Shame, and Moral Transformation," *Political Theory*, 50.2 (2022): 305–336, first published June 17, 2021. Available at: https://doi.org/10.1177/00905917211021796; Meena Krishnamurthy, "(White) Tyranny and the Democratic Value of Distrust," *The Monist*, 98.4 (2015): 391–406; and Meena Krishnamurthy, "From Shattered Dreams to Dreams in the Making: Martin Luther King Jr. on the Transformative Power of Democratic Disappointment" (work in progress).

PART 1
BACKGROUND

1
Desegregation

In the years before he wrote "The Letter from Birmingham Jail," King was developing a chronology of race relations in the United States, which he saw as having gone through several distinct historical periods before the current movement for Black civil rights and desegregation. The first period, extending from 1619 to 1863, was the era of slavery. The second period, from 1863 to 1954, King called "the period of restricted emancipation."[1] It began when President Abraham Lincoln issued the Emancipation Proclamation on January 1, 1863. King's Letter was written in 1963, the one-hundred-year anniversary of Lincoln's signing of the Emancipation Proclamation, and its spirit and ethos pervaded the Letter. In a sense, King saw the Emancipation Proclamation as a regulative ideal. It concerned the national life and character of the United States—whether it could be "radiantly glorious with all the high and noble virtues" or infamously tarnished forever.[2]

The second period, King said, was an advance over the first because it removed the Black American from the bondage of physical slavery. Yet, despite its high-vaulting aims, the Proclamation did not full bring full freedom to the Black American, for it failed to acknowledge her as a full and equal person, which made it easy for segregation to emerge as an ethos and a practice.[3] King saw

---

[1] Martin Luther King, Jr., "The Future of integration," State University of Iowa, November 11, 1959, 1–13 at 1. Available at: http://natedsanders.com/lot-36943.aspx.

[2] Martin Luther King, Jr., "Draft of Chapter VIII, 'The Death of Evil upon the Seashore,'" in Carson et al. (eds.), *The Papers of Martin Luther King, Jr.*, Volume VI, 504–514. Available at: https://kinginstitute.stanford.edu/king-papers/documents/draft-chapter-viii-death-evil-upon-seashore.

[3] King, "The Future of integration," 2.

segregation as "at bottom a form of slavery covered up with certain niceties of complexity."[4] The segregation ethos was enshrined into law by the *Plessy v. Ferguson* decision (1896), which established the doctrine of separate but equal—the doctrine that shaped race relations throughout the country until the beginning of the third period of race relations in the United States, the Civil Rights Era.

According to King, on May 17, 1954, the decision in *Brown v. Board of Education* ushered in the period of "constructive integration" in the United States.[5] According to him, in this creative period, "men seek to rise to the level of genuine intergroup and interpersonal living."[6] As he explains it, the Supreme Court's decision said that the Plessy doctrine must go, that separate facilities were inherently unequal. The moral challenge was to work passionately for the complete realization of the ideals and principles that were first expressed in the Proclamation and reasserted in this decision.

According to King, to fully realize constructive integration required both *desegregation* and *true integration*.[7] Desegregation is "eliminative" and "negative,"[8] removing the legal barriers to equal access to schools, parks, restaurants, and libraries in order to bring Black and white people together physically in the same spaces.[9] However, as King points out, a desegregated society is not the same as an integrated one; desegregation "leads to 'physical proximity without spiritual affinity.' It gives us a society where

---

[4] Ibid., 2.

[5] Ibid., 2.

[6] Ibid., 2.

[7] King sometimes uses the phrase "true integration" (Martin Luther King, Jr., "A Talk with Martin Luther King," in Carson et al. (eds.), *The Papers of Martin Luther King, Jr.*, Volume V, 569. Available at: https://kinginstitute.stanford.edu/king-papers/documents/talk-martin-luther-king). I will use this terminology to distinguish it from the more general notion of the period of "constructive integration," which includes desegregation as well as true integration.

[8] Martin Luther King, Jr., "The Ethical Demands of Integration," in *Testament of Hope* (New York: Harper One, 1986), 117–125 at 118; hereafter referred to as "TOH."

[9] Martin Luther King, Jr., "Does Segregation Equal Integration?: Interview with Mike Wallace," June 25, 1958, in *Martin Luther King, Jr.: The Last Interview and Other Conversations* (Brooklyn, NY: Melville, 2017), 23–42 at 33.

men are physically desegregated and spiritually segregated, where elbows are together and hearts are apart.... It leaves us with stagnant equality of sameness rather than a constructive equality of oneness."[10]

As King says, a society can be fully desegregated in a legal, material sense without an accompanying moral change. In this situation, he says, white Americans may have daily interactions with Black Americans, yet still view these interactions with fear and ignorance.[11] King argues that this is not enough: white people must change their hearts, treating Black people as equals not because it is the law to do so, but because they actually see them as brothers and equals.[12] Integration, as King defines it, is a "personal and intergroup feeling":[13] it is positive acceptance of desegregation and the "welcomed participation" of Black Americans in "the total range of human activities."[14] King calls this kind of truly integrated society "the beloved community."[15] The beloved community, he says, requires a change of heart among white Americans—something the law cannot legislate or enforce.[16] This is how the period of constructive integration advances upon the prior period of restricted emancipation: it aims to remove not only the physical

---

[10] King, "Ethical Demands of Integration," 118.
[11] King, "Does Segregation Equal Integration?," 33.
[12] Martin Luther King, Jr., "Speech at SMU," March 17, 1966, 1-8 at 3. Transcript available at: https://www.smu.edu/AboutSMU/MLK#transcript.
[13] King. "Ethical Demands of Integration," 118; King, "Does Segregation Equal Integration?," 33.
[14] Ibid., 118.
[15] Martin Luther King, Jr., "The Birth of a New Age," in Clayborne Carson, Stewart Burns, Susan Carson, Dana Powell, and Peter Holloran (eds.), *The Papers of Martin Luther King, Jr*, Volume III: *Birth of a New Age, December 1955–December 1956* (Berkeley and Los Angeles: University of California Press, 1997), 339–346 at 344. Available at: https://kinginstitute.stanford.edu/king-papers/documents/birth-new-age-address-delivered-11-august-1956-fiftieth-anniversary-alpha-phi.
[16] Ibid., 124. King, "Speech at SMU," 3. This isn't to say, however, that legislation cannot help at all. A desegregated society is a necessary step to an integrated one. As King says, "we cannot get to integration before going through the process of desegregation where you have to break down through legal means" (King, "Does Segregation Equal Integration?," 33).

barriers to equality and freedom but also the psychological barriers that remained long after emancipation.[17]

This brings us to the question of *oughtness*. Why ought King and his supporters fight for desegregation and integration? Why is doing so a moral imperative? King answers this question with three core moral arguments: the equal worth and dignity of all persons, the right to freedom for all persons, and the importance of a realistic philosophical view of the world.

The first moral argument against segregation concerns the inherent equal worth and dignity of all persons: for King, there is no graded scale of essential human worth.[18] This belief originates in the Christian tradition, which holds that humanity is created in the image of God, and the image of God is universally shared in equal proportions among all humans.[19] This belief is also, for King, rooted in the foundations of the American dream, for the commitment to the equal dignity and worth of all humans is a central American value, mostly clearly expressed in the Declaration of Independence: "All men ... are created equal. They are endowed by

---

[17] In "Integration, Affirmation, and the Freedom of Life," in Tommie Shelby and Brandon Terry (eds.), *To Shape a New World: Essays on the Political Philosophy of Martin Luther King Jr.* (Cambridge, MA: Harvard University Press, 2018), 146–169, Danielle Allen interprets King as drawing a distinction between positive and negative liberty. In her interpretation, desegregation is a form of "negative liberty," and "integration" is a form of positive liberty. The argument I outline here suggests that this interpretation isn't quite right. Allen draws most of her argument from King's essay, "The Ethical Demands of Integration," which was published in 1962. Despite the fact that Isaiah Berlin's essay, "Two Concepts of Liberty" (where the distinction between positive and negative liberty is claimed to have first appeared) had already been published (in 1958), King never explicitly uses the terms "negative" and "positive" liberty in his essay (which came after Berlin's), nor does he use these terms in any of the speeches he gave on integration between 1959 and 1966. Rather, he explicitly draws a distinction between "physical" barriers to integration and "spiritual" ("Ethical Demands for Integration," 118) or "psychological" barriers (King, "Does Segregation Equal Integration?," 64). In "Ethical Demands" and later pieces, he continues, implicitly, to build on this framework (see his "Speech at SMU," March 17, 1966, 3).
[18] King, "Ethical Demands for Integration," 119.
[19] This commitment stems from King's personalism. For a discussion of the connection between dignity and personalism, see Rufus Burrows, *God and Human Dignity: The Personalism, Theology, and Ethics of Martin Luther King, Jr.* (South Bend, IN: University of Notre Dame, 2006). I will say more about the nature of dignity in a later chapter.

their Creator with certain inalienable Rights, that among these are Life, Liberty and the pursuit of Happiness."[20] This is a universalist view: as King writes, "It doesn't say 'some men,' it says 'all men.' It doesn't say 'all white men,' it says 'all men,' which includes Black men,"[21] women, and children, all of whom are equally entitled to dignity.[22]

For King, there are two faces of dignity. There is an inherent worth that all people, including Black Americans, possess by virtue of being the children of God. This aspect of Black dignity can be maintained and remain resilient even in the face of white violence and hatred. Yet, there is another aspect of dignity, which is tied to the recognition and status we receive from others in our social world. In King's view, this type of dignity is nearly unachievable for Black Americans under segregation. There is a tragic realism in his argument, for even when it is difficult to attain, we, as social beings, need and seek the positive regard of others—we are, as King says, "caught up in an inescapable network of mutuality."

Segregation debases this second aspect of the dignity of Black people, and is therefore morally objectionable.[23] Following Kant, King argues that full recognition of the inherent worth and dignity of all men requires that "all men must be treated as ends and never as mere means."[24] Segregation violates this categorical (moral) imperative, because it treats Black men and women as mere means rather than as ends in themselves, thereby reducing Black Americans to things rather than persons. King reminds us that the

---

[20] Quoted in ibid., 199.

[21] He elaborates on this idea in his speech "The American Dream," in Clayborne Carson and Peter Holloran (eds.), *A Knock at Midnight: Inspiration from the Great Sermons of Reverend Martin Luther King, Jr.* (New York: IPM, 2000), 79–100.

[22] Martin Luther King, Jr., "The Crisis of the Modern Family," in Carson et al. (eds.), *The Papers of Martin Luther King, Jr.*, Volume VI, 209–213. Available at: https://kinginstitute.stanford.edu/king-papers/documents/crisis-modern-family-sermon-dexter-avenue-baptist-church.

[23] For an argument that inequality in voting rights damages dignity and self-respect, see Derrick Darby, "A Vindication of Voting Rights," in Terry and Shelby (eds.), *To Shape a New World*, 161–183.

[24] King, "The American Dream," 119.

Southern gentry referred to slaves and Black laborers as "hands," emphasizing the "thing-like" quality that was attributed to Black Americans, reducing them to a mindless body part defined only by its ability to accomplish a "purpose" or "job." The slave owner related to enslaved Black laborers not as people but as objects to serve his own economic ends. But, as King argues, "man is not a thing. He must be dealt with, not as an 'animated tool,' but as a person sacred in himself," with inherent dignity and worth.[25]

Like slavery, segregation undermines the dignity and worth of Black Americans. King argues in the Letter that segregation substitutes what Buber called an "I-it" relationship for an "I-Thou" relationship, relegating persons to the status of things.[26] How does segregation do this? By giving a false sense of superiority to the segregator and a false sense of inferiority to the segregated.[27] For King, the sense of inferiority imposed on Black people represents "the slave chains of today."[28]

Indeed, according to King, the whole system of racial segregation in the American South was created to give working class white Americans a sense of elevated social status. Drawing on C. Vann Woodward's book *The Strange Career of Jim Crow*, King argues that racial segregation did not emerge immediately after the Civil War; it was not, as some have thought, a natural consequence of remaining hatred between the races.[29] "It was really a political

---

[25] Ibid., 119.
[26] WWCW, 94.
[27] "Desegregation and the Future," in Carson et al. (eds.), *The Papers of Martin Luther King, Jr.*, Volume III, 471–479 at 474. Available at: https://kinginstitute.stanford.edu/king-papers/documents/desegregation-and-future-address-delivered-annual-lunch eon-national-committee.
[28] Martin Luther King, Jr., *All Labor Has Dignity* (Boston, MA: Beacon Press, 1963), 92. He also talks about Black Americans as "victims of the slavery of segregation." See Martin Luther King, Jr., "Guidelines for a Constructive Church," in Clayborne Carson and Peter Holloran (eds.), *A Knock at Midnight*, 105–115 at 112. Available at: https://kinginstitute.stanford.edu/king-papers/publications/knock-midnight-inspiration-great-sermons-reverend-martin-luther-king-jr-5.
[29] C. Vann Woodward's book, *The Strange Career of Jim Crow* (Oxford: Oxford University Press, 1955).

stratagem employed by the emerging Bourbon interests in the South," created to divide the Southern masses and suppress the cost of Southern labor.[30] In King's view, the myth of racial inferiority gave credence to lifelong patterns of exploitation that allowed the rich to get richer by making profit out of exploited labor. He explains:

> You see, it was a simple thing to keep the poor white masses working for near-starvation wages in the years that followed the Civil War. Why, if the poor white plantation or mill worker became dissatisfied with his low wages, the plantation or mill owner would merely threaten to fire him and hire former Negro slaves and pay him even less. Thus, the southern wage level was kept almost unbearably low.
>
> …
>
> If it may be said of the slavery era that the white man took the world and gave the Negro Jesus, then it may be said of the Reconstruction era that the southern aristocracy took the world and gave the poor white man Jim Crow. (Yes, sir) He gave him Jim Crow. (Uh huh) And when his wrinkled stomach cried out for the food that his empty pockets could not provide, (Yes, sir) he ate Jim Crow, a psychological bird that told him that no matter how bad off he was, at least he was a white man, better than the black man. (Right sir) And he ate Jim Crow. (Uh huh) And when his undernourished children cried out for the necessities that his low wages could not provide, he showed them the Jim Crow signs on the buses and in the stores, on the streets and in the public buildings. (Yes, sir) And his children, too, learned to feed upon Jim Crow, (Speak) their last outpost of psychological oblivion. (Yes, sir)

---

[30] Martin Luther King, Jr., "Our God Is Marching On." Available at: https://kinginstitute.stanford.edu/our-god-marching.

In King's view, racial segregation and its grounding myth of inferiority were created to support an exploitative economic system—what he sometimes referred to as "the system of slavery in the twentieth century." Following W. E. B. Du Bois, King argues that working class white Americans gain a *psychological* wage from segregation: "the satisfaction of your skin being white, and ... thinking that you are somebody big because you are white."[31] This psychological wage serves as compensation for the low economic wage enforced by racial segregation. The economic system of exploitation that racial segregation enables leaves many white workers starving and Black Americans even worse off, with lower wages and lower social status. Racial segregation also prevents white workers from forming coalitions with Black workers and banding together to overturn the economic system that instrumentalizes both Black and white workers.

The moral badness of racial segregation affects all Black Americans. As an example, King recounts his own experience of being delayed in the airport in Atlanta, Georgia.[32] Like the other passengers, he was given a voucher for a free lunch in the airport restaurant. However, unlike the white passengers from his flight, when he arrived at the restaurant, he was led to a compartment in the back. He waited while everyone else ordered and was served their meals. When he complained to a manager about the delay, he was assured that he would receive the same food and the same service as everyone else. Given that King's meal was already later than the others', this claim was clearly false. King noted other dissimilarities; for example, unlike the white patrons, he wasn't seated near beautiful pictures on the wall; and, unlike the others, he wasn't able to continue his conversation with the (white) people he left the plane with. In these ways, Black people like King are confronted daily with white people's belief in their inequality. The

---

[31] Martin Luther King, Jr., "Drum Major Instinct," in *A Knock at Midnight*, 165–186.
[32] King, "Desegregation and the Future," 474.

system of racial segregation says to him and other Black people, over and over again, "you are not equal to; you do not belong; you cannot be."[33] This is true even for middle class Black Americans, like King, who embody the so-called values of racial uplift.

As King writes, "the segregated becomes a thing to be used, not a person to be respected."[34] Despite his lunch voucher, an economic benefit, King is not treated as the others are treated. In this way, King—like all Black Americans, especially the masses—becomes a mere "cog in a vast economic machine."[35] He is simply a source of profit: his money and labor may be valued within the system of racial segregation insofar as it leads to profit, but he is not valued (or treated) as a person, as an end in himself. This is why racial segregation must be immediately ended: it threatens the dignity of all Black Americans.

The second moral argument against segregation concerns freedom. King argues that a denial of freedom is a denial of life itself. In King's view, the ability to make choices is key to avoiding "thinghood."[36] For King, freedom requires "the capacity to deliberate or weigh alternatives"—"Shall I be a teacher or a lawyer?"[37] It also "expresses itself in decision";[38] to make a decision is to make a choice between alternatives, and when we are not able to choose, we descend into thinghood and mass mind. In consequence, the "expression of freedom is responsibility,"[39] for when a person makes a free choice, she must also be accountable for that choice. Segregation is the absence of freedom: it "cuts off one's capacity to deliberate, decide, and respond."[40] When I can't choose what I shall do or where I shall live or how I shall survive, I am robbed of

---

[33] Ibid., 474.
[34] Ibid., 474.
[35] Ibid., 474.
[36] Ibid., 120.
[37] King, "Ethical Demand for Integration," 120.
[38] Ibid., 120.
[39] Ibid., 120.
[40] Ibid., 120.

the kind of freedom that is the basic quality of person-ness; some person or system has already made those decisions for me, and I cannot assume responsibility for my life, because I play no part in the decisions that constitute it. I am therefore reduced to a mere thing, for as King writes, without freedom, "I do not live. I merely exist."[41]

The Black masses inherently understood how racial segregation undermines freedom. Too often, they were not free to pursue a decent education, meaningful work, and appropriate housing. While the Black middle class certainly had options to choose from, they were still constricted: despite having the economic means, they couldn't go to just any college in the United States or live in just any neighborhood in the American South, for example. The basic character of the personhood of Black Americans, as choice makers, was diminished by the system of racial segregation.

According to King, both the lack of dignity and the lack of freedom imposed by racial segregation are psychologically wounding to Black Americans. This is another reason that segregation is morally wrong, and a topic to which he returns in the Letter. King says that only a Black American "can understand the social leprosy that segregation inflicts upon him. The suppressed fears and resentments, and the expressed anxieties and sensitivities make each day of life turmoil. Every confrontation with the restrictions imposed is another emotional battle in a never-ending war. He is shackled in his waking moments to tip toe stance, never quite knowing what to expect next and in his subconscious he wrestles with this added demon."[42] King argues that the psychological toll of racial segregation undermines the "true reserves" of Black Americans and degrades their overall "life-quality."[43]

---

[41] Ibid., 120.
[42] Ibid., 121. As Danielle Allen notes, King outlines the material consequences of what Phillip Pettit has called "domination"—being subject to the arbitrary interference of another ("Integration, Affirmation, and the Freedom of Life," 152).
[43] King, "Ethical Demand for Integration," 121.

Given his definition of freedom, which emphasizes life-quality-enhancing freedom, King makes clear that desegregation is not enough to ensure freedom in its fullest sense. Only true integration—creating and entering into the beloved community—can do this. Desegregation can break down legal barriers and bring people together physically, but it cannot fully the dismantle the psychological barriers that Black Americans face. Legal desegregation alone will not end the white "fears, prejudice, pride, and irrationality" that reinforce the social stigma (or "leprosy," in King's words) experienced by Black Americans under racial segregation.[44] In order to heal the psychological impacts of segregation, white people must have a change of heart; they must bring Black and white people together, not because it is legally required, but because it is morally right.[45] So long as white people continue in their old way of thinking—which leads them to think of themselves as "somebodies" and of Black Americans as "nobodies," as things to be exploited for their own benefit—then Black Americans will still be subject to psychological harms by being denied access to life-quality-enhancing freedom. This is why integration—not merely desegregation—is morally required. Morally speaking, then, true integration was King's "ultimate goal" for the civil rights movement,[46] but you wouldn't know it from reading the Letter, where he only mentions the word "integration" twice. While King longs to hear white Americans declare, "integration is morally right . . . because the Negro is your brother,"[47] in the Letter his focus is on "the disease of segregation."[48]

If true integration was his "dream" for the United States, why did King focus in the Letter only on ending segregation? It was partly a strategic decision. This brings us to the third argument regarding

---

[44] Ibid., 124.
[45] Ibid., 124.
[46] Ibid., 118.
[47] WWCW, 105.
[48] Ibid., 103.

what we ought to do about integration and segregation. In the years before the Letter, King claimed that, in almost all areas, desegregation would be achieved in a matter of ten to fifteen years, but that integration would "take much longer,"[49] although he rarely discussed a timeline for true integration. For example, in an interview with Alex Haley for *Playboy* magazine, King said of integration, "I confess I do not believe this day is around the corner. The concept of supremacy is so imbedded in the white society that it will take many years for color to cease to be a judgmental factor. But it is certainly my hope and dream. Indeed, it is the keystone of my faith in the future that we will someday achieve a thoroughly integrated society. I believe that before the turn of the century, if trends continue to move and develop as presently, we will have moved a long, long way toward such a society."[50]

Why was King skeptical about the achievement of true integration? Because he was a "realist."[51] As mentioned above, desegregation simply involves removing legal and customary barriers that separate groups and individuals—concrete, external barriers such as laws and "For Whites Only" signs.[52] True integration is much more difficult to achieve, for it is "much more subtle and internal [. . . and] involves attitudes of mutual acceptance" and creating friendship across "the psychological color line."[53] Because King

---

[49] Martin Luther King, Jr., "Interview on 'Front Page Challenge,'" in Carson et al. (eds.), *The Papers of Martin Luther King, Jr.*, Volume V, 192. Available at: https://kinginstitute.stanford.edu/king-papers/documents/interview-front-page-challenge. King repeats this claim elsewhere. For example, he wrote that "the main campaigns of desegregation struggle will be won before the end of the current decade" (King, "After Desegregation—What?," 1–6 at 3).

[50] Martin Luther King, Jr., "Playboy: Interview: Martin Luther King, Jr." in James M. Washington (ed.), TOH (New York: Harper Collins, 1986), 340–377 at 375. King repeats a similar idea when he writes, "before the turn of the century we will have moved a great deal toward an integrated society" (Martin Luther King Jr., "A Talk with Martin Luther King," in Carson et al. (eds.), *The Papers of Martin Luther King, Jr.*, Volume V, 569. Available at: https://kinginstitute.stanford.edu/king-papers/documents/talk-martin-luther-king).

[51] King, "Does Segregation Equal Integration?," 39.
[52] King, "After Desegregation—What?," 3.
[53] Ibid., 3.

was a realist, he recognized that true integration would take time and a lot of hard work, for, through the periods of slavery and segregation, certain racist attitudes had taken hold in the minds of white Americans. It would take much time and effort to overcome these psychological barriers to true integration. Desegregation was only the first step, and the move from desegregation to true integration "is not automatic."[54]

According to King, there are three basic attitudes we can take toward the question of progress toward racial integration, with realism being the best.[55] The first attitude is one of extreme or "superficial" optimism, where one concludes that the problem is just about to be resolved.[56] From this, a person concludes that we can sit comfortably by the wayside and wait for the coming of what is inevitable. In King's eyes, this is too often the position of Black and white moderates. The second attitude is one of extreme pessimism, where one holds that we have only made minor progress regarding race relations. In this view, which is based in either orthodox theology or psychology, the person thinks either that the taint of original sin is essential and inescapable or that certain habit structures are instilled at an early age and are near-impossible to root out. This person concludes that we can do nothing to make progress in race relations, for at bottom, human nature is unchangeable.

The extreme optimist and the pessimist have something in common. As King frames it, "the optimist says do nothing because integration is inevitable. The pessimist says do nothing because

---

[54] Ibid., 3.
[55] Martin Luther King, Jr., "A Realistic Look at the Question of Progress in the Area of Race Relations," in Clayborne Carson, Susan Carson, Adrienne Clay, Virginia Shadron, and Kieran Taylor (eds.), *The Papers of Martin Luther King, Jr.*, Volume IV: *Symbol of the Movement, January 1957–December 1958* (Berkeley and Los Angeles: University of California Press, 2000), 167–179 at 169. Available at: https://kinginstitute.stanford.edu/king-papers/documents/realistic-look-question-progress-area-race-relations-address-delivered-st.
[56] Martin Luther King, Jr., "The Peril of Superficial Optimism in the Area of Race Relations," in Carson et al. (eds.), *The Papers of Martin Luther King, Jr.*, Volume VI, 214–215. Available at: https://kinginstitute.stanford.edu/king-papers/documents/peril-superficial-optimism-area-race-relations.

integration is impossible."[57] King argues that instead, we should adopt a third attitude: the realistic attitude, which attempts "to reconcile the truths of the two opposites and avoid the extremes of both."[58] The realist agrees with the optimist that "we have come a long way," evidenced by the move from slavery to restricted emancipation; and, she agrees with the pessimist that "we still have a long way to go."[59] From this realistic perspective, King believes we can take positive steps toward integration, whether or not it will ever be fully realized.

The demands of integration concern inner attitudes and expressions of respect that law books and jails cannot instill or rectify.[60] Since the demands of integration are not enforceable, true integration is difficult, if not impossible, to achieve and maintain:[61] the "dark and demonic responses" of racial prejudice can only be fully eliminated when people willingly come to accept the moral law that all people, Black and white, are equal,[62] and "true integration" can only be "achieved by true neighbors who are willingly obedient to unenforceable obligations."[63] This is a big ask, and the realistic attitude accounts for the fact that racial prejudice can "creep back in" at any time.[64] As King puts it, "so long as one spark of prejudice lies in the heart of any white American, there is possibility for it to develop into a ... flame of intolerance."[65]

---

[57] King, "A Realistic Look," 169.
[58] Ibid., 169.
[59] Ibid., 169.
[60] It is important to note that these early views about integration, which are very psychological in nature, change over time as King is influenced by his interactions with Kwame Ture (Stokely Carmichael) and Charles V. Hamilton. King retained his view that true integration is mutual acceptance and brotherhood, but he also came to think that integration required "the mutual sharing of power" (Martin Luther King, Jr., *Where Do We Go from Here: Chaos or Community* (Boston, MA: Beacon, 1968), 64). For a brief discussion of this transition in King's thought, see Rose's discussion in *The Drum Major Instinct*, 29–31. For a discussion of the role of power in King's theory of civil disobedience, see Livingston, "Power for the Powerless," 700–713.
[61] King, "Ethical Demand for Integration," 123.
[62] Ibid., 124.
[63] Ibid., 124.
[64] King, "The Peril of Superficial Optimism in the Area of Race Relations," 215.
[65] Ibid., 215.

The periods of slavery and segregation deeply inculcated attitudes of prejudice and superiority among white Americans—attitudes that are very difficult to undo, for in King's view, they are concrete expressions of more general human tendencies toward self-centeredness.

Self-centeredness is the sin of living in an "eternal 'I'" and lacking "the capacity to project the 'I' into the 'Thou'"[66]—precisely the sin of white supremacy and racial prejudice. King follows the three major figures in modern psychiatry in his definitions of self-centeredness, which he sees as the result of the desire to be loved (Freud), to be secure (Jung), and—most notably—the desire to belong, to feel significant and important (Adler). These, he says, are the fundamental desires that "human beings have and that they long for and that they seek at any cost."[67] Because attitudes of prejudice and supremacy are seated within these desires (particularly the desire for security, which can be gained at the expense of another, and the desire to feel belonging and feel significant, which can be satisfied through placing others into an out-group and the self into an in-group), they are very difficult to overcome. They can be diminished, but as King suggests, they can rearise at any "unpredictable" moment.[68]

King says little about how true integration can be achieved or how the psychological barriers to integration, including self-centeredness, can be overcome. In part, this may be because the means can only become clear after desegregation is fully established. Primarily, though, it is because King believes that this is something that each person has to solve for herself.[69] In any case,

---

[66] Martin Luther King, Jr., "Conquering Self-Centeredness," in Carson et al. (eds.), *The Papers of Martin Luther King, Jr.*, Volume IV, 248–259 at 250. Available at: https://kinginstitute.stanford.edu/king-papers/documents/conquering-self-centeredness-sermon-delivered-dexter-avenue-baptist-church.

[67] Ibid., 253.

[68] "The Peril of Superficial Optimism," 215.

[69] While King gives some suggestions about how to overcome self-centeredness, he suggests this is something that he cannot fully explain how to fix: "you will have to solve it, in many points, for yourself" ("Conquering Self-Centeredness," 252). As I discuss in

for the time being, King focuses his attention on desegregation. He does so not only because it is an achievable precondition for integration but because it is right in itself; the law cannot change internal feelings, but it can certainly "control behavior"[70]—it can "control the external effects of those internal feelings that are prejudiced."[71] The law cannot make white people love Black people. It can, however, keep them from lynching Black Americans, or from refusing to rent to them or hire them or allow them to patronize businesses simply because of the color of their skin.[72]

King is optimistic about the realization of desegregation. He sees the *Brown v. Board of Education* decision—which ruled that racial segregation of schools was unconstitutional—and other federal court decrees as clear evidence of progress toward the end of racial segregation.

These laws had already changed transportation, education, and public parks, and King believed that further change was possible, even imminent. But he notes that as segregation becomes illegal in more and more areas of life, (white) backlash has emerged: "many states have risen up in open defiance" to the decision,[73] and a modern version of the Ku Klux Klan, the White Citizens Councils (WCC), appeared. The WCC sought to block and delay desegregation by using litigation and court cases, as well as by physically threatening and economically intimidating Black men and women.

Despite the progress toward legal equality, violence against Black Americans was still rampant in the United States. As King notes,

---

a later chapter ("Fear"), King suggests that individuals ought to find something outside themselves. As I suggest later, King is optimistic that Black Americans can overcome selfishness through other-directed action; he doesn't say much about how to encourage white Americans to do so (ibid., 253).

[70] King, "Desegregation and the Future," 476.
[71] Ibid., 476.
[72] Martin Luther King, Jr., "A Realistic Look at Race Relations," given at NAACP Legal Defense and Educational Fund banquet at New York's Waldorf-Astoria Hotel, May 1956, 6.
[73] King, "Desegregation and the Future," 475.

Black boys, such as Emmett Till, were still being murdered. Black men and women were still being shot merely for expressing their desire to stand up and vote. The homes of Black ministers and community leaders—including King's—were still being bombed. The wages of Black Americans across the country continued to be far below those of white Americans. Segregation was still a conspicuous fact in the United States—glaring in the South and perhaps subtler in the North. "First class citizenship" for Black Americans was still a long way off and would require concerted work to achieve. King believed that for the time being, Black Americans must focus their efforts on ensuring that the courts enforce the laws on the books.[74] Black Americans would have to fight for desegregation, since white Americans weren't going to willingly hand it over. As King makes clear in the Letter, the best way of fighting for the enforcement of existing anti-segregation laws was to engage in nonviolent direct action. This, he felt, was the only way to create the crisis required to force white Americans to act: to "no longer ignore" the issue of desegregation but to "confront" it directly.

---

[74] Ibid., 475.

2
Self-Reliance

As discussed in the Introduction to this book, Martin Luther King Jr. was arrested in Birmingham, Alabama, on April 12, 1963, for violating an injunction against "mass street parades or mass processions or like demonstrations without a permit." It was during his time in jail that King wrote the famous "Letter from Birmingham Jail." While the Letter was ostensibly written in response to the "Call for Unity" made by eight white clergymen, published in the Birmingham paper, it was equally written to other moderates. These audiences included Birmingham's Black businessmen, who had chosen not to support the demonstrations, and the white moderates across the nation, who King felt needed to be spurred to use their political power. These white moderates were people such as William Faulkner,[1] members of the Kennedy administration, and writers and editors at major newspapers and magazines such as the *New York Times* and *Time* magazine. These white moderates were counseling those already in the movement not to demonstrate—indeed, not to do anything outside of engaging in "open and honest" discussion and waiting patiently for

---

[1] In "Our Struggle," King takes William Faulkner to task for encouraging Black Americans to wait: "Writing in *Life*, William Faulkner, Nobel prize-winning author from Mississippi, recently urged the NAACP to 'stop now for a moment.' That is to say, he encouraged Negroes to accept injustice, exploitation and indignity for a while longer. It is hardly a moral act to encourage others patiently to accept injustice which he himself does not endure" (Martin Luther King, Jr., "Our Struggle," in Carson et al. (eds.), *The Papers of Martin Luther King, Jr.*, Volume III, 236–241. Available at https://okra.stanford.edu/transcription/document_images/Vol03Scans/236_Apr-1956_Our%20Struggle.pdf. King was also speaking here to all of those moderate white Americans who were unable to see the urgency of political action.

the courts to end racial segregation.[2] For King this was tantamount to asking him to continue to patiently accept injustice, exploitation, and indignity—hardly a moral act, in King's view.

King was deeply disappointed by these white moderates. In coming to Birmingham, King had wanted and expected[3] the white moderates to not only support the movement but to engage in direct political action in service to the cause of ending racial segregation:

> I came to Birmingham with the hope that the white religious leadership of this community would see the justice of our cause and, with deep moral concern, would serve as the channel through which our just grievances could reach the power structure. I had hoped that each of you would understand. But again I have been disappointed.[4]

The white moderates of Birmingham had explicitly committed to ending racial segregation in the retail sector, removing signs saying "whites only" and the like. King had taken the white moderate merchants at their word. He had expected the white moderates to

---

[2] See "Call for Unity"; see also "Poorly Timed Protest," p. 43; "Editorial," *New York Times*, April 17, 1963, p. A40.

[3] This is the "orthodox definition" of hope (see Adrienne Martin, *How We Hope: A Moral Psychology* (Princeton, NJ: Princeton University Press, 2013), 11). R. S. Downie's is a central example of this sort of position. Downie writes, "There are two criteria which are independently necessary and jointly sufficient for 'hope that.' The first is that the object of hope must be desired by the hoper. [...] The second [...] is that the object of hope falls within a range of physical possibility which includes the improbable but excludes the certain and the merely logically possible" (R. S. Downie, "Hope," *Philosophy and Phenomenological Research*, 24.2 (1963): 248–251 at 248f). Similarly, J. P. Day writes, "*A* hopes that *p*" is true if "*A* wishes that *p*, and *A* thinks that *p* has some degree of probability, however small" is true (J. P. Day, "Hope," *American Philosophical Quarterly*, 6.2 (1969): 89–102 at 89).

[4] WWCW, 105. King was also quoted as saying, "I was confident that the white ministers, priests, and rabbis of the South would prove strong allies in our just cause. But some became open adversaries, some cautiously shrank from the issue, and others hid behind silence. My optimism about help from the white church was shattered; on too many occasions since, my hopes for the white church have been dashed" (Martin Luther King Jr., "Interview by Martin Agronsky for 'Look Here'").

materially support the movement for Black civil rights. But they failed to meet this expectation.

Why? At times, King supposed that their inaction came from different views about political tactics: while both King and the white moderates believed the way forward was through "open discussion," they disagreed about how best to stimulate this discussion. As Jonathan Reider explains, King's calls for direct action were "not a repudiation of negotiation but their midwife."[5] King believed that nonviolent direct action in Birmingham was necessary to bring about negotiation and peaceful discussion.[6] For him, this was the purpose of direct action: it forced the hand of those who constantly refused to confront racism by dramatizing the issue so that it could no longer be ignored.[7]

In response, the white moderates said they saw King's "activity in Birmingham as extreme."[8] However, King's nonviolent direct action was anything but extreme: it was designed to offer a middle path between acceptance of the (insupportable and immoral) status quo and armed revolution.[9]

> I stand in the middle of two opposing forces in the Negro community. One is a force of complacency, made up in part of Negroes who, as a result of long years of oppression, are so drained of self respect and a sense of "somebodiness" that they have adjusted to segregation; and in part of a few middle-class

---

[5] Rieder, *Gospel of Freedom*, 53.
[6] WWCW, 89.
[7] Ibid., 89.
[8] Ibid., 99.
[9] He wrote, "You may well ask: 'Why direct action? Why sit ins, marches and so forth? Isn't negotiation a better path?' You are quite right in calling for negotiation. Indeed, this is the very purpose of direct action. Nonviolent direct action seeks to create such a crisis and foster such a tension that a community which has constantly refused to negotiate is forced to confront the issue. It seeks so to dramatize the issue that it can no longer be ignored.... The purpose of our direct action program is to create a situation so crisis packed that it will inevitably open the door to negotiation. I therefore concur with you in your call for negotiation. Too long has our beloved Southland been bogged down in a tragic effort to live in monologue rather than dialogue" (WWCW, 89–90).

Negroes who, because of a degree of academic and economic security and because in some ways they profit by segregation, have become insensitive to the problems of the masses. The other force is one of bitterness and hatred, and it comes perilously close to advocating violence. It is expressed in the various black nationalist groups that are springing up across the nation, the largest and best known being Elijah Muhammad's Muslim movement... . I have tried to stand between these two forces.[10]

King saw himself as advocating for a method that was both active and healing: nonviolence is the "sword that heals"—it is a powerful force for transformation that does not wound others.

King came to believe that the white moderates were looking for reasons not to act. This belief was reinforced by other justifications from whites. Some argued that when nonviolent resistance provoked violent responses (from Bull Connor and other representatives of the racist state), this responsive violence invalidated the peacefulness of the resistance itself—a notion that King found absurd. Others argued that Black people should be patient, should wait for justice. For example, King received a letter saying, "All Christians know that the colored people will receive equal rights eventually, but it is possible that you are in too great a religious hurry. It has taken Christianity almost two thousand years to accomplish what it has. The teachings of Christ take time to come to earth."[11] King saw this idea that the arc of history bends *unaided* toward justice as "a tragic misconception of time"; he called "strangely irrational" the "notion that there is something in the very flow of time that will inevitably cure all ills," for "time itself is neutral; it can be used either destructively or constructively."[12] Only political action across time—not the passage of time itself—would

---

[10] Ibid., 99–100.
[11] Ibid., 99.
[12] Ibid., 99.

bring about justice.[13] Indeed, King came to believe that the white moderates' suggestion to "slow down" really meant "never": "For years now I have heard the word 'Wait!' [. . .] This 'Wait!' has almost always meant 'Never.' As one of our distinguished jurists said, 'Justice too long delayed is justice denied.'"[14]

Some might suppose that, at its heart, the conflict between King and the white moderates was about the morality of racial segregation—about whether the white moderates, like King, really believed that racial segregation was wrong. This was not the problem. King took the white moderates at their word when they said that they believed that racial segregation was wrong and that they were committed to its end.[15] Others might believe that the disagreement was about tactics—about which actions should be taken to end racial segregation. Again, this was not what King saw as the problem. In fact, what King took issue with was the white moderates' political inaction, plain and simple—their counsel to "wait" until justice somehow accomplished itself: "For years now I have heard the word 'Wait!' It rings in the ear of every Negro with piercing familiarity. This 'Wait!' has almost always meant 'Never.'

---

[13] He wrote, "Human progress never rolls in on wheels of inevitability; it comes through the tireless efforts of men willing to be co workers with God, and without this hard work, time itself becomes an ally of the forces of social stagnation" (Ibid., 99).

[14] Ibid., 91.

[15] In some cases, this blind spot was the result of not knowing the moral facts. Some people, such as Birmingham Police Commissioner Bull Connor, genuinely didn't seem to know that racism was wrong. They believed that the white race was in fact superior and that whites ought to have the privileges they had. King sometimes referred to this sort of "blindness" as "intellectual and spiritual blindness" (*Strength to Love* [hereafter STL], 35). Like other types of ignorance, King argued, this real, deeply held belief in white racial superiority was just a form of rationalization—a way of giving moral sanction to systems that benefited white Americans (STL, 37). King did not focus on trying to change people who were mired in this type of ignorance and were explicit in their committment to racial segregation, however. In part, this was because he knew he was unlikely to change the hearts and minds of people with such deeply seated and explicitly held racist beliefs. But it was largely because, like Du Bois, King believed that many (if not most) white Americans already knew that slavery and racial segregation were morally wrong and that these people were both more reachable and more numerous than the virulent racists. This seems right, at least with respect to the white moderates. According to their own testimony, the white moderates already knew that racial segregation was morally wrong; they were simply unmoved to act upon this knowledge.

As one of our distinguished jurists said, 'Justice too long delayed is justice denied.'"[16]

What explained the white moderates' inaction? King runs through several possibilities. Perhaps the white moderates knew that segregation was wrong but simply *did not know how wrong it was*. In works written after the Letter, such as *Where Do We Go from Here*, he suggests that if they knew how wrong it was, they would have known that *immediate* political action to end racial segregation was morally required.[17] But it seems impossible that they did not know: mandated segregation of public schools, public transportation, and public spaces such as restrooms, restaurants, and drinking fountains were all highly visible every day, and all seem clear evidence of the moral rot at the basis of racial segregation.

King considers that some Southern whites may not have understood the full wrongness of segregation, because Black people they were in contact with strategically performed acceptance of racial segregation. King understood why Black people might engage in such performances—their lives and livelihoods were often at stake—but he worried that these performances inadvertently shored up the ideological mystification of Jim Crow, allowing whites to believe that resistance to racial segregation must be the work not of the seemingly content Black people they knew but of "outside agitators."[18] This is, in part, why King believed so fervently in engaging in creative "nonconformity" rather than submission or acquiescence—and perhaps part of why he sought to bring the Black community of Birmingham on board with the demonstrations. After the Freedom Rides, sit-ins, boycotts, and marches, King thought, white Americans must be able to see that Jim Crow was wrong and in need of urgent remedy.

---

[16] WWCW, 91.

[17] Martin Luther King Jr., *Where Do We Go from Here: Chaos or Community?* (Boston: Beacon Press, 1994), 90; hereafter referred to as WDWGH.

[18] WWCW, 19. While King doesn't say this explicitly, it is also implied in some of his lectures in *Strength to Love* (STL, 11–20; 31–41).

Yet, even in the face of this growing civil rights movement, many white moderates continued to counsel patience. This led King to conclude that they were genuinely ignorant—but that this ignorance was not at all innocent. Instead, it was profoundly informed by motivated reasoning and ideology.[19] This is to say, on some level, the white moderates apprehended how wrong racial segregation was, but they couldn't accept and internalize this information without damning themselves and all white people.[20] As Alexander Livingston and Erin Pineda argue, for King, privileged people are psychologically invested in maintaining a sense of the self as ethical and innocent.[21] As King put this idea, "it seems to be a fact of life that human nature cannot continue to do wrong without eventually reaching out for some rationalization which will help to clothe an obvious wrong in the beautiful garments of righteousness."[22] To avoid the shame and guilt associated with the continuation of racial segregation, white moderates blinded themselves to the truth about how wrong racial segregation was and thereby rationalized their inaction. King explained:

> Slavery in America was perpetuated not merely by human badness but also by human blindness. True, the causal basis for the

---

[19] For a related discussion of the moral psychology of white ignorance as it appears in King, see Alexander Livingston, "'Tough Love': The Political Theology of Civil Disobedience," *Perspectives on Politics*, 18.3 (2020): 851–866. His discussion links white ignorance with fear, arguing that it is bolstered by self-induced and irrational fear of Black Americans: "Desegregation is a screen whites project their fear onto" in order to disavow their complicity in and responsibility to eliminate segregation (859). See also Erin Pineda, *Seeing like an Activist* (Oxford: Oxford University Press, 2021), who conceives of white ignorance as a way of seeing or as habits of interpretation that are cultivated in the context of a white state among citizens and policymakers (see, especially, 20–21, 162–163). Pineda argues that white ignorance is something that is maintained ("it resists"; "fights back" and "refuses to go quietly") and can be resilient even in the face of the disruptive challenges that are posed by direct action (175).

[20] In Krishnamurthy, "Democratic Propaganda," I suggest that this is a form of bad faith.

[21] Livingston, "Tough Love," 859; Pineda, *Seeing like an Activist*, 161–162, 175.

[22] Martin Luther King Jr., "A Realistic Approach to Race Relations" May 17, 1956, 3. http://thekingcenter.org/archive/document/realistic-look-race-relations#.

system of slavery must to a large extent be traced back to the economic factor. Men convinced themselves that a system that was so economically profitable must be morally justifiable. They formulated elaborate theories of racial superiority. [. . .] This tragic attempt to give moral sanction to an economically profitable system gave rise to the doctrine of white supremacy.[23]

King suggested that like the slave owners, segregationists created a narrative about the inferiority of Black people to justify their own inaction.[24] They "refused" to know that the inferiority of the Black race had been scientifically and morally refuted.[25] They "blindly believe[d] in the eternal validity of an evil called segregation and the timeless truth of a myth called white supremacy."[26] And this intentional ignorance allowed white people—both the active segregationists and the passive moderates who refused to act—to continue to believe in their own good moral characters, even as they perpetuated and enabled the oppression of other human beings.[27]

King, who is concerned with white moderates' *lack* of positive action to end racial segregation, suggests at times that the white moderates' passivity in fact became a damaging form of action. Just as refusing to decide has the same effect as deciding to say no, refusing to fight segregation has the same effect as supporting it. Why did the white moderates choose not to act? Primarily because

---

[23] STL, 37.
[24] Ibid., 38.
[25] Ibid., 38.
[26] Ibid., 38.
[27] King put it this way: "In their relations with Negroes, white people discovered that they had rejected the very center of their own ethical professions. They could not face the triumph of their lesser instincts and simultaneously have peace within. And so, to gain it, they rationalized—insisting that the unfortunate Negro, being less than human, deserved and even enjoyed second class status. They argued that his inferior social, economic and political position was good for him. He was incapable of advancing beyond a fixed position and would therefore be happier if encouraged not to attempt the impossible" (King, "Interview on 'Front Page Challenge,'" in Carson et al. (eds.), *The Papers of Martin Luther King, Jr.*, Volume V, 75).

they had material preferences for "social order" over justice. They had paternalistic beliefs about their own power and authority over Black Americans, believing that they should decide the tactics and timetable for racial progress. These beliefs manifested themselves not only in reluctance to take positive action to end racial segregation but in an active stance *against* such action. They not only stayed out of the fray and refused to dirty their hands by getting involved in the movement; they also intervened by saying "wait," and, in so doing, they ensured that it meant "never." They were constantly "advising" the movement to use different tactics, to delay until a better time, and to accept token concessions.[28] In taking these stances over and over again, the white moderates actively produced the outcomes they said they abhorred and rejected: violence, hatred, and anger. As he concluded his long litany of complaints against the white moderate, King wrote, "if our white brothers dismiss as 'rabble rousers' and 'outside agitators' those of us who employ nonviolent direct action, and if they refuse to support our nonviolent efforts, millions of Negroes will, out of frustration and despair, seek solace and security in black-nationalist ideologies— development that would inevitably lead to a frightening racial nightmare."[29] Ultimately, white moderates' stance was not a fully passive one; they were much more like the segregationists who actively worked against racial segregation than they might like to think.

Indeed, in some discussions of white moderates before he penned the "Letter," King did not clearly distinguish between the "white moderates" and the "segregationists." This may be because he thought their behavior was rooted in the same impulses and desires. In an interview with *Playboy Magazine*, a few years before the "Letter," King's use of the term "white 'moderates'" contains scare quotes around the term "moderates," suggesting that the

---

[28] WWCW, 109.
[29] Ibid., 101.

interviewer, at least, found some irony in his tone or gestures as he used the phrase. Did King believe that white moderates were truly moderate?[30]

Similarly, in later writings about the backlash from white moderates in the North, King made explicit connections between white moderates and white segregationists.[31] He suggested that, although white moderates blinded themselves to this fact, many of them were as committed to white supremacy as the slave owners and the segregationists of the South, because they (like all white people) benefited from white supremacy. He often talked about white moderates as having a "strange duality," for while they professed to believe that racism in its various forms was wrong, they failed to take immediate political action toward achieving integration—and at times even actively worked against it.[32] As King put it, "often white liberals are unaware of their latent prejudices."[33] Like the segregationists, they had self-interested reasons for remaining unaware. As discussed earlier, under racial segregation, white Americans—moderates and segregationists alike—continued to benefit from a system of economic exploitation and political dominance that was premised and reliant on the subordination of the Black race.

This was true across the nation, not only in the South where racial segregation was the law of the land. As King came to see, even in the North, where segregation was strictly prohibited by the law, it existed in practice in the form of segregated housing, racialized poverty, and the underfunding of public schools. King recognized that it would be difficult to root out racial prejudice in America—to fully enter into the beloved community—because white people's

---

[30] These quotation marks appear in the printed interview, which renders King's words thus: "Over the past several years, I must say, I have been gravely disappointed with such white 'moderates'" (King, "Playboy Interview," 355).
[31] WDWGH, ch. 3.
[32] Ibid., 82.
[33] Ibid., 94.

belief in themselves as both superior *and moral* demanded the continued subjugation of Black people: "we can see the developing dilemma of white America: the haunting ambivalence, the intellectual and moral recognition that slavery is wrong, but the emotional tie to the system so deep and pervasive that it imposes an inflexible unwillingness to root it out."[34] Though on some level, they must have known how wrong racial segregation was, the white moderates' so-called fear of "social disorder" and "social ostracism" (which reflects their deeply repressed *guilt* and *desire* for continued material benefits) caused them to continue to waver, to not take political action.

Indeed, in discussing the deep-rooted white supremacist ideology that was present in all white people, even white moderates, King used the example of Abraham Lincoln, the Great Emancipator himself. King noted that as early as 1837, when he was a state legislator, Lincoln was already referring to the injustice and impracticality of slavery. Yet, even as he vacillated about what to do about the problem, Lincoln expressed some of the white supremacist doctrines of his day, writing about physical differences between Black people and white people and making it clear that he felt that white people were the superior race.[35] Lincoln did, of course, famously go on to take political action toward dismantling slavery, but even he spent years wavering about what he should do and whether the cost of action would be too high. This is what ideologies such as white supremacy do: they manage contradictions. The white moderates knew that

---

[34] Ibid., 81.

[35] Frederick Douglass had similar views of Lincoln: "It must be admitted, truth compels me to admit, even here in the presence of the monument we have erected to his memory, Abraham Lincoln was not, in the fullest sense of the word, either our man or our model. In his interests, in his associations, in his habits of thought, and in his prejudices, he was a white man. He was preeminently the white man's President, entirely devoted to the welfare of white men. He was ready and willing at any time during the first years of his administration to deny, postpone, and sacrifice the rights of humanity in the colored people to promote the welfare of the white people of this country" (Frederick Douglass, "Oration in Memory of Abraham Lincoln," April 14, 1876. Available at: http://teachingamericanhistory.org/library/document/oration-in-memory-of-abraham-lincoln/).

racial segregation was wrong, but, on a deeper emotional level, they refused to recognize the depth of its wrongness so that they could justify refusing to take immediate political action to upset the system that they lived comfortably within and benefited from.

Despite white people's emotional ties to white supremacy, the ideology did not in fact offer real material benefits to all white Americans. King consistently argued that racial segregation was bad for working-class white Americans because it prevented any type of labor solidarity with Black workers, enabling business owners to economically exploit both groups. If poor white workers expressed dissatisfaction with low wages, the plantation or mill owner could simply threaten to fire him and replace him with formerly enslaved Black people, whom the owner could pay even less. Why, then, would white moderates of the working class not support political action to end racial segregation in order to end wage suppression? What did Jim Crow offer white workers that was more valuable than better wages? As discussed earlier (in Chapter 1), white workers of the South and the North were paid a *psychological* wage: they benefited not materially but socially and emotionally from the social status or privilege conferred to them by their whiteness—privilege that depended on the system of racial segregation. White working-class moderates thus served their own self-interest when they denied or ignored the urgency of the political action needed to end segregation, whether legal or de facto.

The political inaction of the white moderates—upper, middle, and working class—was an ongoing and important problem for King, for they held the keys to political power. King knew that without the support and participation of the white moderates, political change was unlikely.[36] But how could he challenge the ideology

---

[36] Though King never gave up on the possibility that whites would undergo moral transformation and create permanent peace for the right reasons, over time he became more solid in his belief that cooperation based on pragmatic changes that would change people's actions and habits of life was the mostly likely way forward. For example, King wrote in his later work that "the cooperation of Negro and white based on the solid

and motivated reasoning that prevented the white moderates from supporting and joining the movement? While King never stopped hoping that the "best" of white America could be persuaded to join the movement based on ethical reasons alone, he knew that without constant prodding, they were more likely to remain settled in their complacency.[37] He believed that:

> if first-class citizenship is to become a reality for the Negro he must assume the primary responsibility for making it so. The Negro must not be victimized with the delusion of thinking that others should be more concerned than himself about his citizenship rights. Neither the white liberal nor the federal government will pass out the Negroes' rights on a silver platter.[38]

He knew "through painful experience that freedom is never voluntarily given by the oppressor; it must be demanded by the oppressed."[39] "The negro," he argued, had not gained "a single right in America without persistent pressure and agitation."[40] This is why he refused to wait—why he advocated for what he called "nonviolent pressure"[41] and "constructive coercion."[42]

King believed that, though their reasons were their own, the Black middle class was, like white moderates, prone to

ground of honest conscience and proper self-interest can continue to grow in scope and influence" (WDWGH, 53).

[37] Ibid., 9.
[38] Martin Luther King, Jr., "The Rising Tide of Racial Consciousness," in Carson et al. (eds.), *The Papers of Martin Luther King, Jr.*, Volume V, 499–508, at 504. Available at: https://kinginstitute.stanford.edu/king-papers/documents/rising-tide-racial-consciousness-address-golden-anniversary-conference.
[39] WWCW, 91.
[40] Ibid., 96.
[41] Ibid., 91.
[42] Ibid., 96. He advocates for the use of "coercion" as early as 1955 (Autobiography, ch. 7) and as late as 1967 (WDWGH, 91) and endorses "putting pressure where it really hurts" in 1968 ("I've Been to the Mountaintop," in *Call to Conscience* (New York: Grand Central Publishing, 2001)).

rationalizations and complacency. They, too, were benefiting from the existing system; they did not wish to rock the boat, and so they counseled the same continued patience and political inaction as white moderates did. King believed the Black middle class, who also benefited from racial segregation, tried too often to "identify with the white majority, the white middle class," driven in part by internalized white supremacy and an unconscious hatred of themselves.[43] He believed that "psychologically" they rejected anything that reminded them of their heritage, of Africa, or of "the masses of Negroes."[44] Blinded by ideologies of white supremacy (the root of the politics of Black respectability), the Black middle class chose ignorance, becoming "insensitive to the problems of the masses."[45][46] As we will see throughout this book, King hoped that, with the right levers, they could be persuaded to join the Black masses.

As Justin Rose has argued, King—much to the chagrin of other Black preachers, like those he addressed upon arriving in Birmingham—believed that *all* Americans, and especially Black Americans, had a moral duty to engage in "transformative political service by 'putting their bodies and souls in motion'" to collectively

---

[43] Martin Luther King, Jr., "Who Speaks for the Negro," in *Martin Luther King, Jr.: The Last Interview and Other Conversations* (New York: Melville House, 2017), 65. King, WWCW, 99.

[44] King, Jr., "Who Speaks for the Negro," 65. WWCW, 99.

[45] WWCW, 99.

[46] Malcolm X often charged King with operating in bad faith, arguing that King's work toward integration through appeals to whites were bad faith evasions of his own role in encouraging Black "moderation" (in the form of nonviolence), which emanated from an inferiority complex of his own. This raises the question of whether King can be sure that he is not—like the white moderate—in the grips of rationalization and bad faith judgments. The short answer is that he can't be certain. As Gandhi noted, all people, Black, white, and Brown, may be subject to bad faith. This is, in part, why Gandhi supported nonviolent tactics as the right path to moral progress: nonviolence comes from a commitment to humility, and since we can never be certain that we are not in the grips of bad faith, the best we can do is aim not to harm others through violence as we push for what we want. Gandhi writes, "if this kind of [nonviolent] force is used in a cause that is unjust, only the person using it suffers. He does not make others suffer for his mistakes" (Mohandas Karamchand Gandhi, *Hind Swaraj and Other Writings*, ed. Anthony Parel (Cambridge: Cambridge University Press, 2009), 89).

resist racial oppression.[47] As I will discuss later (Chapter 6), King believed that Black Americans had a duty to engage in collective action—a duty both to the self, as collective action expressed as a believed and felt sense of self-respect, and to others, for collective action put into practice the moral requirement that we love our friends and enemies alike. In King's view, to fulfill this duty to self and others, Black Americans needed to transform themselves. Through Black self-transformation, he argued, the best of white America could also be transformed, and Black and white Americans together could transform the political structures of America.

King knew it would be difficult to address the deeply ingrained white supremacist ideology in the South head-on, and so his political campaigns in the South were often crafted to instead draw out the sympathy of white moderates in the North, who did not directly benefit from the racial segregation of the South and carried less guilt about their own role in racial oppression. King believed that Northern white moderates were more open to sympathizing with Black Americans in the South, for they could separate themselves from the atrocities that occurred there; in contrast, white Southerners who directly benefited from racial segregation—socially, politically, economically, and psychologically—were more likely to cling to these benefits and their deeply held beliefs.

For example, Wyatt Tee Walker has said that he and King intentionally sought to create conditions in Birmingham that would draw out the virulence of the racism there, making it impossible for white moderates in the North to ignore the violence inherent in America's racist systems. Walker, who planned the tactics of King's demonstrations, said that he targeted Birmingham for the campaign because of Bull Connor's tendency toward violence:

> My theory was that if we mounted a strong nonviolent movement, the opposition would surely do something to attract the

---

[47] Rose, *The Drum Major Instinct*, 17.

media, and in turn induce *national sympathy and attention* to the everyday segregated circumstance of a person living in the Deep South.[48]

Walker sought to reveal—and to have documented in images—the violence in Birmingham in order to break through the complacency of white moderates in the North. Seeing Black children being punched, chased, and hosed down had a significant impact on these white moderates. Until the violence was made visible to them, it had been easy for white Northerners to believe white Southerners' claims that race relations in the South were amicable. Seeing children being beaten broke their complacent ignorance, awakening their sympathy with Black Americans.[49] They were forced to imagine what it was like to be the target of racist violence, and to imagine their own children being treated so—and, continuing that line of reasoning, to imagine themselves and their children being treated unequally, in the ways that had prompted the demonstrations in the first place. The images of Black children made it easier for white viewers in the North to enter the subjective mode, to imaginatively experience the suffering of Black Americans. Yet, as King knew, there were limitations to the sympathy of white Northerners, who benefited in their own subtle ways from white privilege and were ultimately disinclined to urgently act toward political transformation that would directly affect their own lives in the North. As the push for equality grew, King was forced to turn his efforts North and push for full economic integration there, but his appeals to sympathy would prove less effective when they called on Northern white moderates to see and act in response to their own complicity in the racist systems of America.

---

[48] Bass, *Blessed Are the Peacemakers*, 96; my italics.
[49] King wrote, "Every attempt to end the protest by intimidation, by encouraging Negroes to inform, by force and violence, further cemented the Negro community and brought sympathy for our cause from men of good will all over the world" ("Our Struggle," 236–237).

King saw the 1964 adoption of the Civil Rights Act and the Voting Rights Act as completing only the "first phase" of the freedom movement. In the "second phase" of the movement, King planned to work for "economic equality," which would ensure that everyone—not only Black people—had a basic level of income and reasonable healthcare, education, and housing. King released a "Freedom Budget" for all Americans, which proposed a second New Deal to promote job growth at living wages and to meet his other economic goals. This second phase received little support from those in the North. In the white communities in Chicago where marches for fair housing were taking place, King's liberal friends cried out in "horror" and "dismay," claiming that King was creating "hostility" and "hatred," telling him, "you are only developing a white backlash."[50] In King's view, these types of conflict were unavoidable, because as we have discussed above, reaching true equality would require difficult adjustments in the lives of many white people, and not only in the South.[51]

This backlash did not surprise King; he believed it was simply the surfacing of the same old prejudices, hostilities, ambivalences, and rationalizations that had always characterized white America's attitude to racial justice.[52] His plan to secure decent jobs, housing, and income for *all* Americans—not just Black Americans—threatened the economic and social interests of the middle- and upper-class white Northern moderates, who were just as invested in a labor underclass made up of both Black and white people as white Southerners were, and reacted just as Southerners had to abolitionist and anti-segregationist movements—including using violence. Famously, during a march in Marquette Park in Chicago, King was attacked by an angry white mob.[53]

---

[50] WDWGH, 96.
[51] Ibid., 101.
[52] Ibid., 72.
[53] David Bernstein, "The Longest March," *Chicago Magazine*, July 25, 2016. Available at: http://www.chicagomag.com/Chicago-Magazine/August-2016/Martin-Luther-King-Chicago-Freedom-Movement/.

Despite this, King never completely gave up on the power of sympathy. According to Ralph Abernathy, the head of the SCLC (which carried out the campaign after King's demise), the intention of the second phase of the movement, known as the Poor People's Campaign, was to create sympathy between Black and white Americans by dramatizing the plight of America's poor of all races and making very clear that they are sick and tired of waiting for a better life. King's plan was similar to the one he used in Birmingham: he planned to bring the American poor of all races to Washington, D.C., forcing politicians to see them and sympathize with their plight. As with the Birmingham march, King planned to show the bad effects of poverty on children in order to tug at politicians' heartstrings. He wrote:

> If you are, let's say, from rural Mississippi, and have never had medical attention, and your children are undernourished and unhealthy, you can take those little children into the Washington hospitals and stay with them there until the medical workers cope with their needs, and in showing it your children you will have shown this country a sight that will make it stop in its busy tracks and think hard about what it has done.[54]

After spending time in Chicago, King had a healthy skepticism about how committed the white moderates of the North were to racial equality. He knew that Chicagoans, like Southerners, would look out for their own self-interest, which would make sympathizing with impoverished Black people difficult. This is why he saw nonviolent coercion as crucial: he believed that, even when sympathy was unlikely, nonviolent pressure and coercion could be used to steer the white moderates in the right way to produce effective policy change.

---

[54] Martin Luther King, Jr., "Nonviolence and Social Change," in Cornel West (ed.), *Radical King* (Boston, MA: Beacon Press, 2015), 152.

For this reason, King sometimes played to self-interest as a strategy, as a precondition for creating unlikely sympathy. Even before the Birmingham campaign, King rolled out an economic boycott of the Montgomery bus system. It was designed to make it uncomfortable for white people to continue as they had; it sought to provoke action by appealing to people's social and economic self-interests, which he felt would trump their psychological self-interest in feeling superior. In Montgomery, 75 percent of passengers on the bus were Black. Without these passengers, the bus company faced serious financial losses and likely bankruptcy. The economic boycott made the costs of inaction higher than the costs of action, and the buses were eventually desegregated.

King appealed to self-interest in the hope that it would create the conditions for sympathy to emerge. Nonviolent coercion jeopardizes, at least temporarily, some of the material and psychological benefits desired by the white moderate—benefits that were guarded and secured through white supremacy. As Reinhold Niebuhr notes, nonviolence robs "the opponent of the moral conceit by which he identifies his interests with peace and order of society."[55] Typically, nonviolent protestors (like those boycotting the Montgomery bus system) are categorized as enemies of public order, as criminals inducing violence, while those supporting the status quo (such as the bus company owners) are portrayed neutrally. But the plausibility of this moral picture is destroyed when the protestors refuse to engage in violence. In the face of the nonviolence of protestors' actions, the status quo does not have its usual plausible moral unction, and sympathy can at least become possible.

It is possible that economic boycotts similar to the Montgomery bus boycott could have worked in the North as part of King's "second wave." We will never know. King was assassinated on

---

[55] Reinhold Niebuhr, *Moral Man and Immoral Society: A Study in Ethics and Politics* (Louisville, KY: Westminster John Knox Press, 2013), 250.

April 4, 1968, in Memphis, Tennessee—before his "Poor People's Campaign" had its first march. During the frantic search for his assassin, James Earl Ray, riots erupted across the country, movement leaders fought over who would take the helm, and the Campaign came to an early end.

If the white moderates are unlikely to be moved by emotive appeals—and more likely to be moved by appeals to self-interest and by the coercive power of nonviolent boycott—why did King continue to address them in the Letter, which was ultimately an emotive appeal? There, King notably and repeatedly registers his disappointment in the white moderates:

> I must confess that over the past few years I have been gravely disappointed with the white moderate. I have almost reached the regrettable conclusion that the Negro's great stumbling block in his stride toward freedom is not the White Citizens' Counciler or the Ku Klux Klanner, but the white moderate, who is more devoted to "order" than to justice; who prefers a negative peace which is the absence of tension to a positive peace which is the presence of justice; who constantly says: "I agree with you in the goal you seek, but I cannot agree with your methods of direct action"; who paternalistically believes he can set the timetable for another man's freedom; who lives by a mythical concept of time and who constantly advises the Negro to wait for a "more convenient season." Shallow understanding from people of good will is more frustrating than absolute misunderstanding from people of ill will. Lukewarm acceptance is much more bewildering than outright rejection.[56]

King directly addresses the white moderates because they claim to share in the same moral commitments as he does, and to value a relationship with him as part of a moral community. The white

[56] WWCW, 96–97.

moderates are supposed to be partners in the work of the church here on earth and in the political projects of racial equality and democracy in the United States. King is disappointed in the white moderates for failing to act on their moral commitments. As Jonathan Reider suggests, "disappointment" is King's "euphemism" for moral rage and fury.[57] King's "disappointment" here is infused with a sense of righteous indignation, which, as we will see, is a moral emotion that is driven by the sense that justice has been violated. King is indignant at the white moderates for not acting on their stated moral principles of racial equality. In an important sense, by expressing his indignant disappointment, King is calling the white moderates to account, inviting them to recognize their own moral failings and to do better. King's disappointment is meant to evoke white moderates' sense of shame and to make them feel "the fierce urgency of now," leading them to join the movement.[58]

We might also wonder why King continues to speak to the Black moderates here, and whether he really believes they can be moved to act. After all, he expresses the same indignant disappointment to the Black moderates as he does to the white moderates. Even though Black moderates share in the indignities and fears of the Black masses, caused by white supremacy, they are skeptical that political action will end racial segregation. Black moderates engage in uplift politics not only as form of resistance but also as a way of securing the material and social benefits of their own class status. The irony is that, in seeking to push back against Black stereotypes, Black moderates engage in what King refers to as "conformity" or what is sometimes called "accommodation": they give into white preferences and aspirations by mirroring, adopting, and

---

[57] Rieder, *Gospel of Freedom*, 76.
[58] Martin Luther King Jr., "I Have a Dream," in James M. Washington (ed.), *A Testament of Hope: The Essential Writings and Speeches of Martin Luther King Jr.* (New York: Harper Collins, 1991), 217–220. For a detailed account of King's attempt to shame and call the white moderates to account, see Krishnamurthy, "Democratic Propaganda."

taking them on. This is why King was disappointed in the Black moderates: because they are acting just like the white moderates. They too are insensitive to the problems of the masses. They too have privileges that are both desired and are a source of guilt. They too fail to engage in political action to end racial segregation. And, in King's view, they too should be ashamed of their actions.

King spoke directly to the moderates—white and Black—for at least two reasons. The first reason is largely pragmatic. King insists that the battle is more than half won—that the old order is ending, "no matter what Bastilles remain"—when the oppressed realize they have the power to engage in action to make themselves free.[59] But Bastilles nevertheless do remain, especially in the form of the moderates, both white and Black. King knows that the stubbornness and endurance of the moderates in the face of Black struggle had become its own source of exhaustion, demoralization, and demotivation. King hopes to overcome these motivational barriers. King tells us something about how the moderates, as the target and audience of Black nonviolent action, ought to be conceived of: as *those who must be moved*, even against their own immediate wishes and material interests, for the sake of both desegregation and the future horizon of integration.

The second reason King addressed the moderates has to do with his own sense of moral duty. He believed he was duty-bound to minister in a way that would transform those individuals who can be transformed. King believed that all humans are created in the image of God and therefore have the capacity for moral transformation, but this capacity to transform is not fully actualized in the real world because of material conditions. Because of these earthly conditions, King thought, it was the masses who were most likely to undergo transformation, and the moderates—Black and then white moderates—who were next most likely. King repeats twelve times in the Letter that he is disappointed in the white moderates,

---

[59] WWCW, 135.

because he *seeks to create an audience that doesn't exist yet*. His disappointment is an expression of faith on his part that there is an audience that will take his disappointment seriously, and heed his call to them to become the kind of people who would honor and act upon the commitments they say they already have. Grace Lee Boggs, who was King's contemporary and friend, articulated the point in this way: "nonviolence is a way of respecting the capacity of human beings to grow—it gives them the opportunity to grow their souls and we owe that to each other."[60] As we will see, dignity is a central value for King. And, as Boggs suggests, when we appeal to those who seem unmovable or unreliable, we are in fact respecting their inherent dignity—giving them the opportunity to be the moral people we believe they could be.

However, King had a well-grounded skepticism of the white and Black moderates, and he thought them unlikely to be moved through mere emotional appeal. Because of his faith in the power of the Black masses, though, King believed that the moderates—white and Black—could and should be morally pressured into supporting the movement by nonviolent coercion. Ultimately, King believed that it was the efforts of the Black masses that would bring the moderates on board and eventually make political progress possible. This is why his primary audience and focus in the Letter is ultimately the Black masses.

---

[60] Grace Lee Boggs, "Grace Lee Boggs in Conversation with Angela Davis," Making Contact, Radio Stories and Voices to Take Action, February 20, 2012. Available at: https://www.radioproject.org/2012/02/grace-lee-boggs-berkeley/.

3
Sensible Sermon

King believed racial progress in the United States would only occur through pressure exerted by Black people. He was largely skeptical about whether white Americans would or could do what was right on their own, but he had faith in Black people—particularly in the ability of the Black masses to put moral pressure on white Americans. This gave him hope that white people would change, and that racial progress was possible.

However, not all Black Americans were interested in applying the kind of moral pressure King saw as necessary, and he recognized that there were important barriers to political action by Black Americans. Like white Americans, middle- and upper-class Black Americans benefited from the system of racial segregation, and sometimes they too were blinded by ideologies of white supremacy and Black respectability,[1] among other things.[2] This blindness, in King's view, could lead the Black middle and upper classes to become "insensitive to the problems of the masses."[3]

As discussed earlier, King believed that the Black masses, who had never been content with racial segregation, were the most likely to "rise up" and to begin to "cry out" for justice.[4] However,

---

[1] The term "respectability politics" was coined by Evelyn Brooks Higginbotham in her book *Righteous Discontent* (Cambridge, MA: Harvard University Press, 1993). In this context, "respectability" refers to the practice of adopting the manners and morality of white Americans in order to resist stereotypically negative views about Black individuals.

[2] Richard Wright discusses this phenomenon in detail in *Black Boy: A Record of Childhood and Youth* (New York: Harper & Row, 1966).

[3] WWCW, 99.

[4] He wrote: "Many men have vested interests in Egypt, and they are slow to leave. Egypt makes it profitable to them, some people profit by Egypt. The vast majority, the

as we will see in more detail in later chapters, the masses, too, faced barriers to political action. King argued that some, as a result of long years of enforced oppression, were "so drained of self-respect and a sense of 'somebodiness'"[5] that they "lost faith in themselves and came to believe that perhaps they were inferior."[6] Others lost trust in white Americans and were "caught up in the clutches of the injustices surrounding them"; these people had "come to the conclusion that the problem can't be solved [from] within."[7]

Another central barrier to political action—a very rational one, shared by Black Americans of all classes and backgrounds—was fear. Of course, King says, Black people never liked racial segregation, but they were "afraid to say it" because of the consequences of speaking out.[8] For Black people, King says, engaging in political action to end racism "is always costly and never altogether comfortable." The consequences could be social and economic—"walking through the valley of the shadow of suffering, losing a job, or having a six-year-old daughter ask, 'Daddy, why do you have to go to jail so much.'"[9] Or they might be physical, material, violent—being beaten or lynched. Fear of these outcomes led some to political passivity and others to radicalism, turning them into "extremists," overcome with "bitterness and hatred," who came "perilously close to advocating violence."[10] Violence was anathema to King, who, as we will see, believed that it was both immoral and

---

masses of people never profit by Egypt, and they are never content with it. And eventually they rise up and begin to cry out for Canaan's land" (Martin Luther King, Jr., "The Birth of a New Nation," in Carson et al. (eds.), *The Papers of Martin Luther King, Jr.*, Volume IV, 157. Available at: https://kinginstitute.stanford.edu/king-papers/documents/birth-new-nation-sermon-delivered-dexter-avenue-baptist-church.

[5] WWCW, 100.
[6] King, "A Realistic Approach to Race Relations," 3.
[7] Ibid., 3.
[8] Ibid., 7.
[9] STL, 19
[10] WWCW, 100.

deeply impractical.[11] He believed that violence was more likely to lead to the extermination of Black people in America than to racial justice.[12]

King was confident that the only way forward was through nonviolent direct action, led by Black Americans. He knew that he would need to find ways to foster courage and determined action among Black Americans. How might King motivate Black Americans to engage in the nonviolent action needed for political progress? He considers two options: *intellectualism* and *emotionalism*, the two modes of motivation used in the Christian church. Intellectualism is, roughly, the view that all that is needed for moral motivation is propositional knowledge; emotionalism is the view that, in addition to propositional knowledge, political motivation requires emotions or desires.

King believed that toughminded "intellectualism" was not enough to motivate nonviolent action.[13] It was too cold and too detached to enlist the masses, who had other, more pressing concerns, such as meeting their basic needs.[14] He also knew that

---

[11] In his *Autobiography*, King wrote, "you come to see that tactically as well as morally it is better to be nonviolent. Even if one didn't want to deal with the moral question, it would just be impractical for the Negro to talk about making his struggle violent" (*Autobiography*, 266). King also wrote, "One of the main questions that the Negro must confront in his pursuit of freedom is that of effectiveness," he then argues that violence is deeply ineffective (WDWGH, 58).

[12] WDWGH, 58.

[13] See the postscript for further discussion of intellectualism and emotionalism in Black political thought.

[14] King was influenced in his views on these matters by S. Radhakrishnan. In a paper for a course on the "History of Living Religions," King wrote about the strengths of Hinyana and Mahayana Buddhism. Drawing heavily on Radhakrishnan's work, King argued that "Hinyana could never become a popular religion. Its cold, passionless metaphysics could never inspire a real emotional uplifting. . . . As Buddhism spread throughout India and even beyond it, it had to adjust itself to new modes of thought. It had to present its message in language understandable to the masses. This challenge was met by Mahayana Buddhism. Mahayanism was able to capture the minds of the masses by giving up the icy coldness of some forms of early Buddhism and framing a religion that could appeal to the inner emotions." See Martin Luther King, Jr., "The Chief Characteristics and Doctrines of Mahayana Buddhism," in Clayborne Carson, Ralph Luker, Penny A. Russell (eds.), *The Papers of Martin Luther King, Jr.* Volume I: *Called to Serve*, January 1929–June 1951 (Berkeley and Los Angeles: University of California

while tenderhearted emotionalism could be "uplifting,"[15] leading to bold and determined action, even when it required tremendous sacrifice, excessive focus on emotion was too often irrational and led people down the wrong path.[16]

Ultimately, King saw the strengths and weaknesses of both these positions, and he chose to use the strengths of both: he believed that the path forward required bringing together head and heart, and this was his formula for action.[17] He wrote:

> Jesus reminds us that the good life combines the toughness of the serpent and the tenderness of the dove. To have serpentlike

---

Press, 1992)., 314–315. Available at: https://kinginstitute.stanford.edu/king-papers/documents/chief-characteristics-and-doctrines-mahayana-buddhism.

[15] Ibid.

[16] For example, King believed that people's learned disgust for interracial marriage created a knee-jerk emotional response that was very difficult to overcome with any amount of rational reasoning. King wrote, "the religious convictions and social customs of the South have become so crystallized against interracial marriages that it is very difficult to get any rational thinking on the subject. Indeed, the whole question of intermarriage has developed many irrational fears within the white south. It is a subject in which sheer emotionalism takes over and rationality is pushed entirely in the background" (Martin Luther King Jr., "Advice for Living," in Carson et al. (eds.), *The Papers of Martin Luther King, Jr.*, Volume IV, 375. Available at: https://kinginstitute.stanford.edu/king-papers/documents/advice-living-6). Similarly, he wrote that "only the misguided reactionary clothed in the thin garments of irrational emotionalism will seek to defend" segregation, which "is both rationally inexplicable and morally unjustifiable" (Martin Luther King, Jr., "Desegregation and the Future," in Carson et al. (eds.), *The Papers of Martin Luther King, Jr.*, Volume III, 472. Available at: https://kinginstitute.stanford.edu/king-papers/documents/desegregation-and-future-address-delivered-annual-luncheon-national-committee). King found a strong strain of emotionalism within the Black church, which he felt was not properly balanced by rationalism; he said, "I revolted, too, against the emotionalism of much Negro religion" (*Autobiography*, 15), and asserted that in the Black church, emotionalism could become an end in itself, transforming worship into a kind of spectacle or entertainment: "the very people who make worship an entertaining center are the people who are convinced that their actions reveal the holy spirit. They have confused overt emotionalism with the true holy spirit." He contrasted this with the balanced approach he advocated for, pointing out that "[t]his misinterpretation of the holy spirit has caused many to fail to see value of a sensible sermon" (Martin Luther King, Jr., "Worship," in Carson et al. (eds.), *The Papers of Martin Luther King, Jr.*, Volume VI, 222–225 at 223. Available at: https://kinginstitute.stanford.edu/king-papers/documents/worship-sermon-dexter-avenue-baptist-church).

[17] STL, 2.

qualities devoid of dovelike qualities is to be passionless, mean, and selfish. To have dovelike qualities without serpentlike qualities is to be sentimental, anemic, and aimless. We must combine strongly marked antitheses.[18]

While King does acknowledge that employing both qualities in proper balance may be difficult, he believes that this is the ideal we ought to aim for, even if we never fully realize it.

King put this belief into action in his concept of the "sensible sermon," which sought to bring together people's hearts and minds. He used the sensible sermon to *persuade* his audiences of the immediate need for direct action (intellectualism), while also *moving* them to participate in the movement (emotionalism). King laid out his ideas for the sensible sermon in several of his writings. With his sensible sermons, King hoped "to get people to see, do, or be something."[19] For King, sermons can be understood not only as a form of worship on his part but also as an attempt to foster appropriate worship on the part of others. Appropriate worship—"worship at its best"[20]—has three components, on King's view. It has an "upward look" toward God, an "inward look" toward ourselves in relation to God, and an "outward look," which involves "service" to others. For King, worship was not merely a private affair but was something to be directed toward others and made material through service. In support of this idea, King quotes the Bible: "What doth the Lord requ[i]re of thee but to do justly, love[, and show] mercy."[21] Combining emotionalism and

---

[18] STL, 6.

[19] Martin Luther King, Jr., "Sermon Sketches," in Carson et al. (eds.), *The Papers of Martin Luther King, Jr.*, Volume VI, 81, fn 1. Quoting from King, Class notes, Preparation of the Sermon, 30 November 1948–16 February 1949. Available at: https://kinginstitute.stanford.edu/king-papers/documents/sermon-sketches.

[20] Martin Luther King, Jr., "Worship at Its Best," in Carson et al. (eds.), *The Papers of Martin Luther King, Jr.*, Volume VI, 350–351 at 351. Available at: https://kinginstitute.stanford.edu/king-papers/documents/worship-its-best-sermon-dexter-avenue-baptist-church.

[21] Ibid., 351.

intellectualism, King's sermons helped people to attain an upward and inward look and to engage in service toward others—which, for him, was most perfectly expressed in the fight to obtain justice for others. King's goal was to use his sermons to create an emotional impact to move people toward the realization of justice and truth in this world.

Because it emphasizes the use of emotion to move people to act, King's sermonizing can be understood as a form of *propaganda*.[22] The term "propaganda" was originally associated not with lying or manipulation for political ends but with "propagating," or spreading, the Christian faith.[23] King himself framed the sermon as a form of propaganda. At Dexter Avenue Baptist Church, in a sermon titled "Propagandizing Christianity," King preached that "for the average person, the word propaganda has evil and vicious overtones,"[24] but that propaganda is not necessarily "evil": "There is a noble sense in which propaganda can be used."[25] According to King, "propaganda is simply an attempt to disseminate principles or ideas by organized effort," and he argued that when Jesus asked Christians to bear witness to the "uttermost part of the earth," he was calling upon his "disciples to be true propagandizers."[26] Christians are obligated to disseminate Christianity to every tribe, race, nation, and village, and Christ requires Christians "to go out and talk" about—to propagandize or sermonize about—Christianity.[27] When King endorsed the use of propaganda, he reminded us that

---

[22] See Krishnamurthy, "Democratic Propaganda," 305–336.

[23] The word was coined by Pope Gregory XV in 1622 to refer to the *congregiode propaganda*, which was an organization of the Roman curia that had jurisdiction over missionary territories. See Sheryl Ross Tuttle, "Understanding Propaganda: The Epistemic Merit Model and Its Application to Art," *Journal of Aesthetic Education*, 36.1 (2002): 16–30 at 16–17.

[24] Martin Luther King Jr., "Propagandizing Christianity," in Carson et al. (eds.), *The Papers of Martin Luther King, Jr.*, Volume VI, 184–187 at 184. Available at: https://kinginstitute.stanford.edu/king-papers/documents/propagandizing-christianity-sermon-dexter-avenue-baptist-church.

[25] Ibid., 184.

[26] Ibid., 185.

[27] Ibid., 185.

Christians were commanded by Christ to use propaganda to spread the moral truth:

> Never under estimate the power of words. (Adve[r]tizing has discovered it; Hitler discove[r]ed it). If Hitler could do all of this with an evil idea it seems that we could rock the world with the truth of the saving power of the gospel. If the advertizers can convince the men that they can't do without their products, we ought to be able to convince men of the productive power of God in Christ.[28]

In this definition, propaganda is talk of a certain type and for a certain purpose: talk imbued with emotion and designed to arouse similar emotions in its hearers in order to change and shape their behavior—to move them to engage in social, political, and economic action.

If King's political propagandizing is intended to appeal to the emotions to move hearers to action, we must ask: what is an emotion? Many modern philosophers are working on this question. Most view each emotion as having multiple components. Consider an episode of intense fear due to the sudden appearance of the police while you are walking down the street. This fear has a *cognitive* component (to be afraid, you must believe the police are dangerous), a *physiological* component (your heart rate and blood pressure increase), a *phenomenological* component (a sense that you are undergoing something unpleasant), an *expressive* component (your upper eyelids raise and your jaw drops open), a *behavioral* component (you experience an overwhelming urge to react in some way—e.g., to flee), and a *mental* component (your attention focuses as a result of an adrenaline dump).[29]

---

[28] Ibid., 185.
[29] Andrea Scarantino and Ronald de Sousa, "Emotion," in *The Stanford Encyclopedia of Philosophy* (Summer 2021 Edition), Edward N. Zalta (ed.), https://plato.stanford.edu/archives/sum2021/entries/emotion/.

King himself seems uninterested in theorizing what an emotion is in a systematic way, unlike contemporary theorists of emotion. Contemporary theorists tend to focus on a limited set of questions: which components are essential to emotion; how we distinguish emotions from one another; how we distinguish emotions from things that are not emotions; and whether and how emotions motivate behavior. King is rightly concerned with different questions. He takes for granted that emotions motivate behavior—this is precisely why he is interested in them. The question he is interested in is: how do we arouse the emotions and use them to motivate nonviolent direct action—a specific kind of political behavior? This is perhaps why King does not always go into detail about the various components of the emotions or explain how they hang together. As we will see, he rarely discusses the physiological, expressive, or mental components of the emotions he is concerned with, tending instead to focus on the cognitive, phenomenological, and behavioral components. This is because he is primarily concerned with shaping the political environment within which the emotions arise and in deliberately evoking certain emotions in order to motivate people to transform an unjust structure through collective action.

This brings us back to propaganda. For King, propaganda—facts plus emotion—shapes the immediate political environment; it invokes specific emotions in readers and exhorts them to funnel those emotions into a particular type of action. According to King, propaganda itself is neither inherently good nor bad. Its value depends on the merit of the cause being urged.[30] When it is used for truth and justice, then it is morally good.[31] King argued that propaganda was a useful tool, especially when used for essentially democratic purposes—to lead people to work toward racial justice and

---

[30] King, "Propagandizing Christianity," 184–187.
[31] The two men's views on propaganda seem to differ only in the fact that King's views stemmed from his Christianity and Du Bois's did not.

to end racial oppression. King explicitly said that even propaganda from the government could be used to forward the inherently democratic aim of integration, writing, "when our government takes this matter seriously it will continue to use its constitutional authority to end the system of segregation. But it will go beyond this. Through the Department of Health, Welfare and Education it will carry on an active program of propaganda to promote the idea of integration."[32]

For King, integration and desegregation were the proper cornerstones of a society that was founded on the democratic principle that all men are created equal. This principle, expressed in the Declaration of Independence, is the true and "sacred recognition" of the inherent worth and dignity of the human personality.[33] According to this principle (which is both political and religious), there is no graded scale of worth, no divine right of one race that differs from the other,[34] for every individual was created in the image of God and has etched in her personality the "indelible stamp of the Creator."[35] In King's view, slavery and segregation stand in diametric opposition to this principle of the sacredness of human individuality;[36] these twin evils prevent our "democratic and Christian health from being realized."[37] As King sees it, Christians have a moral duty to promote racial integration and desegregation, and they can be urged to fulfill this moral duty through the sensible sermon as propaganda.

While others have noted that the Letter is a form of sermon, it has not previously been interpreted in relation to King's views on propaganda.[38] When we do read the Letter this way, we can

---

[32] Martin Luther King, Jr., "The Rising Tide of Racial Consciousness," in Carson et al. (eds.), *The Papers of Martin Luther King, Jr.*, Volume V, 499–508 at 507.
[33] Martin Luther King, Jr. "The Ethical Demands of Integration," 117–125 at 118.
[34] Ibid., 119.
[35] Ibid., 119.
[36] Ibid., 119.
[37] Martin Luther King, Jr., "Rising Tide," 507.
[38] A few others have suggested that the "Letter" was a form of sermon. See Wesley T. Mott, "The Rhetoric of Martin Luther King, Jr.: Letter from Birmingham Jail,"

see it as more than a rational argument for engaging in direct action to end racial segregation: it is a "sensible sermon" to the readers and, in King's terms, a piece of propaganda, designed to bring about real change in feeling and action. We can now see how King achieved a middle position between emotionalism and intellectualism. Through his Christian notion of truthful propaganda, King found a way to guide "the people's" emotions with the moral truth, avoiding both the irrationality of pure emotionalism and the cold-heartedness and detachment of pure intellectualism. By using the sermon as a form of truthful propaganda, he could bring together hearts and minds; he could move Black (and, to a lesser extent, white) Americans to join the movement for civil rights.

As a "sensible sermon," the Letter was written in language the masses could understand; it aimed to convey moral truth in a lively and vivacious way, not only convincing readers of the truth but also stirring their souls and rousing them to action. The Letter was King's way of infecting his readers with the very feelings—dignity, indignation, fear, faith, courage, and love—that drove his own political action. While he never stopped hoping that the "best" of his white readers would sympathize with him and the cause after reading the Letter, he wrote it in large part for his fellow Black citizens, especially the Black masses—those he believed were most likely to feel the same way as he did and to let those feelings drive them to political action.

King's views on propaganda were influenced by the thinkers he admired most, in particular Gandhi and W. E. B. DuBois.[39] Gandhi had explicitly argued that propaganda should first be used to rouse

---

Phylon, 36.4 (1975): 411–421, and Malinda Snow, "Martin Luther King's 'Letter from Birmingham Jail' as Pauline Epistle," *Quarterly Journal of Speech*, 71 (1985): 318–334, especially 327–332. One exception, that interprets the Letter as propaganda, is my own work, Krishnamurthy, "Democratic Propaganda," 305–336.

[39] King read only two books while he was imprisoned in Birmingham, one of which was Du Bois's classic, *Souls of Black Folks* (Rieder, *Gospel of Freedom*, 104).

"the people," and once it has taken its effect among the oppressed, it can be used on the oppressors. Then, if the propaganda was not effective among the oppressors, the oppressed masses, assembled by the propaganda, would have available to them other options for resistance, such as nonviolent coercion.

King was introduced to Gandhi's nonviolent method through CORE (Congress on Racial Equality). Early CORE activists such as Bayard Rustin and James Farmer were deeply influenced by Gandhi's disciple Krishnalal Shridharani, who had worked alongside Gandhi in the Indian independence movement. Early CORE writings on nonviolence drew heavily from Shridharani's *War without Violence* (1939),[40] which described the step-by-step procedures for organizing nonviolent resistance. Of the twelve steps needed to build a nonviolent movement, propaganda ("agitation") is the second.[41] It is deployed after direct negotiation with leaders of the opposition has failed, when one must "launch activities in the opposite direction" and "go to the people."[42] The goal of propaganda is to generate "cause consciousness" by starting a campaign of agitation among the people who are the most "directly affected" by the injustice at hand.[43] According to Shridharani, the use of multiple types of media—songs, catchy slogans, interviews, speeches, group meetings, debates, radio, and cinema—is vital to the "machine of mass propaganda."[44]

In Gandhi's thinking, propaganda has a dual function. It is used both to ensure the "contagious spreading" of the ideology of Swaraj (self-government) and to encourage "the people" to join the movement through appeal to their emotions.[45] Gandhi makes clear from

---

[40] Taylor Branch suggests that Shridharani's book was the "semiofficial bible of CORE" (Branch, *Parting the Waters*, 171).

[41] Krishnalal Shridharani, *War Without Violence* (New York: Harcourt and Brace, 1939), 10.

[42] Krishnalal Shridharani, *My India My America*, (New York: Duell, Sloan, and Pearce, 1941), 285.

[43] Shridharani, *My India My America*, 285; Shridharani, *War Without Violence*, 10.

[44] Shridharani, *My India My America*, 285.

[45] Shridharani, *War Without Violence*, 11.

the first page of his political treatise *Hind Swaraj* that the book itself is a form of truthful propaganda, written to expose the defects of the colonial system and to "arouse among the people certain desirable sentiments"—sentiments that would lead his Indian readers (and, later, sympathetic English readers) to support and join the Independence movement.[46] *Hind Swaraj* was first published in the *Indian Opinion*, a paper for the Indian masses whose mission was to deliver news about Indians in the colonies (especially South Africa) to the Indian public. Gandhi wrote for the masses, who were the most likely to rise up against the British. King did the same: remember that the Letter was first circulated in Black churches before it hit the mainstream media.

King's thinking combined Gandhi's ideas about political propaganda with those of W. E. B. Du Bois, who saw propaganda as an emotional appeal to win the reader's sympathy, which he defined as a fundamentally democratic sentiment designed to connect disparate people.[47] According to Melvin Rogers,[48] Jason Stanley,[49] and Robert Gooding-Williams,[50] Du Bois held that propaganda has a distinctively "democratic" character. According to Rogers, Stanley, and Gooding-Williams, Du Bois saw democratic propaganda as

---

[46] Mohandas Karamchand Gandhi, Anthony Parel (ed.), *"Hind Swaraj" and Other Writings* (Cambridge: Cambridge University Press, 2009), 13. Gandhi published *Hind Swaraj*, his treatise on Indian Independence, in English one year after he had published it in Gujarti in his Indian newspaper.

[47] Marcus Garvey did something similar, referring to UNIA's activity as "twenty-five years of propaganda activity"; he said, "the man who is to lead must be from the shock battalion, he must be able to, by his force and personality arrest the attention of men by shocking or daring deeds or expressions" (Marcus Garvey, "Universal Negro Improvement Association," in Robert A. Hill (ed.), *The Marcus Garvey and University Negro Improvement Association Papers, Vol. 1: 1826–August 1919*, lxxxviii, fn. 174 (Berkeley: University of California Press, 2023). Here, Garvey suggests that propaganda can be a way of shocking people's moral conscience and motivating political action.

[48] Melvin Lee Rogers, "The People, Rhetoric, and Affect: On the Political Force of Du Bois's *The Souls of Black Folk*," *American Political Science Review*, 106.1 (2012): 188–203.

[49] Jason Stanley, *How Propaganda Works* (Princeton, NJ: Princeton University Press, 2015).

[50] Robert Gooding-Williams, "Beauty as Propaganda: On the Political Aesthetics of W.E.B. Du Bois," The 2021 Dewey Lecture in Law and Philosophy, University of Chicago Law School, Chicago, IL, February 10, 2021.

expanding people's moral horizons, offering them a wider view of the world and their place in it. These scholars read *Souls of Black Folk* as this kind of democratic propaganda, arguing that Du Bois attempts to expand "the people's" view of themselves. In "Criteria of Negro Art," Du Bois explicitly states, "Art is propaganda and ever must be."[51] This is because artists produce and disseminate a *moral* vision, depicting "goodness in all its aspects of justice, honor and right . . . as the one true method of gaining sympathy and human interest."[52]

Like Gandhi, and like King after him, Du Bois sought to reach both the oppressor and the oppressed. Although, as Rogers has argued, Du Bois hoped to transform white America's moral and political sensibilities through his writing, expanding white people's sense of "the people" to include a multiracial coalition of individual citizens, Du Bois also knew that propaganda or art promoting justice for Black Americans was unlikely to be of much interest to white readers. According to Du Bois, most white readers preferred "literary and pictorial racial prejudgment which deliberately distorts Truth and Justice, as far as colored races are concerned."[53] Du Bois knew that the sort of propaganda that he hoped to write would be of greater interest to Black Americans, and he wrote at least in part, if not primarily, for them.

For Du Bois, art is an especially potent form of propaganda, for it combines aesthetics and politics, using truth as the "one true method of gaining sympathy and human interest."[54] Du Bois's own work exemplified the power of this combination of aesthetics and politics, for his literary works are also always powerful political statements. As Robert Gooding-Williams argues, the *Souls of Black Folk* is "both a call to arms and an aesthetic event, at once

---

[51] Du Bois, "Criteria of Negro Art," 26. Available at: http://www.webdubois.org/dbCriteriaNArt.html.
[52] Ibid., 26.
[53] Ibid., 26.
[54] Ibid., 26.

a manifesto and electrifying sound and light—thus, a book that demands to be read equally as political argument and literary art."[55] Du Bois's work was successful propaganda precisely because of this blend of art and truth, emotion and action, aesthetics and politics. As Lawrie Balfour notes, "Du Bois's flights of imagination [in his novel *Darkwater*] reveal a conviction that political ideas may exceed the limits of analytical expression and that they must be advanced in a way that produces receptivity in the men and women to whom they are directed."[56] In other words, for art to successfully convey political ideas and bring about political change, it must ignite emotion in its readers.

King's propaganda campaign for the Civil Rights Movement drew upon not only Gandhi and Du Bois's ideas about propaganda and the creation of sympathy but also those of Leo Tolstoy. As one writer notes, "Martin Luther King looked to Tolstoy as a kind of moral hero, a man in touch with the inner workings of the spirit."[57] Tolstoy famously claimed that art had the power to infect others with feelings previously experienced by the artist: art is, he said, a human activity where "one man consciously, by means of certain external signs, hands on to others feelings he has lived through, and ... other people are infected by these feelings and also experience them."[58] Because of its power to evoke sympathy among disparate people, Tolstoy believed, art is essential to social progress. It is "a means of union among men, joining them together in the same feelings, and indispensable for the life and progress toward the well-being of individuals and of humanity."[59]

---

[55] Robert Gooding-Williams, "Du Bois, Politics, Aesthetics: An Introduction," *Public Culture*, 17 (Spring 2005): 203–215 at 204.

[56] Lawrie Balfour, "Darkwater's Democratic Vision," *Political Theory*, 38.4 (2010): 537–563 at 541.

[57] Jay Parini, "There's More to Tolstoy than War and Peace," *The Guardian*, January 6, 2010. Available at: https://www.theguardian.com/books/booksblog/2010/jan/06/more-to-tolstoy-war-peace.

[58] Leo Tolstoy, *What Is Art?* (New York: Thomas Crowell & Co. Publishers, 1899), 42.

[59] Ibid., 43.

While King supported and engaged in a variety of art forms (musical, pictorial, and theatrical) as part of his work in the movement, none was more important to him than literary art—textual art, in the form of oratory, letters, and essays. Influenced by his time in the church, King came to believe with Tolstoy that literary art, especially oratory and writing, were the best ways of stimulating sympathy—of spreading emotions to others. For King, the sermon was the cornerstone of his motivational apparatus.

King identified with the calling and practice of preaching, reporting, "I am fundamentally a clergyman, a Baptist preacher. This is my being."[60] As Andrew Young noted, "The only way Martin could have answered [his critics] was in writing. But if he had been given a chance to go preach it [the Letter] to them, he probably would have done that."[61] King always preached sermons; even his political speeches and writings were sermons. King preferred sermons, in part, because he was a skilled sermonizer. He was charismatic. He knew how to navigate a diverse audience. This ability was, in many respects, a collective production. King grew up listening to sermons. He absorbed techniques and learned how to navigate the audience from watching his father at Ebenezer Baptist Church. His father was an old-school preacher who used cadence and gesture to the communicate emotive qualities of his message. King used all the techniques he heard and saw.[62]

King honed these skills at Morehouse University, the renowned historically Black institution where he did his undergraduate studies. After this, he entered the world of white education, attending Crozer Theological Seminary and Boston University Divinity School, where he earned a doctorate in systemic theology. Here, he formally learned the foundations of a good sermon—song,

---

[60] Quoted in Maurice O. Wallace, *King's Vibrato: Modernism, Blackness, and the Sonic Life of Martin Luther King, Jr.* (Durham, NC: Duke University Press, 2022), 111.
[61] Rieder, *Gospel of Freedom*, xix.
[62] Jonathan Rieder, *The Word of the Lord Is Upon Me: The Righteous Performance of Martin Luther King, Jr.* (Cambridge, MA: Belknap, 2008), 11.

argument, homily, citation, inflection, philosophy, rhythm, examples, authors, theology, and ideas. He developed a knack for integrating commonly quoted passages of scripture, formulaic phrases, and even lyrics from hymns and Black spirituals into his sermons.[63] As Keith D. Miller has shown, the Letter itself borrowed ideas, themes, and arguments from Henry Fosdick, H. H. Crane, Harris Wofford, George Kelsey, and Howard Thurman—"familiar influences of the black folk pulpit."[64] All of these tactics made King's sermon accessible to a broad audience, and especially his Black audience.

As I have mentioned, King ultimately preferred the sermon because it could both convey a rational, analytical moral message and carry an emotional appeal. The sermon is King's moral argument—conceptual and justificatory—rendered to persuade and move his audience by appealing to both their hearts and their minds. The sermon does this work largely because of its delivery—its cadence, rhythm, and tone. As Hortense Spillers argues, it is not only about the analysis that King offers; it is also about "the word as King delivers it."[65] King's delivery was more about euphony, she writes, than gesture.[66]

King's delivery of the sermon was inspired by the music of the Black religious tradition, which was often used to set the stage for the sermon—to create a heightened sense of expectation in the listener so that maximum attention is corralled for the upcoming sermon. He himself began singing at the age of six at church groups and conventions, beside his organ-playing mother, Alberta King. He grew up hearing people such as Mahalia Jackson—a friend of his father's—sing at Ebenezer Baptist Church.[67] This music spoke

---

[63] Keith D. Miller, *Voice of Deliverance* (Athens: University of Georgie Press, 2008), ch. 5.
[64] Miller, *Voice of Deliverance*, 162; Rieder, *The World of the Lord*, 8–9.
[65] Spillers, "Martin Luther King and the Style of the Black Sermon," 15.
[66] Ibid., xx.
[67] Ibid., 12.

to a broad audience, but especially to the experiences of the Black masses, and, as Wyatt T. Walker wrote, to "their hearts and souls."[68] Spillers suggests that Black religious music helped the intellectuals and the masses to not only understand the moral message of King's sermons but to feel together.[69]

Black freedom songs are made of clever phrases that can be used to ignite a campaign, but for King they were more than this. They were also invocations of the richness of Black history, inherited from Black ancestors who had the stamina and moral fiber to free themselves from racial oppression.[70] The Black freedom songs are adaptations of the sorrow songs, the shouts for joy, and the battle hymns sung by the enslaved. King wrote that the mere words of these songs, like "Woke Up This Morning with My Mind Stayed on Freedom," inspire people; they need no music to convince. King sought to channel the energy of Black freedom songs into the delivery of his sermons.[71]

While King believed that in his sermons, the simple words and sonorous rhythms of Black freedom songs could inspire the masses, he also knew that singing the songs had a special power to encourage hope and determination, for those who sing together as they march are bound together by collective courage. King wrote in Birmingham that it is through music that "the Negro is able to dip down into wells of a deeply pessimistic situation and danger-fraught circumstances and to bring forth a marvelous, sparkling, fluid optimism. He knows it is still dark in his world, but somehow, he finds a ray of light."[72] King drew inspiration for his views about the importance of music from the most important women in his life: his wife, Coretta Scott King, and his mother, Alberta King.

---

[68] Wyatt T. Walker, "Introduction," in Birmingham, Alabama, 1963, Mass Meeting, Album no. FD5487 Folkway Records, Broadway, New York. Available at: https://www.crmvet.org/crmpics/albums/63_bham_liner.pdf.
[69] Spillers, "Martin Luther King and the Style of the Black Sermon," 27.
[70] King, *Autobiography*, 177–178.
[71] King, *Autobiography*, 177.
[72] Ibid., 178.

Both women believed in the power of song. They often performed Freedom Songs together, at meetings, conventions, rallies, marches, and protests. This music played a crucial role in inspiring, mobilizing, and sustaining the movement.

Wyatt T. Walker explained the importance of music to mass meetings, which moved from community to community to provide information about the campaigns, encourage support, and draw people into the movement. He wrote:

> It is important to note that on the very day that demonstrations were launched in Birmingham, the city bus system went on strike. Without public transportation, it was thought that the infant movement was doomed. Yet for thirty nine nights, without interruption, the rallies were held in support of one of the most significant struggles in the South. A great deal of the stimulus for the sustained rallies was the quality of the music that made the mass meetings attractive in spite of the transportation dilemma.

Even when they were tired or overworked, music drew people to the rallies, mass meetings, and marches. It eased their souls and restored their energy. Through music, the people were able to pull themselves out of exhaustion, pessimism, and fear and bring forth a bold and energetic faith that sustained their activity in the movement.

Many of the key figures of the movement were skilled singers, including Andrew Young, Dorothy Cotton, James Bevel, Fred Shuttlesworth, and Ralph Abernathy. During the Albany movement, King said that "the freedom songs are playing a strong and vital role in our struggle."[73] Quoting King, Robert Shelton reported in the *New York Times* that these songs "give the people new courage

---

[73] Robert Shelton, "Songs a Weapon in Rights Battle," *New York Times*, August 20, 1962, p. 1

and a sense of unity. I think they keep alive a faith, a radiant hope, in the future, particularly in our most trying hours."[74]

The themes, rhythms, and phrases of the freedom songs run through King's sermons and oral addresses. King brought his musical sensibilities to the platform and to all of his oral sermons, and in turn to the Letter, one of King's most eloquent utterances.[75] Indeed, King's written style is only a slightly more formalized version of his platform style.[76] The Letter's rational and intellectual appeal is carefully constructed: it is an inductive argument for nonviolent direct action, a multi-premise refutation of the arguments against this action, structured as a box-within-a-box.[77] It skillfully interlaces this argument with themes from the sermons of American pastors Harry Fosdick and H. H. Crane, as well as from speeches by Harris Wofford and George Kelsey (whom he had known since his days at Morehouse).[78] The Letter invokes multiple moral authorities, with philosophers such as Paul Tillich, Reinhold Niebuhr, and Martin Buber held up alongside heroes of the movement, such as James Meredith and the Black women who "decided not to ride segregated buses."[79] It moves from appealing to the sacred notion of time to rich biblical images and Pauline allusions, all while drawing out King's own personal story of suffering.

The Letter balances this intellectual appeal with its emotional appeal, much of it achieved through rhythm and cadence working together to create an emotional effect. He develops rhythm through repetition, recurrent rhetorical questions, and formalized dialogue and narrative. Mott argues that "the raw emotional power of King's Letter arises simply from the increasing tempo and from the relentless force of repetition and parallelism. The first few paragraphs,

---

[74] Ibid, 1
[75] Mott, "The Rhetoric of Martin Luther King, Jr.," 412.
[76] Ibid., 412.
[77] Miller, *Voice of Deliverance*, 167.
[78] Ibid.
[79] WWCW, 110.

which establish the speaker's personality and the text, contain relatively short sentences presented matter-of-factly; but as it proceeds, the Letter accelerates a strong rhythm, the sentences become longer in key emotional passages."[80] For example, King repeats the phrase "when you," and the sentences that follow that introductory phrase slowly become longer and longer ("when you have seen vicious mobs" and "hate-filled policemen" and "twenty million Negro brothers smothering in an airtight cage"; "when you seek to explain to your six-year-old daughter why she can't go to the public amusement park"; "when you are humiliated day in and day out"), ratcheting up the emotion as each successive clause builds higher. As Rieder writes, in this moment, the Letter reaches an emotional height, and "[t]he poise and patience have vanished in a flood of emotion."[81] Through this rhythmic building, King communicates what he fears (violence) and suffers (indignities) as a Black man in the United States, as well as the sense of indignation he feels as a result of these experiences. It is perhaps one of the most memorable and moving passages of the Letter.

Tonality, timbre, cadence, and rhythm were techniques that King polished during his time at Crozer and Boston University. Maurice O. Wallace argues that "King's sermonic voice boasts a musical quality."[82] As Richard Lischer writes, King's voice "is a beautiful voice . . . with breathtaking range"; his voice moves from "husky reflection" to the "peaks of ecstasy. Like a good singer, he will open his mouth wide to hit the notes but will not reach or strain. His voice never breaks."[83] King's voice was emotive, full throated and pitched to the habits of Black hearing.[84] King preached with an intent to sound the Word, not merely speak it.

---

[80] Mott, "The Rhetoric of Martin Luther King, Jr.," 414.
[81] Rieder, *Gospel of Freedom*, 60.
[82] Wallace, *King's Vibrato*.
[83] Quoted in ibid., p. 10. See Richard Lischer, *The Preacher King: Martin Luther King, Jr. and the Word That Moved America* (New York: Oxford University Press, 1995), 133.
[84] Wallace, *King's Vibrato*, 107.

For those who had heard King speak, especially his sermons at mass meetings, it would have been almost impossible to not hear King's voice—what Maurice O. Wallace refers to as his "vibrato"—ringing throughout the Letter. King's vibrato—the trembling, throbbing quality of his voice—was deeply inspired by the organ playing of his mother Alberta. The vibrato sound is clearly heard in all of King's preaching—his musical speech making—and it also inflects the text, creating its own emotional impact. Returning to that famous passage, the reader can almost hear King repeatedly sing-say, in his baritone, "when you...."

King supported and engaged in a variety of art forms and propaganda as part of his work in the movement, including musical, pictorial, theatrical, literary, and textual art, in the form of oratory, letters, and essays. However, the sermon, which included elements of many of these art forms, was his preferred form of propaganda. He was a skilled orator who hoped to bring his message to his existing Black audience and beyond. The rhythm that King established in the Letter—through tone, cadence, and vibrato—is all-important to conveying the insurgent Black emotions—fear, dignity, indignation, courage, faith, and love—that are key to King's emotional appeal. He hoped the souls of the Black folk who read it would be moved by this rhythm and that they would join him on the streets.

PART 2
EMOTIONS

4
Fear and Fearlessness

For King, fear was the emotion that troubled the human personality more than any other.[1] In the Letter, King famously writes that Black Americans in particular "are plagued with inner fears."[2] They are "harried by day and haunted by night" by the fact that they are Black in America, "living constantly at tiptoe stance, never quite knowing what to expect next."[3] In his view, it was this (very rational!) fear that stood in the way of Black self-reliance and political action. According to King, fear takes a variety of forms—personal, social, and even existential—and all of these types of fear are shaped and intensified by the history, social structures, culture, and politics of the world we live in.[4]

An example of personal fear is the fear of ourselves; self-fear can produce feelings of insecurity, lack of self-confidence, and a sense of personal failure—what King, following other psychologists of the time, calls an "inferiority complex."[5] According to King, because of their historical circumstances, Black people sometimes

---

[1] Martin Luther King, Jr., "The Mastery of Fear, Sermon Notes," in Carson et al. (eds.), *The Papers of Martin Luther King, Jr.*, Volume VI, 317–318 at 318.

[2] WWCW, 93.

[3] Ibid., 93.

[4] For a discussion of King's later views on fear, especially on the link between fear, manhood, and militarism (and violence), see Shatema Threadcraft and Brandon M. Terry, "Gender Trouble: Manhood, Inclusion, and Justice," in Shelby and Terry (eds.), *To Shape a New World*, 137–204. For a discussion of white fear, see Brandon M. Terry, "Requiem for a Dream: The Problem-Space of Black Power," in *To Shape a New World*, 290–324.

[5] Martin Luther King, Jr., "Draft of Chapter XIV, 'The Mastery of Fear or Antidotes for Fear,'" in Carson et al. (eds.), *The Papers of Martin Luther King, Jr.*, Volume VI, 535–545 at 535. Available at: https://kinginstitute.stanford.edu/king-papers/documents/draft-chapter-xiv-mastery-fear-or-antidotes-fear#:~:text = We%20can%20master%20fear%20not,affirmation%20of%20one%27s%20essential%20nature.

experience inferiority complexes. Living under the conditions of slavery created self-fear in some Black Americans, who lost faith in themselves, and who perhaps felt that they were less than human because white society forcefully reiterated that message—through law and practice—every day.[6] Of course, not every Black American had a sense of self-fear. Despite the messages sent by white America, King notes that his own father and mother maintained a sense of their own humanity and dignity. The point perhaps—as Michele Moody-Adams has articulated and which we will revisit in the next chapter—is that maintaining this sense of oneself can be very difficult under unjust circumstances,[7] leaving room for self-fear to arise. When it does, says King, self-fear can block our latent creative energy, because we are occupied by trying to be someone we are not.[8] Here, King builds on his earlier criticisms of the Black middle class and their racial uplift ideology: in his view, it is self-fear that is leading them to embrace white (rather than Black) values and standards.

Social fears come from living under specific political and economic institutions and policies. As an example of a social fear, King discusses the economic fear caused by "living in a competitive society,"[9] which (following the German American psychoanalyst Karen Horney) King sees as the cause of most of today's psychological problems. This fear affects everyone, at all income levels, even "Captains of industry," who are fearful of the possible failure of their business and the uncertainty of the stock market.[10]

---

[6] Martin Luther King, Jr., "The Rising Tide of Racial Consciousness," in Carson et al. (eds.), *The Papers of Martin Luther King, Jr.*, Volume V, 499–508 at 500.

[7] Michele Moody-Adams, "Race, Class and the Social Construction of Self-Respect," *The Philosophical Forum*, 24.1–3 (1992–1993): 251–266.

[8] Martin Luther King, Jr., "Overcoming an Inferiority Complex," in Carson et al. (eds.), *The Papers of Martin Luther King, Jr.*, Volume VI, 303–316 at 307. Available at: https://kinginstitute.stanford.edu/king-papers/documents/overcoming-inferiority-complex-sermon-delivered-dexter-avenue-baptist-church#:~:text = Now%20it%20seems%20to%20me,my%20inherited%20abilities%20and%20handicaps.

[9] King, "Draft of Chapter XIV, 'The Mastery of Fear or Antidotes for Fear,'" 536.

[10] Ibid., 536.

The fear is strongest, though, for workers—"the laboring men and women whose sweat and skills keep the wheels of industry rolling"[11]—who must worry about unemployment, automation, and the collapse of their industry.[12] Many Black Americans were already among the most vulnerable of workers—the lowest paid and with the least job security. As mentioned earlier, King believed that discrimination and lack of opportunities for education worked together to confine Black Americans to unskilled and semi-skilled jobs—exactly the types of jobs in which human workers are most likely to be replaced by technology. When this happened, Black employees had little hope of accessing retraining, and many had very little economic margin that would allow them to weather periods of unemployment; Black employees were hired at pay below a living standard, with pay rates for Black employees being especially low in the American South.[13] As King notes, because of these economic conditions, Black people of the middle and working class harbored the deep and reasonable fear that it would be impossible for them to build financial security for themselves and their families.

The third type of fear that King addressed is existential (religious or ontological) fear. In the 1960s, the world had witnessed the devastating power of the atomic bomb, and nuclear proliferation was well underway. People worried about death, nonbeing, and racial annihilation,[14] as well as the tense global political climate, in which a small diplomatic error could result in nuclear warfare. According to King, material attempts to alleviate these existential fears (such as building fallout shelters) only increased the fear, since existential

---

[11] Martin Luther King, Jr. "Draft of Chapter III: 'On Being a Good Neighbor,'" in Carson et al. (eds.), *The Papers of Martin Luther King, Jr.*, Volume VI, 78–486 at 480. Available at: https://kinginstitute.stanford.edu/king-papers/documents/draft-chapter-iii-being-good-neighbor.
[12] King, "Draft of Chapter XIV, 'The Mastery of Fear or Antidotes for Fear,'" 536.
[13] WWCW, 13.
[14] He only uses the phrase "racial annihilation" in the final draft of "Antidotes to Fear," which appears in STL.

fears cannot be erased through material solutions (fallout shelters would in fact be of little use in the event of an atomic bomb).

The form of existential fear that King is most concerned with is the fear of suffering. In the 1960s, during the Cold War, the existential fear of nuclear war and the suffering and death it would bring was shared by all Americans. But Black Americans had a unique existential fear: the fear of white Americans and the suffering they could cause for Black people who sought to desegregate the South.[15] The fear of white backlash could paralyze potential Black activists, who sometimes strategically remained silent about desegregation. This, King pointed out, helped to reinforce white people's mistaken view that there was no need for change—that most Black people were perfectly happy with the status quo.

Of course, as King says, in fact, Black people never like racial segregation; sometimes, they are just "afraid to say it."[16] Taking a stand against segregation is, for Black people, "always costly and never altogether comfortable"; it always runs the risk of "walking through the valley of the shadow of suffering" in some form, whether by "losing a job, or having a six-year-old daughter ask, 'Daddy, why do you have to go to jail so much,'"[17] or even physical suffering or death—being beaten or lynched or having your house bombed. King knows that Black Americans would suffer economic reprisals, boycotts, threats, and intimidation for visibly working toward desegregation. As Justin Rose notes, King himself "had been stabbed and brutally assaulted, his house has been bombed several times, and he was subject to death threats on a daily basis."[18]

---

[15] Martin Luther King, Jr., "Mastering Our Fears," in Carson et al. (eds.), *The Papers of Martin Luther King, Jr.*, Volume VI, 319–321 at 319. See also Martin Luther King, Jr., "The Mastery of Fear, Sermon Outlines," in Carson et al. (eds.), *The Papers of Martin Luther King, Jr.*, Volume VI, 318–319. Available at: https://kinginstitute.stanford.edu/king-papers/documents/mastery-fear.

[16] Martin Luther King, Jr., "A Realistic Look at Race Relations," given at NAACP Legal Defense and Educational Fund banquet at New York's Waldorf-Astoria Hotel, May 1956, p. 7.

[17] STL, 19.

[18] Rose, *The Drum Major Instinct*, 63.

Black Americans' fear of taking a stand against segregation was (and is) always present. Indeed, the fear of white backlash is particularly paralyzing because it combines all three types of fear: personal fear, social fear, and the existential fear of suffering. In his discussion of the fear of white backlash, King draws on the ideas of Howard Thurman, whose book *Jesus Disinherited* accompanied him on many of his journeys.[19] Thurman's influence is typically overlooked, but his work is central to understanding King's views on fear.

Thurman begins his second chapter, "Fear," by noting how Black people were "hounded by day and harrowed by night" by fear—phrasing that King echoes in the Letter. Thurman attributes this peculiarly Black fear to a sense of "isolation and helplessness" in the face of violence. As Thurman notes, there is something special about white violence against Black people: "it is violence that is devoid of the element of contest."[20] When two men are equally matched, violence is terrible, but each has a fair chance. When power—and the instruments of violence—belong to only one of the two combatants, the other person has no protection or recourse from violence; the fear that results from this helplessness is deeply terrifying.[21] In American society, white people have unarguable and enormous advantages over Black people, and Black people are highly aware of this disadvantage. They know they cannot fight back effectively to protect themselves without significant backlash, nor can they demand protection from a white supremacist society.

According to Thurman, it is not fear of death or physical suffering that is doing most of the work here: "It is the deep humiliation arising from dying without a benefit of cause or purpose.... It is merely being killed or being beaten in utter wrath or indifferent sadism without the dignity of being on the receiving end of a

---

[19] Vincent Harding, "Foreword" in Howard Thurman, *Jesus and the Disinherited* (Boston: Beacon Press, 1996), xii.
[20] Thurman, *Jesus and the Disinherited*, 27.
[21] Ibid., 27.

premeditated act."[22] In the Jim Crow South, Black people lived with the day-to-day fear that any small insult, vague frustration, or whim could trigger violence. Black fear comes from whites' ability to arbitrarily exert white power and violence against Black people at any moment. This experience, Thurman argues, attacks Black men and women's sense of self-respect and personal dignity.

As Corey Robins sees it, for King, fear is the apprehension of harm or the belief that something is harmful, where harm is understood as the deprivation of some good to the individual. Those who are empowered can arouse fear simply by threatening an individual's enjoyment of that good. As King shows us, Black fear results from quotidian repressions. Whites have a large catalog of fears by which they rule over Black Americans:

> when you have seen vicious mobs lynch your mothers and fathers at will and drown your sisters and brothers at whim; when you have seen hate-filled policemen curse, kick, brutalize, and even kill your black brothers and sisters with impunity ... when you are humiliated day in and day out by nagging signs reading "white" men and "colored"; when your first name becomes "n*****" and your middle name becomes "boy" (however old you are) and your last name becomes "John," and when your wife and mother are never given the respected title of "Mrs."

King makes clear that these small acts—even the mere threat of them—"hover quietly" over the relationship between white and Black Americans, subtly influencing everyday conduct by inducing fear without requiring much in the way of physical intimidation.[23]

As Robins explains, generating fear in this way across time and space requires a specific political ideology and culture and a particular set of laws and policies. It also requires the cooperation of the

---

[22] Ibid., 28.
[23] Ibid., 19.

entire society: elites and collaborators actively cause fear through their actions, and bystanders passively accept the behavior, paving the path for the elites and their collaborators to act. This is why Robins argues that, for King, fear of white backlash is not just a private experience but is also something more public.[24] Black fear is an emotion that takes place within and is structured by a specific political environment, Jim Crow, and each element of Black fear is a symptom of the American experience under legalized racial segregation.

Like Thurman, King is concerned with the harm to personal dignity that arises from being "harried by day and haunted by night" and "not knowing what to expect next."[25] He builds on Thurman's discussion of fear, suggesting that the everyday fear Black Americans experienced was magnified many times over when they were actively working to disarm white power through nonviolent resistance. This is in part because these acts of resistance bring to the surface the inequality in power articulated by Thurman. In cases of white backlash, white power is expressed not just through individual acts of retribution (whether premeditated or impulsive) but also through the actions of the state—a Goliath which holds *all* the power in any contest. The actions of the state are not merely a counter-response to Black resistance, as with individual actions; they are a resounding statement that "Black Lives Don't Matter." When the state acts to suppress Black civil rights and Black demonstrations for those civil rights, it asserts that Black lives are not of equal value. As Frederick Douglass suggests, the state's expression of this belief is a greater threat to Black dignity than individual expressions of it could ever be. The broader political environment is not only created and reinforced by individuals (elites, collaborators, bystanders, and victims)

---

[24] Corey Robins, *Fear: The History of a Political Idea* (Oxford: Oxford University Press, 2004), 19.
[25] WWCW, 92.

but is coercively imposed through the potentially lethal force of the state.

As King sees it, the fear of the "white backlash" to Black resistance combines all aspects of fear: personal, social, and existential. Black fear is thus especially overwhelming, pervading entire lives, leaving people "psychologically wrecked and spiritually dejected."[26] Because "it drains one's energy and depletes one's resources," it leaves some utterly exhausted, without the energy to fight, especially against the overwhelming power of the state.[27] Like all the fears, it can lead to what King calls "stand-stillism" and "do-nothingism."[28]

Of course, it is neither possible nor desirable to get rid of all fear. Some fears are adaptive, protecting us; King calls these "normal" fears. These are necessary and constructive; only "abnormal" fears are destructive. Drawing on the American pastor Harry Emerson Fosdick, King saw fear as an "indispensable elemen[t] of the human make-up," a result of our evolutionary past[29]— the "elemental alarm system"[30] that warns us of danger. King uses an example from Freud, pointing out that "a person tramping through the heart of an African jungle . . . should quite properly be afraid of snakes."[31] To avoid the real danger that snakes pose, we cultivate behaviors that will reduce our risk.[32] Without this kind of fear,

---

[26] King, "Draft of Chapter XIV, 'The Mastery of Fear or Antidotes for Fear,'" 535–545 at 536. Available at: https://kinginstitute.stanford.edu/king-papers/documents/draft-chapter-xiv-mastery-fear-or-antidotes-fear.

[27] King, "The Rising Tide of Racial Consciousness," 536. According to King, in the face of fear, some people flee to a world of illusion and fantasy, where they imagine they are doing the things they are afraid to do (or cannot do) in the real world—a dangerous method of getting away from fear. See King, "Overcoming an Inferiority Complex," 305.

[28] Martin Luther King, Jr., "A Realistic Look at the Question of Progress in the Area of Race Relations," in Carson et al. (eds.), *The Papers of Martin Luther King, Jr.*, Volume IV, 167–179 at 175. Available at: https://kinginstitute.stanford.edu/king-papers/docume nts/realistic-look-question-progress-area-race-relations-address-delivered-st.

[29] Fosdick, *On Being a Real Person* (New York: Harper & Brothers, 1943), 110.

[30] Harry Emerson Fosdick, "Conquest of Fear," in his *The Hope of the World* (New York: Harpers, 1933), 59–68 at 59.

[31] King, "Draft of Chapter XIV, 'The Mastery of Fear or Antidotes for Fear,'" 535–545.

[32] Thurman, *Jesus and the Disinherited*, 30.

humans would not have survived the primitive world. Following Freud, King says that fears become normal or abnormal through context: it is normal to fear snakes in the jungle, but "if a person suddenly begins to fear that snakes are under the carpet of his city apartment, then his fear is abnormal, neurotic."[33] King draws out this distinction between "normal" and "abnormal" fears, which he calls "personal anxieties."[34] Unlike personal anxieties (which King says must be addressed through psychiatry), normal fear "can be faced, analyzed, attacked and endured," because "unlike anxiety, [fear] has a definite object" in the material world.[35]

This distinction between normal fear and personal anxiety is important for King. He wishes to establish that Black fear is legitimate and rational, unlike the white fear that drives the "whole system of racial segregation," which "is buttressed by a series of irrational fears—fear of losing a preferred economic position, fear of losing social status, fear of intermarriage, fear of adjusting to a new situation."[36] King believes that "all race prejudice is a product of fear that is usually groundless."[37] Groundless fear—fear disconnected from reality—cannot be a normal and productive fear. Yet numerous white people spend sleepless nights and haggard days attempting to fight these corroding fears.[38] According to King, these attempts to fight irrational personal anxieties brings for white people "deeper and more pathological fears, fears that leave the victims inflicted with strange psychoses and peculiar cases of paranoia."[39] Like all

---

[33] King, "Draft of Chapter XIV, 'The Mastery of Fear or Antidotes for Fear,'" 537. As Myisha Cherry argues, normal fear represents the world accurately. Myisha Cherry, *The Case for Rage* (Oxford: Oxford University Press, 2021), 38.

[34] This distinction between fear and personal anxiety appears in Martin Luther King, Jr., "Draft of Chapter XIV, 'The Mastery of Fear or Antidotes for Fear,'" 537. The distinction does not appear in earlier drafts of the chapter (Martin Luther King, Jr., "Mastering Our Fears," in Carson et al. (eds.), *The Papers of Martin Luther King, Jr.*, Volume VI, 319–321) or later drafts ("Antidotes to Fear" in STL, 119–132) versions of the speech.

[35] King, "Draft of Chapter XIV, 'The Mastery of Fear,'", 538–539.

[36] Ibid., 540–541.

[37] Martin Luther King, Jr., *Stride Toward Freedom: The Montgomery Story* (Boston: Beacon Press, 1958), 200.

[38] King, "Draft of Chapter XIV, 'The Mastery of Fear,'" 541.

[39] Ibid., 541.

personal anxieties, this is best treated with psychiatric help, but as we will see later (Chapter 6), King also believes that loving action carried out with goodwill by Black Americans can help some white people overcome some of their fearful prejudice.[40]

According to Martha Nussbaum, fear is something that should be overcome and transitioned out of, since, in her view, fear is "intensely narcissistic"—it pushes out all thoughts of other people.[41] She takes a developmental approach to fear and the selfishness it produces. Infants, she says, are primarily concerned with ensuring that their basic needs are met, and through expressions of fear, infants aim to control the humans around them to help meet these needs. Just as a fearful infant focuses on her own needs, so do fearful adults, whose fear drives away concerns for others. For example, she writes, "soldiers describe their experience of fear in combat as involving a vivid inward focus on their whole body, which becomes their whole world."[42] For her, "fear is the emotion of an absolute monarch, who cares about nothing and nobody else," and the monarch can only be satisfied by instrumentalizing others to get what he needs to overcome his fear.[43] Nussbaum sees fear as largely immoral, because it leads us to ignore the concerns of others.

Nussbaum thinks that fear is also impractical because it can lead to "retributive anger"—an objectionable form of anger that seeks payback for perceived wrongdoing. Following Lucretius, she believes that retributive anger can arise out of fear of our own human vulnerabilities,[44] such as "infantile helplessness" and "its adult cousin the fear of death."[45] When we are fearful that our needs are being neglected by others—and, relatedly, when we are fearful of our own death—we can become angry at other people,

---

[40] Ibid., 541.
[41] Martha Nussbaum, *The Monarchy of Fear: A Philosopher Looks at Our Political Crisis* (New York: Simon & Schuster, 2018), 29.
[42] Ibid., 29.
[43] Ibid., 30.
[44] Ibid., 68.
[45] Ibid., 68.

driving us to seek retribution from them. Nussbaum argues that anger of this sort is not only immoral but can and often does lead to violence—which in turn produces more fear, which brings about more violence, ad infinitum.

While King likely shares Nussbaum's views of white fear, he sees Black fear (especially fear of white violence) as a legitimate and rational response to the personal, social, and existential conditions under which Black Americans live. In the face of white supremacy, only a fool would be unafraid. Black fear has a real object—white power, as expressed in individual and state actions—and being fearful of it is rational. While King sees this rational Black fear as a barrier to political action, King follows Fosdick and departs from Nussbaum in his belief that fear can be turned into something productive; our goal ought not be to eliminate fear altogether, he says, but "to harness it" and "master it."[46]

King believes that fear can lead us in a positive direction, pushing us to come up with creative solutions to the real problems we face. Invention, he suggests, often comes from the motivation to escape something we dread: the fear of darkness led to the invention of electricity; the fear of pain led to the development of medicines; and the fear of ignorance led to the creation of great institutions of learning.[47] In short, "normal fear motivates us to improve our individual and collective welfare; abnormal fear . . . constantly poisons and distorts our inner lives."[48] We need to fear what is truly to be feared in order to be motivated to overcome it, but we must channel our fear in ways that are constructive and that promote the common good. Ultimately, King agrees with Fosdick's assertion that fear can be given "intelligent implementation."[49] Unlike Nussbaum, King does not think that fear is inherently narcissistic;

---

[46] King, "The Mastery of Fear, Sermon Notes," 320. Here, King is again following Fosdick, "Conquest of Fear," 60.
[47] King, "Draft of Chapter XIV, 'The Mastery of Fear,'", 537.
[48] Ibid., 538.
[49] Fosdick, *On Being a Real Person*, 110.

because of their shared history and their social position within the system of racial segregation, Black Americans share their (well-grounded) fear of white violence and retaliation. King believes that this shared fear can bring Black Americans together in action to ensure racial justice—an action whose benefits are collective, not individual. King does not think that fear necessarily devolves into Nussbaum's retributive anger but that, when channeled through love, fear can take a useful shape.

As I will show in Chapter 5, to appropriately channel Black Americans' legitimate fear, King turns to the idea of righteous indignation. According to King, racial progress can be made by transforming the exhaustion caused by fear and the "do-nothingism" it feeds into something productive. The antidote to this exhaustion is righteous indignation. In addition, the endless exhaustion and pain of fear can itself create its own antidote: King writes that "*as a result of their tiredness* they decided to rise up and protest.... As a result of their rising up colored peoples of the world have broken aloose from colonialism and imperialism"[50] [emphasis added]. This is what was taking place in the U.S. civil rights movement. The fear and exhaustion resulting from the racist status quo began to outweigh the fear of white violence. As King said of the Montgomery bus boycott,

> there comes a time, my friends, when people get tired of being plunged across the abyss of humiliation, where they experience the bleakness of nagging despair. There comes a time when people get tired of being pushed out of the glittering sunlight of life's July and left standing amid the piercing chill of an alpine November.... We are here, we are here this evening because we're tired now.[51]

---

[50] King, "A Realistic Look at the Question of Progress in the Area of Race Relations," 175–176.
[51] Martin Luther King, Jr., "Montgomery Bus Boycott," in Josh Gottheimer (ed.), *Ripples of Hope: Great American Civil Rights Speeches* (New York: Basic Civitas Books, 2003), 210–216 at 212.

One of the great questions King addresses in his writings is *how to harness fear*. King suggests that to move through fear, we must face it squarely and try to understand it, in all its manifestations. The more we try to avoid, ignore, or repress our fears, he says, the more damage they do. First, we must ask ourselves why we are afraid. In some cases, he says, we may sometimes find that our fears are the product of our imaginations, not of reality—a recognition that can help to reduce our fears. Indeed, even if they are real, when we get our fears out in the open, we can begin to laugh at them. This is good, King explains, because ridicule is often "the master cure" for fear.[52] King put this into practice in his own life; during his time working with the SCLC, King literally laughed at death.[53] Just before the March in Birmingham began, King greeted his close friends with "Y'all boys ready to go to Bombingham?!" He cracked jokes about the racial terror that he and the other demonstrators faced as a way of defusing their very legitimate fear of violent retaliation, minimizing the police dogs, fire hoses, jail time, and armed members of the national guard by joking about them in order to reduce the demonstrators' fear and make it more manageable. King had a well-known reputation as a jokester, and perhaps this helps us understand why: King was constantly faced with fear, and joking was a way of mastering it.

In other cases, King suggests that when we ask ourselves why we are afraid, we may see that our fears arise from some childhood need or apprehension.[54] King often recounted the story of a particularly fearful man, telling it both to his Black congregations at Dexter and to audiences during his travels. According to King, this man was plagued with a sense of social inferiority and

---

[52] King, "Draft of Chapter XIV, 'The Mastery of Fear,'", 538. Here, King follows Fosdick, *On Being a Real Person*, 132.

[53] This story was told by Darien Pollock on June 27, 2020 in a post on Facebook (a copy of which is with the author). Pollock was told this story by Andrew Young during his time as an intern at the Andrew Young Center for Global Research at Morehouse.

[54] King, "Draft of Chapter XIV, 'The Mastery of Fear,'" 538.

rejection. When he looked at his fear squarely, he found that it was rooted in his childhood experience of rejection. According to King, his mother was self-centered and his father was busy, and both quietly rejected the child. This rejection led to bitterness; the bitterness produced resentment; the resentment was expressed in tantrums; and the tantrums simply evoked punishment and further rejection. Over time, he learned that he could only get appropriate attention if he "concealed his bitterness."[55] Because his childhood attempts to express himself were met with rejection and punishment, the man transformed himself into a "dependent, subservient creature who always concealed his true feelings."[56] King suggests that when the man looked at himself clearly, he could see that his fears were rooted in his childhood experiences and unexpressed resentment. It was only by looking at his fears in the light that he was able to deal with them appropriately and change his behavior.

Why would King tell and retell this story to Black audiences? According to King, the man's psychological "adjustment" to the negative conditions of his childhood can help us understand Black people's "adjustment" to a racist system. This adjustment, which he often calls "conformity," is a common barrier to Black political action, in King's view. According to King, people sometimes try to solve problems by learning to conform to "what is": they feel that "if they will only think and act like other people they will achieve mental and emotional adjustment."[57]

However, King adamantly believes that there are some things in our social system to which we must not adjust. We need not always conform to "what is"; sometimes we must work toward "what

---

[55] Ibid., 538.
[56] Ibid., 538.
[57] Martin Luther King, Jr. "Draft Chapter II: 'Transformed Nonconformist,'" in Carson et al. (eds.), *The Papers of Martin Luther King, Jr.*, Volume VI, 466–476 at 467. Available at: https://kinginstitute.stanford.edu/king-papers/documents/draft-chapter-ii-transformed-nonconformist.

should be." King calls on Black people, especially Black Christians, to be nonconformists: "we are called to be people of conviction not conformity; people of moral nobility and not social respectability. We are called to a higher loyalty, to a more excellent way."[58] In his attempts to rouse Black people to action, King explicitly called upon people to become "maladjusted" to the unjust conditions in the United States.[59] According to him, Black people must never respond to fear by "adjust[ing] to the evils of segregation and the crippling effects of discrimination" or to the "economic conditions which take necessities from the many to give luxuries to the few" or to the "madness of militarism and the self-defeating method of physical violence."[60] King believes that the "salvation of the world lies in the hands of the maladjusted."[61]

King links maladaptation and nonconformity to the mastering of fear—here, the fear of being associated with a minority idea. Mastering this fear, he says, requires Black Americans to challenge both racial segregation and the other systems that support and reinforce it, including the economic system. American society, he argues, convinces us that happiness is found in impressive automobiles and fancy houses and expensive clothes, but Black Americans should have higher aspirations. Here, King is speaking directly to the Black upper and middle classes, challenging their consumerist, conformist values, telling them not to participate in the "compassionless detachment" and "arrogant individualism" of American culture that leads the privileged to ignore the needs of the underprivileged masses.[62] King calls on all Black Americans, and especially on economically privileged Black Americans, to "stall conformity" and instead follow the moral imperative to live differently; he encourages them to go against the majority of

[58] Ibid., 467.
[59] STL, 11.
[60] Ibid., 11.
[61] Ibid., 11.
[62] King, "Transformed Nonconformist," 469.

Americans by shifting away from rugged individualism and toward real collectivism.[63]

This raises an important question for King: how can we master the fear of maladjustment and nonconformity? How can we become fearless? His answer to this question is that three emotions—courage, faith, and love—can lead us out of fear. Here, I will focus on King's ideas about courage and faith, examining how they help us to move through fear and make it possible for Black Americans to take political action; I leave the detailed discussion of love's role in this process to a later chapter (Chapter 6) of its own, because of its importance in King's views of the emotions.

To understand how to become fearless, we must first understand what fearlessness is. According to King, fearlessness is that quality which enables us to stand up to any fear. It is the inner determination not to be stopped or overwhelmed by any object, to go on despite obstacles, however frightful they may be. It involves standing up to one's fear "amid life and the circumstances of life,"[64] even when that fear is both dangerously present and legitimate. But fearlessness goes beyond merely standing up in the face of what one fears. In his writings about his own life, King says he has never met someone more "fearless and courageous" than his father,[65] who "never feared the autocratic and brutal person in the white community. If they said something that was insulting, he made it clear in no uncertain terms that he didn't like it."[66] Here, King links fearlessness with not only facing fear and standing up, but with taking a stand for *what is right*, despite the consequences. King says something similar about his mother's fearlessness, her willingness to refuse to participate in the social systems that reinforce

---

[63] Ibid., 470.
[64] Martin Luther King, Jr., "Unfulfilled Hopes, Sermon," in Carson et al. (eds.), *The Papers of Martin Luther King, Jr.*, Volume VI, 359–367 at 362. Available at: https://kinginstitute.stanford.edu/king-papers/documents/unfulfilled-hopes-0.
[65] King, *Autobiography*, 4.
[66] King, "Draft of Chapter XIV: 'The Mastery of Fear,'" 539.

individualism over collectivism: "In spite of her relatively comfortable circumstances, my mother never complacently adjusted herself to the system of segregation."[67]

This willingness to stand up for what is right is at the heart of King's discussions of the "creative power of protest." Some of the fear that is inspired by Jim Crow is through the fear of jailing. Children are taught at an early age that if they disobey the rules of racial segregation, they will be arrested. These children learn that when they see "white" and "colored" signs, they dare not defy them, unless they want to get arrested. King seeks to challenge this fearfulness. King writes, "let us not fear going to jail. If the officials threaten to arrest us for standing up for our rights, we must answer by saying we are willing and prepared to fill up the jails of the South. Maybe it will take this willingness to stay in jail to arouse the dozing conscience of man."[68] King hopes that our moral commitments can help us to be fearless. He links fearlessness ("let us not fear going to jail") with standing up for what is right, finding creative and productive ways to face fear.

The sit-in campaigns of 1960 and the subsequent creation of the Student Nonviolent Coordinating Committee (SNCC) demonstrated the fearless and creative potential of grassroots organizing. The sit-ins began on February 1, 1960: four Black students from North Carolina A & T College sat down at a Woolworth lunch counter that was reserved for white customers in Greensboro, North Carolina. When the waitress asked them to leave, the students refused to do so. By the end of April, Black students organized sit-ins in more than thirty locations in seven states with more than 50,000 students participating.[69] As King

---

[67] King, *Autobiography*, 3.
[68] Martin Luther King, Jr., "A Creative Protest," in Carson et al. (eds.), *The Papers of Martin Luther King, Jr.*, Volume V, 367–270 at 369. Available at: https://kinginstitute.stanford.edu/king-papers/documents/creative-protest.
[69] "Sit Ins," in Carson Clayborne (ed.), *Martin Luther King Jr. Encyclopedia*. Available at: https://kinginstitute.stanford.edu/encyclopedia/sit-ins.

planned the Birmingham campaign, he thought of these Black students demonstrating at lunch counters across the South, refusing (like his father and mother) to adjust to racial segregation, using creative ways to challenge the idea that Black Americans preferred segregation or that justice would achieve itself if the victims of injustice would just wait patiently enough. King's concept of fearlessness requires a willingness to suffer and sacrifice for what is right; he believed that with a commitment to moral fearlessness—to standing up for what is right, defending a minority idea, and challenging the status quo—you must sometimes be willing to face the fear of physical suffering, willingly taking blows and bites and blasts from fire hoses.

Pain and death, as King writes, are a "stark, grim, inevitable reality."[70] Nevertheless, King says, the forces that threaten Black life ought to be met with the daring "courage to be"[71]—to live in defiance of the forces that seek to empty out joy and self-determination and zest for life. King suggests that fearfulness breeds self-abnegation: a fearful person loses his will to live in the face of the uncertainties of life. Fearlessness is, in part, self-affirmation—affirmation of the worth of Black life and its continuance. A fearless person has a zest for life because of her belief in her own worth. To fully affirm her life, a person must also overcome the kind of inferiority complex that King believes can sometimes sit at the center of fear, and that results from living under Jim Crow. In King's view, the key is "self-acceptance":[72] an individual should seek to accept herself, with all her limitations and her endowments, just as God made her.

How does someone begin to do this? King suggests that every individual should begin by praying, "Lord help me to accept myself."[73] For King, Christian faith was the solution to the problem of fear of all kinds. It was designed to teach and encourage its

---

[70] King, "Draft of Chapter XIV, 'The Mastery of Fear,'" 539.
[71] Ibid., 539.
[72] King, "Overcoming an Inferiority Complex," 307.
[73] Ibid., 307.

followers to push their individual selves—their desires and egos—to the background and focus on larger questions: higher forces (such as God), brotherhood, and human striving for good. According to King, this is the best way to overcome an inferiority complex, for when the ego is subordinated to larger forces, it is much more difficult to damage. Many people have inferiority complexes, he says, because they do not think about higher things at all; they spend most of their time working, coming home, and thinking about themselves. "Their life is lived in a mirror room" that reflects society's view of them back to themselves.[74] In the case of Black Americans, the view reflected back is one of inferiority. To avoid this kind of self-negating reflection, King encourages people to become absorbed in great causes, ideals, and principles that are bigger than themselves.[75]

This is why King saw faith as the most powerful remedy for fearfulness. As we know, King was not afraid of failure; he believed that desegregation would be accomplished within ten to fifteen years, and he wrote, "I have no fear about the outcome of our struggle in Birmingham."[76] However, like any other human being, King himself had experienced some personal and existential fears and the "do-nothingness" that they can produce. He was able to move through them only with faith. In his autobiographical writings, King tells us of a moment where fear overcame him. King received an angry telephone call that threatened his life, and it pushed him over the edge. Fear turned into despair. He felt alone and as if he could not continue in his work, and he began looking for ways to "move out of the picture."[77] But, says King, his faith revived him: "my fears began to pass from me. My uncertainty disappeared. I was ready to face anything. The outer situation remained the same, but God had

---

[74] Ibid., 314.
[75] Ibid., 309.
[76] WWCW, 108.
[77] STL, 117.

given me inner calm."[78] King's faith buffered the negative psychological and emotional effects of fear.

King initially presents faith as consisting, in part, of particular *affective* attitudes that he felt could motivate political action. Without the feelings of confidence, courage, and inner peace that resulted from his belief in God, King would not have had the determination to go on, to keep fighting the good fight, to resist fear and despair "in spite of" the pervasiveness of injustice.[79] The affective components of faith played a key role in moving King to overcome the existential fear of death posed by white people and continue to engage in political action.

But faith is linked with these affective states by way of something deeper: the recognition of the quintessentially moral nature of faith in God. For King, God was the ground of moral progress, and King overcame his fear through God's power. The feeling of God at his side reminded him that moral progress requires action:

> God is at work in his universe... he is striving with our striving...
> As we struggle to defeat the forces of evil, the God of the universe struggles with us. Evil dies on the sea shore not merely because of man's endless struggle against it, but because of God's power to defeat it.[80]

In King's view, God does not strive *for* us but *alongside* us. King's is no passive faith; he strongly cautioned against the "fallacy of thinking that God will cast evil from the earth, even if man does nothing except to sit complacently by the wayside."[81] Instead, he argues, we must join our faith with action: "[w]e must pray with unceasing passion for racial justice, but we must also use our minds to develop a program, organize ourselves into mass

---

[78] Ibid., 117.
[79] Ibid., 95.
[80] Ibid., 83.
[81] Ibid., 137.

non-violent action, and employ every resource of our bodies and sounds to bring an end to racial injustice."[82] "Always man must do something."[83]

For King, we are the instruments of God in this moral work; it is our responsibility to work to bring about the beloved community, the Kingdom of Heaven here on earth. King inextricably links the *belief* in God with the *action* of surrendering the self to God, asserting that they must work together to bring about the beloved community: "One [part of faith] may be called the mind's faith, wherein the intellect assents to a belief that God exists. The other may be referred to as the heart's faith whereby the whole man is involved in a trusting act of self-surrender."[84]

For King, faith and belief in God's existence are connected with four "essential matters":

1. The nature of God: He is a personal spirit.
2. The character of God: He is perfectly good.
3. The relation of God to all other existence: He creates, sustains, and orders all.
4. The motive of God in his relation to all other existence: His motive is holy love.

In these matters of faith, belief in God's existence is conjoined with, among other things, a belief in God's goodness, which is linked with belief in the world's goodness and our own (relative) personal goodness. This belief feels pleasant and calming, and it is conjoined with feelings of confidence. The idea that God is mindful of individuals—is a *personal* spirit who cares for and is concerned with the well-being of individuals—helps with self-fear, or the inferiority complex: it gives one a sense of value and worth, and a sense

---

[82] Ibid., 138.
[83] Ibid., 139.
[84] Ibid., 141.

of belonging and at-homeness in the universe, which also helps one feel less alone in the world and, in turn, less despairing.

Faith in God is not self-executing, however; humans must choose to act. This is why King argues that faith is also linked with an act of self-surrender that allows us to become "instruments of God"[85]—God's means to justice and the end of evil. Through prayer, an act of self-surrender, King argues, the soul of man becomes united with the life of God. To acknowledge that God exists is to understand that God is not "wholly other."[86] By identifying ourselves, through prayer, with an all-good God, our wills will somehow become his will. King writes, "we will be just, because God is justice; we will love, because God is love; we will be good, because God is goodness; we will be wise, because God is wisdom."[87] For King, this kind of self-surrender to God—as a move outward and away from ourselves—is one strategy for overcoming fear.

King's moral and philosophical conception of faith in God also underwrote what Ryan Preston-Roedder has called his sense of "faith in humanity,"[88] which fostered his belief that Black Americans would transcend their fear in order to work for justice. This faith in humanity, says Preston-Roedder, is a forward-looking and optimistic attitude: when someone has faith, she "forms expectations about people's future attitudes or actions,"[89] and "when someone who has faith in humanity forms such expectations, she tends to judge, even in the face of reasons for doubt, that people will act decently, provided that they receive the right forms of encouragement."[90] This is central to how King saw faith as motivating

---

[85] Ibid., 142.

[86] Martin Luther King, Jr., "Mastering Our Evil Selves"/"Mastering Ourselves," in Carson et al. (eds.), *The Papers of Martin Luther King, Jr.*, Volume VI, 94–97 at 97. Available at: https://kinginstitute.stanford.edu/king-papers/documents/mastering-our-evil-selves-mastering-ourselves.

[87] Ibid., 97

[88] Ryan Preston-Roedder, "Faith in Humanity," *Philosophy and Phenomenological Research* 87.3 (2013): 664–687.

[89] Ibid., 668.

[90] Ibid., 668.

political action—as encouraging people to act fearlessly, even in the presence of fear. King believed in God's goodness and power and also in people, all of whom were made in God's image and had the capacity for goodness. This was not a naïve or uncritical belief. His faith gave him confidence that right action was attainable—a real and live possibility for all people, Black and white, moderate and conservative, middle and working class—with the right kind of encouragement from King and his supporters.[91]

It is this faith in humanity that King referenced when he spoke of faith in others' work toward political progress. He wrote of a trip to India that, he said, "had a great impact upon me personally," for on this trip he saw that "the amazing results of a non-violent campaign" were brought about not by Gandhi alone but by all the people who engaged in that nonviolence alongside Gandhi—"his son, his grandsons, his cousin and other relatives [. . . and] his close comrades."[92] King says, "I left India more convinced than ever before that non-violent resistance is the most potent weapon available to oppressed people in their struggle for freedom. It was a marvelous thing to see the amazing results of a non-violent campaign."[93] This is an expression of faith in the power of nonviolent human action, which "leads to redemption and the creation of the beloved community."[94]

King's faith in humanity was reinforced by the political efforts of—and progress produced by—the Black students' movement in Montgomery, which he saw as "based on hope"; in a speech given to the Fellowship of the Concerned of the Southern Regional Council, he called it "a movement based on faith in the future," on "the possibility of the future bringing to being something

---

[91] Ibid., 668.
[92] Martin Luther King Jr., "My Trip to the Land of Gandhi," in Carson et al. (eds.), *The Papers of Martin Luther King, Jr.*, Volume V, 231–238 at 233. Available at: https://kinginstitute.stanford.edu/king-papers/documents/my-trip-land-gandhi.
[93] Ibid., 233.
[94] Ibid., 233.

real and meaningful."⁹⁵ He then repeated the lyrics of "We Shall Overcome," the hymn adopted by the Black students' movement, which went on to become one of the theme songs for the Civil Rights Movement as a whole. The hymn itself is an expression of hope and optimism. There is no room for fear or doubt in the assertion "we *shall* overcome." Hope and optimism are contagious; King's faith in the students—inspired by their own faith in progress and collective political action—was an antidote to despair, and the students' courage to stand up for what is right in the face of potential suffering encouraged those in the movement to continue to move forward and work together in the face of overwhelming obstacles. He said, "it is out of this deep faith in the future that they are able to move out and adjourn the councils of despair, and to bring new light in the dark chambers of pessimism" in which some fearful Black Americans had dwelled.⁹⁶

Both the Indian demonstrators and the Black students believed in and acted with faith in the movement and the future. This faith passed to King himself, allowing him to see their goodness and, by extension, the goodness of all who were participating—and even the potential goodness of those who were not yet participating, such as the Black and white moderates. According to Preston-Roedder, King's faith made him ever aware of the goodness in others: "when someone who has such faith makes judgments about people's past or current attitudes or actions, she tends to be acutely sensitive to evidence of people's decency, including evidence that others are likely to overlook."⁹⁷

King's faith in the future—that there will be a future and that it will be different—was grounded in the evidence of the past. He kept always in mind the great pain of the struggles of his ancestors, who managed to survive terrible circumstances, never losing their

---

[95] Martin Luther King, Jr. "Love, Law, and Civil Disobedience," in Bill Blaisdell (ed.), *Essays on Civil Disobedience* (Minneapolis, MN: Dover, 2016), 120–131 at 130.
[96] Ibid., 130.
[97] Preston-Roedder, "Faith in Humanity," 668.

hope for the future. They passed this hope down to King himself. As he put it in the Letter:

> I have no despair about the future. I have no fear about the outcome of our struggle in Birmingham, even if our motives are at present misunderstood. We will reach the goal of freedom in Birmingham and all over the nation, because the goal of America is freedom. Abused and scorned though we may be, our destiny is tied up with America's destiny. Before the pilgrims landed at Plymouth, we were here. Before the pen of Jefferson etched the majestic words of the Declaration of Independence across the pages of history, we were here. For more than two centuries our forebears labored in this country without wages; they made cotton king; they built the homes of their masters while suffering gross injustice and shameful humiliation—and yet out of a bottomless vitality they continued to thrive and develop. If the inexpressible cruelties of slavery could not stop us, the opposition we now face will surely fail.[98]

The faith in humanity that King expresses here comes from the struggle of the Black people who came before him, and their ability to survive and thrive despite their circumstances. Even as King looks toward the past, he is orienting himself and his audience toward the future. Looking to the past—with an openness to evidence of goodness or progress—is one way to fortify ourselves in the present. King drew sustenance from the indomitable spirit of his ancestors, a spirit which enabled them to make progress in the midst of the most crippling forms of racial oppression.

Just as Christ is the center of King's faith in God, the people King knew and admired are the center of his faith in humanity. King believed that humans support causes based not on ideologies but on personalities, for it is "persons that most deeply influence

---

[98] WWCW, 108–109.

our lives."[99] King's faith in humanity—the Black students, the demonstrators in India, his family, and especially his ancestors—served to mitigate his despair and helped him to move through his legitimate fear of white people and the existential threat they posed. All of this evidence gave him hope, for he saw that all across the long arc of history, the racially oppressed had continued to fight and make progress in spite of the fierce resistance of the white oppressor. This recognition helped King to face his fear of white people and the threat they posed to his life, and to carry on in the movement despite this fear.

Before signing off, King closed the Letter with a reminder that Black people were even then "courageously and nonviolently" sitting in at lunch counters, willingly going to jail for "conscience sake."[100] Like James Meredith, who had organized the "March against Fear" in Mississippi (1966), students were bravely "fac[ing] jeering and hostile mobs."[101] "Battered Negro women" were standing up, quite literally; one weary seventy-two-year-old explained her boycott of the segregated buses by saying, "My feets is tired, but my soul is at rest."[102] King's faith in Black people—in their capacity for goodness and hard work—was a humanitarian faith that, in combination with his faith in God, helped him overcome his existential fear. It also helped him to believe in himself and in the goodness of humanity more generally, which moved him to meet his own commitment to ending racial segregation.

One might wonder, as Harry Fosdick did, what happens when faith in humanity is not fulfilled—when good people "die or betray trust, personal possibilities peter out, creative work confronts failure, building a better world seems dubious."[103] Indeed, King

---

[99] Martin Luther King, Jr., "Christ, the Center of Our Faith," in Carson et al. (eds.), *The Papers of Martin Luther King, Jr.*, Volume VI, 201–202 at 202. Available at: https://kinginstitute.stanford.edu/king-papers/documents/christ-center-our-faith.
[100] WWCW, 110.
[101] Ibid., 110.
[102] Ibid., 110.
[103] Fodsick, *On Being a Real Person*, 131.

suggests that in the modern world, it is easy for man to lose faith in man. He refers to two recent events as seeming to give reason for pessimism about "the nature and destiny of man": the 1955 lynching of Emmett Till and the rioting at the University of Alabama in response to the admission of the school's first Black American student, Autherine Lucy.[104]

In the face of events such as these, which foster pessimism about man's ability and willingness to act on his inherent goodness, how can we go on? Fosdick suggests that without a belief in God, pessimism leads us to either moral nihilism, "which is fatal to society," or to "spiritual despair," which is fatal to the individual victim.[105] He argues that these outcomes can only be avoided through faith in God. Here, Fosdick means faith in two senses—both a belief in God's existence and feelings of confidence and trust in God's goodness and power. For Fosdick, only these beliefs and feelings can cast out fear. King agrees with Fosdick that faith in humanity is inextricably intertwined with faith in God. The insistence that there is hope for man is a central tenet of King's Christian faith. He writes, "Christianity has always insisted that man's plight is never so low that it can[']t be better."[106] Humans contain an ocean of infinite possibilities and potentialities.[107] While King urges us to remain aware of the evil potential of human nature, he also insists that we maintain faith in the individual's ability to rise above the limitations of heredity, environment, and injustice.

However, King also turns Fosdick's claim on its head. King boldly claims that not only does our faith in God sustain our faith in our fellow man, but that our faith in our fellow man sustains our faith in God. When we look outward at other people and see them

---

[104] Martin Luther King, Jr., "Faith in Man," in Carson et al. (eds.), *The Papers of Martin Luther King, Jr.*, Volume VI, 253–255 at 254. Available at: https://kinginstitute.stanford.edu/king-papers/documents/faith-man.
[105] Fodsick, *On Being a Real Person*, 131.
[106] King, "Faith in Man," 254.
[107] Ibid., 254.

doing God's work, standing up for what is right even when it causes them great suffering, our own faith in God's goodness and power increases. For King, the fact that humans continue to work to build a better world, despite the personal cost, confirms that God exists and is good, for their efforts are an expression of God's existence and true nature. King articulates a vision of faith in which faith in God and faith in humanity are deeply intertwined and together work to master fear in the face of white backlash and violence.

5
Dignity and Indignation

Near the end of the Letter, King writes that the real heroes of the civil rights movement are those who "rose up with a sense of dignity."[1] According to King, the growing movement for racial justice was explained, in part, by a "revolutionary change" in the way that Black Americans viewed themselves, their "nature and destiny," and their "determination to struggle and sacrifice" for desegregation.[2] King asserts that "once [the Black American had] thought of himself as an inferior and patiently accepted injustice and exploitation. Those days are gone."[3] As the last chapter showed, this new self-view required Black people to take stock of their fears and work through them, but once those self-fears were mastered, "a new negro" emerged, with a "new sense of self-respect and new sense of dignity."[4] King makes this point explicitly in an interview with Richard D. Heffner, when he is asked to explain who exactly the New Negro is: "the new Negro is a person with a new sense of dignity and destiny with a new self-respect; along with that is this lack of fear which once characterized the Negro, this willingness to stand up courageously for what he feels is just and what he feels he

---

[1] WWCW, 110.
[2] Martin Luther King, Jr., "Remaining Awake Through a Great Revolution," in Carson et al. (eds.), *The Papers of Martin Luther King, Jr.*, Volume V, 219–226 at 223. Available at: https://kinginstitute.stanford.edu/king-papers/documents/remaining-awake-through-great-revolution-address-morehouse-college.
[3] Martin Luther King, Jr., "Nonviolence and Racial Justice," in Carson et al. (eds.), *The Papers of Martin Luther King, Jr.*, Volume IV, 118–119 at 118. Available at: https://kinginstitute.stanford.edu/king-papers/documents/nonviolence-and-racial-justice.
[4] King, "Remaining Awake Through a Great Revolution," 222.

deserves on the basis of the laws of the land. I think also included would be this self-assertive attitude."⁵

King here reminds us of the psychological impact of American racism: the practices of American slavery and, later, racial segregation had forced Black people into performing subservience and the acceptance of their assigned social place, and this strategic performance eventually became internalized leading some Black Americans to lose "faith" in themselves and "to feel that perhaps they were less than human."⁶ Black Americans, "forced patiently to submit to insult, injustice and exploitation," had lived in what King calls a negative peace—an absence of conflict—rather than a positive peace, which is grounded in a true sense of justice, good will, and brotherhood among the people.⁷ As time passed, this negative peace became more and more fragile. Large changes in society, the economy, and politics came together, and Black Americans took a "new look" at themselves, both individually and as a group.⁸ King writes that Black Americans rooted out the "self-depreciation" that had been forced upon them and replaced it "with dignity."⁹

King was not the first to use the term "New Negro." It had been used by many people, including Booker T. Washington, but it is most closely linked with Alain Locke's writings. In Locke's view, the "Old Negro" was more myth than man, a creation of the white imagination, a passive reflection generated by conditions of forced

---

⁵ Martin Luther King, Jr. "Interview by Richard D. Heffner for 'The Open Mind,'" in Carson et al. (eds.), *The Papers of Martin Luther King, Jr.*, Volume IV, 126–131 at 126. Available at: https://kinginstitute.stanford.edu/king-papers/documents/interview-richard-d-heffner-open-mind.

⁶ King, "The Rising Tide of Racial Consciousness," in Carson et al. (eds.), *The Papers of Martin Luther King, Jr.*, Volume V, 500. Available at: https://kinginstitute.stanford.edu/king-papers/documents/rising-tide-racial-consciousness-address-golden-anniversary-conference. See also King, "Nonviolence and Racial Justice," 119.

⁷ King, "Nonviolence and Racial Justice," 119.

⁸ Ibid., 119.

⁹ Martin Luther King, Jr., "Our Struggle," in Carson et al. (eds.), *The Papers of Martin Luther King, Jr.*, Volume III, 236–241 at 237. Available at: https://kinginstitute.stanford.edu/king-papers/documents/our-struggle.

dependence. It was the result of protective social mimicry and strategic acquiescence that was performed by Black people to survive in these conditions of forced dependence. In Locke's view, the "New Negro" is a being who sees herself anew, no longer obscured by the perception of others. She has an invigorated sense of self-understanding, self-acceptance, and, in turn, a new sense of self-respect. The new negro is also an agent who acts rather than is acted upon. Locke suggests that historical processes are key to this transformation. He believed that the great migration of Black Americans (1910–1925), when Black people moved in massive numbers from the South to the North and especially into urban city centers like Harlem, helped create the conditions for the "New Negro" to be born.

Locke's account of the emergence of the "New Negro" is very similar to King's. Like Locke, King believes that several historical processes came together to cause Black Americans to take a new look at themselves and to embrace their sense of dignity and self-respect more deeply. First, the country was modernizing: with the spread of automobiles, Black Americans who previously had little ability or reason to leave the South traveled more and saw that violent segregation was not the norm everywhere. Second, the Depression and the upheaval caused by the two world wars led many Black Americans to move from the rural South to urban industrial communities, where their lives began to improve: their purchasing power increased, their housing conditions improved, and they had better access to education. During this period, literacy rates among Black Americans dramatically increased, and more Black students were earning academic degrees, including graduate degrees. These new travel and educational experiences gave Black Americans a broadened outlook on the world—and on themselves. According to King, these changes drove Black Americans to change their self-image.

Third, the Supreme Court's decision outlawing segregation in public schools also played a pivotal role in this change. As King put it, the law was a public statement that "'separate but equal' facilities are inherently unequal, and that to segregate a child on the basis of his race is to deny that child equal protection of the law."[10] This decision further engendered a new sense of pride and enhanced Black Americans' sense of dignity and self-worth. Fourth was the effect of global news, communication, and travel, which allowed Black Americans to see that their struggle for freedom was just one part of the larger "worldwide struggle" for racial and economic justice that was being carried out by subjugated people.[11] Contemporary anti-colonial movements in Asia and Africa were succeeding, and they deeply influenced Black thinking, including that of King and the other organizers of the Civil Rights Movement in America. King writes, "Fourteen years ago the British Empire had under her domination more than six hundred million people in Asia and Africa. But that number will be reduced to less than forty million (40,000,000) after Nigeria receives her independence a few days from now."[12] Black Americans saw that the struggle among the oppressed for dignity was not isolated to the United States; "It is a drama being played on the stage of the world with spectators and supporters from every continent."[13][14]

---

[10] King, "The Rising Tide of Racial Consciousness," 500. See also Martin Luther King, Jr., "A Look to the Future," in Carson et al. (eds.), *The Papers of Martin Luther King, Jr.*, Volume IV, 269–276 at 272. Available at: https://kinginstitute.stanford.edu/king-papers/documents/look-future-address-delivered-highlander-folk-schools-twenty-fifth-anniversary. As noted in the first chapter, King saw Black Americans' sense of self-worth as being continually reinforced by religion, which emphasized a God who loved everyone—"'not his specificity but his fundamentum,' not the texture or the color of his skin but the quality of his soul." King, "The Rising Tide of Racial Consciousness," 507; King, "A Look to the Future," 274.

[11] King, "The Rising Tide of Racial Consciousness," 501.

[12] Ibid., 501.

[13] Ibid., 501.

[14] For more about King's views on the connection between the global movement and the American one, see Martin Luther King, Jr., "Remarks Delivered at Africa Freedom Dinner at Atlanta University," in Carson et al. (eds.), *The Papers of Martin Luther King, Jr.*, Volume V, 197–202. Available at: https://kinginstitute.stanford.edu/king-papers/documents/remarks-delivered-africa-freedom-dinner-atlanta-university.

What does King mean by a sense of dignity? King uses the word in a variety of ways and contexts.[15] He seems to most often use the term to refer to certain types of attitudes and conduct—a specific set of beliefs and feelings that produce behavior that adheres to certain norms. Given my focus here on King's attempts to activate emotion in order to motivate political action, I will in this chapter work primarily with this understanding of dignity in King's work. As we will see, dignity, in this sense, is not the same as Black respectability or as being "adjusted" or "conformist."

For King, when a person has dignity, it means that he "has come to feel that he is somebody. He is no longer ashamed of the color of his skin or the texture of his hair."[16] Because he accepts himself as a part of the race of Black people, he accepts his "[f]leecy locks and Black complexion."[17] In King's view, dignity is a self-regarding attitude. To have a sense of dignity is to have an attitude of self-acceptance—acceptance of one's own self, both physical and nonphysical, just as it is. As we saw in Chapter 4, this kind of self-acceptance is essential to overcoming personal fear.

---

[15] It is sometimes hard to know precisely how King defines "dignity," since he uses the word in a variety of different ways. At times, King sees dignity as an end state—a world where "men will live together as brothers" (Martin Luther King, Jr., "Some Things We Must Do," in Carson et al. (eds.), *The Papers of Martin Luther King, Jr.*, Volume IV, 328–342 at 342. Available at: https://kinginstitute.stanford.edu/king-papers/docume nts/some-things-we-must-do-address-delivered-second-annual-institute-nonviole nce). Derrick Darby argues that King's notion of dignity—as an end state—requires that there be no entrenched social hierarchies, and that law works by publicly leveling the social rank of citizens. In other words, dignity can occur only in a world where everyone's rights are respected, and where law "expresses the content and scope of our commitment to dignity"; universal human rights, such as the right to vote, are one way of publicly expressing a commitment to the equal dignity of all (Derrick Darby, "A Vindication of Voting Rights," in Terry and Shelby (eds.), *To Shape a New World*, 161–183 at 163).

[16] See King, "The Rising Tide of Racial Consciousness," 501; Martin Luther King, Jr., "MIA Mass Meeting at Holt Street Baptist Church," in Clayborne Carson (ed.), *A Call to Conscience: The Landmark Speeches of Martin Luther King, Jr.* (New York: IPM/Warner Books, 2001), 12. Available at: https://kinginstitute.stanford.edu/king-papers/docume nts/mia-mass-meeting-holt-street-baptist-church.

[17] King quotes the phrase "fleecy locks and Black complexion" from a poem by William Cowper, "The Negro's Complaint" (London: Harvey and Darton, 1788). See King, "The Rising Tide of Racial Consciousness," 501; King, "MIA Mass Meeting," 12.

King says that everyone should accept themselves, because everyone has equal "worth" and "significance."[18] As discussed in Chapter 1, King's belief in equal worth originates from his religious beliefs, for in his view, humanity is created in the image of God, and that divine image is universally shared in equal proportions among all humans. He also believes that the commitment to the equal dignity and worth of all humans—including women and children as well—is a founding American value, clearly expressed in the Declaration of Independence, although of course this value has never been fully put to work in the United States.

To have a sense of dignity, a person must believe, as both the Christian and American traditions assert, that she has equal worth and status—that, as a Black American, she is inherently equal to white Americans. To have a sense of dignity, she cannot maintain a belief in her own inferiority.[19] She must believe that she deserves the very same freedoms that white Americans already have. Freedom is bound up with personhood: robbing people of their freedom robs them also of their personhood, disavowing the image of God within them and the values enshrined in the American constitution. To deny someone freedom "means in fact that someone or some system has already made these decisions for me, and I am reduced to an animal."[20] As Derrick Darby notes in his discussion of King's concept of dignity, this type of denial of freedom undermines our capacity to make "deliberative choices." In Darby's reading, King regarded this capacity as a central "resource" to humans, one that distinguished them from their animal ancestors.[21] This understanding of dignity links King with other central thinkers in mainstream political philosophy such as

---

[18] King links dignity with both "significance" (King, "Some Things We Must Do," 332) and "worth" (King, "The Crisis in the Modern Family," in Carson et al. (eds.), *The Papers of Martin Luther King, Jr.*, Volume VI, 212).
[19] King, "Some Things We Must Do," 333.
[20] King, WDWGH, 104; quoted in Darby, "Vindication of Voting Rights," 173.
[21] Darby, "Vindication of Voting Rights," 173.

Immanuel Kant and John Rawls, who saw the dignity of humanity as being linked with "rational autonomy."[22] King argues that even when the belief that one is worthy of freedom (and deliberative choice) is submerged by circumstances, there is "a throbbing desire ... an internal desire for freedom within the soul of every man. And it's there; it might not break forth in the beginning, but eventually it breaks out."[23]

Dignity is also affective. For King, it is not just a set of beliefs about one's own worth, but also, as Robert Gooding-Williams puts it, "the felt sense" of one's own worth—an "incipient self-respect."[24] This feeling is how one's belief in one's own worth expresses itself. But, as Gooding-Williams argues, for King, dignity is best—and perhaps even necessarily—expressed not only through feeling but through action. We must express our inwardly felt sense of dignity through action that demands acknowledgment of our inherent worth. More specifically, as Gooding-Williams argues, this felt sense of dignity must manifest itself in resistance to the system that objectifies individuals and denies their equal worth. In King's view, this is one of the defining characteristics of "the new Negro": he is willing to stand up courageously for what he feels is just and what he feels he deserves on the basis of the laws of the land. This willingness is linked to the self-assertive attitude that derives from felt dignity.[25]

With an enlivened sense of self-respect, Black Americans came to believe that freedom was a basic condition of the personhood of which they were now keenly aware. This recognition, King thought, would foster the urgent desire for freedom and the willingness to take political action to achieve it. As King writes, "We

---

[22] For a more detailed discussion of Kant's concept of dignity and how it relates to King's, see Darby, "Vindication of Voting Rights."

[23] King, "Birth of a New Nation," in Carson et al. (eds.), *The Papers of Martin Luther King, Jr.*, Volume IV, 156.

[24] Robert Gooding-Williams, "The Du Bois–Washington Debate and the Idea of Dignity" in Terry and Shelby (eds.), *To Shape a New World*, 19–34.

[25] King, "Interview by Richard D. Heffner," 126.

can't slow up. We can't slow up and have our dignity and self respect."[26] Why? "Men cannot be satisfied with Egypt. They tried to adjust to it for a while. Many men have vested interests in Egypt, and they are slow to leave. Egypt makes it profitable to them, some people profit by Egypt. The vast majority, the masses of people never profit by Egypt, and they are never content with it. And eventually they rise up and begin to cry out for Canaan's land."[27] Black people—especially among the masses—with this new sense of their own dignity now refused to be relegated to second place; they demanded that they be treated equally—that they receive their share of Canaan, which white Americans had for so long kept for themselves.

This self-assertive attitude is accompanied by honesty and truth-telling. In the past, King says, Black Americans strategically used duplicity and deception to survive. Though they didn't like the conditions they lived in, for strategic reasons, they pretended to accept them, giving rise to the negative peace mentioned above. "But now from the housetops, from the kitchens, from the classrooms and from the pulpit, the Negro says in no uncertain terms that he doesn't like the way he's being treated. So at long last the Negro is telling the truth. And I think this is also one of the basic characteristics of the new Negro."[28]

Self-assertion is expressed by taking a stand, even when it might cost us personally. King connects these two things explicitly to the campaign in Montgomery, saying, "I would seek to arouse the group to action by insisting that their self-respect was at stake and that if they accepted such injustices without protesting, they would betray their own sense of dignity and the eternal edicts of God Himself."[29]

---

[26] Martin Luther King, Jr., "Quotable Quotes from Rev. King," in Carson et al. (eds.), *The Papers of Martin Luther King, Jr.*, Volume III, 209–210 at 209. Available at: https://kinginstitute.stanford.edu/king-papers/documents/quotable-quotes-rev-king.

[27] King, "Birth of a New Nation," 156–157.

[28] Ibid., 160.

[29] Martin Luther King, Jr., *Stride Toward Freedom: The Montgomery Story* (Boston: Beacon Press, 1958), 48.

Elsewhere, he called upon all Black Americans, especially those in the South, "to assert their human dignity" and "to seek justice and reject all injustice, especially that in themselves [and to] refuse further cooperation with the evil element which invites them to collude against themselves in return for bits of patronage. We know that such an assertion may cause them persecution; yet no matter how great the obstacles and suffering, we urge all Negroes to reject segregation."[30] Here we see that dignity is, in part, what gives rise to and is expressed in courageous or fearless action—taking a stand and being willing to take on the costs of doing so.

In King's view, *failing* to act against segregation would in fact be an act against the self. According to him, Rosa Parks had a similar view. "When Mrs. Rosa Parks ... was asked why she had refused to move to the rear of a bus, she said: 'It was a matter of dignity; I could not have faced myself and my people if I had moved.'"[31] A failure to act requires one to disregard oneself and one's worth; failure to act means colluding in injustice by accepting morally wrong social conditions such as bus segregation. This is not something a self-respecting and dignified individual can do, in King's view: "It would be more honorable to walk in dignity than ride in humiliation."[32][33] King realizes that "this will mean suffering and sacrifice. It might even mean going to jail.... It might even mean

---

[30] Martin Luther King, Jr., "A Statement to the South and Nation," in Carson et al. (eds.), *The Papers of Martin Luther King, Jr.*, Volume IV, 103–106 at 104. Available at: https://kinginstitute.stanford.edu/king-papers/documents/statement-south-and-nation-issued-southern-negro-leaders-conference.

[31] King, "Our Struggle," 237.

[32] King, "Interview by Martin Agronsky," in Carson et al. (eds.), *The Papers of Martin Luther King, Jr.*, Volume IV, 292.

[33] For a discussion of how King's emphasis on dignity and self-respect creatively synthesizes the two different approaches to the race problem emblematized by W. E. B. Du Bois and Booker T. Washington, see Gooding Williams, "The Du Bois–Washington Debate and the Idea of Dignity," 19–34. For an account of the connection between self-respect and protest, see Bernard R. Boxill, "Self-Respect and Protest," in *Philosophy Born of Struggle*, ed. Leonard Harris, 2nd ed. (Dubuque, IA: Kendall/Hunt, 2000), 312–322. For a discussion (similar to King's) of the ways that racism and discrimination can deeply undermine self-respect, see Moody-Adams, "Race, Class, and the Social Construction of Self-Respect," 251–266.

physical death. But if physical death is the price that some must pay to free their children from a permanent life of psychological death, then nothing could be more honorable."[34] For King, self-respecting individuals are willing to "suffer and sacrifice" for their freedom, both physical and psychological.

Why does self-respect require action? As Darby notes, for King, dignity has both personal and public elements. Systems of segregation, discrimination, and political domination based on race impact how Black individuals see themselves. King suggests that they impose "manacles of self-abnegation" upon Black Americans, which make it much more difficult for them to say, "I am a somebody. I am a person. I am a man with dignity and honor."[35] As Michele Moody-Adams has argued, it is very difficult to maintain a sense of self-respect living under a system of racial segregation.[36] Individual dignity is publicly recognized through a system of laws and policies. When that system recognizes the equal status of all its citizens and establishes legally supported ways of treating them as equals, it becomes easier for everyone to maintain a sense of self-respect. This is why King argued, in Birmingham, that "any law that uplifts the human personality is just. Any law that degrades human personality is unjust."[37] King believed we must lift our laws "from the quicksand of racial injustice to the solid rock of human dignity."[38]

As Gooding-Williams reads King, his discussion of dignity echoes the work of several important Black thinkers. It echoes Du Bois's well-known criticism of Booker T. Washington's politics of strategic acquiescence, which Du Bois sees as voluntarily

---

[34] WWCW, 35.
[35] Martin Luther King, Jr., "Where Do We Go from Here," in Clayborne Carson and Kris Shepard (eds.), *A Call to Conscience: The Landmark Speeches of Martin Luther King, Jr.*, 171–199 at 184. Available at: https://kinginstitute.stanford.edu/where-do-we-go-here. Quoted in Darby, "Vindication of Voting Rights," 177.
[36] Moody-Adams, "Race, Class and the Social Construction of Self-Respect," 251–266.
[37] WWCW, 94.
[38] WWCW, 99.

surrendering the conditions of Black self-respect. It also echoes Frederick Douglass's remarks after his fight with Edward Covey: "A man without force is without essential dignity of humanity. Human nature is so constituted that it cannot honor a helpless man, although it can pity him; and even this it cannot do long, if the signs of power do not arise."[39] Gooding-Williams interprets Douglass as suggesting that a slave who remains helpless in the face of domination will not manifest the dignity that is required to motivate anyone with a human nature, including himself, to accord him the respect he deserves. As Douglass sees it, to manifest dignity, the slave must struggle to resist the practice of objectification. In this tradition of Black political thought, action is essential because it is required to induce respect from others and, especially, oneself. In a similar vein, King argues that, if they fail to protest by demanding that their dignity be acknowledged, then the Black citizens of Montgomery and Birmingham cannot be said to respect themselves. They must, as Gooding-Williams writes, save themselves from their patience and protest their oppression for the sake of their dignity.[40]

Dignity is manifested through action. As Nick Bromell reminds us, Douglass's violent resistance to Covey transforms Douglass, rendering him "unafraid to die." Douglass writes, "I was no longer a servile coward ... trembling under the frown of a brother worm of the dust, but my long-cowed spirit was roused to an attitude of independence. I had reached the point at which I was not afraid to die. This spirit made me a freeman in fact, though I still remained a slave in form."[41] As Gooding-Williams sees it, by battling Covey, Douglass discovers that he is an individual who would rather die than live under conditions of domination and exploitation. The prospect of death ceases to cow Douglass—that is, it ceases to

---

[39] Quoted in Gooding-Williams, "The Du Bois-Washington Debate and the Idea of Dignity," 26.
[40] Ibid., 26.
[41] Nick Bromell, *The Time Is Always Now: Black Thought and the Transformation of US Democracy* (Oxford: Oxford, 2013), 25.

cause fear.⁴² Douglass no longer knows fear of death, in Gooding-Williams's view, because he recognizes that sustaining the struggle matters more than preserving his individual life.⁴³

King holds a related view. For King, fearlessness grows out of acting on and manifesting one's belief in one's dignity—one's belief in one's own worth and that of all those who are living now and who will live. Sustaining the struggle matters because it is a way of ensuring the dignity of all Americans, especially Black Americans. It is, as King notes, imperative that the struggle continue, not only for himself and the people of his time, but for the future and the children who will live in it—to ensure that they too will live in a more just world. For King, dignity drives us to not only look at ourselves and consider what is required for our own dignity, but also to look outward toward others and toward what is required for collective dignity over time.

King's view is a departure from Douglass's in that claiming or sustaining dignity does not require physical force: it can be achieved by nonviolent forceful challenges to the systems that deny Black dignity. In Montgomery, King tells us that he had to "arouse the group to action by insisting their self-respect was at stake and that if they accepted such injustices without protesting, they would betray their own sense of dignity and the eternal edicts of God himself."⁴⁴ Black citizens, in his view, "had no alternative

---

⁴² Robert Gooding-Williams, *In the Shadow of Du Bois: Afro Modern Political Thought in America* (Cambridge, MA: Harvard University Press, 2009), ch. 179.

⁴³ Bromell does not read Douglass's new fearlessness as just a result of his use of physical force, as Gooding-Williams had suggested in some of his earlier work (Gooding-Williams, *In the Shadow of Du Bois*, 179). Bromell argues that action is not the only thing that motivates Douglass's transformation, for one can become fearless without lifting a finger: attitude, not action, is the key, according to Bromell. He grounds this reading in Douglass's acknowledgment that he is just a "worm" living among other human worms. This, Bromell argues, indicates Douglass's acceptance of "the absolute nullity of human life, of its meaningfulness, and of the absurdity, therefore, of his ego's terror of extinction" (Bromell, *The Time Is Always Now*, 26.) In Bromell's view, it is Douglass's acceptance of his wormlike lack of significance, as much as it is his use of force and resistance, that allowed him to claim and reclaim his dignity. Needless to say, [in my reading of him] King would not agree with Bromell's view.

⁴⁴ STF, 48.

but to protest" and needed to be "saved" from their patience—a patience that white people chose to interpret as indicating that Black people liked the way they were being treated.[45] For King, we are all glorified beings, created in the image of God, with equal worth, and equally deserving of the life conditions that give rise to and sustain dignity. For King, Black dignity, understood in this sense, demands immediate self-assertion through collective political action.

Dignity thus requires action, in King's view. But how does dignity give rise to this specifically political action? As King describes it, "righteous indignation"—anger at being subject to indignity—was the driving force behind the Letter, and a matching sense of righteous indignation would drive people who realized their own worth to take political action:

> After I was placed in a cell in solitary confinement, a newspaper was slipped to me. I turned it over and found a kind of advertisement that had been placed there, taken out by eight clergymen of all the major religious faiths in our nation. They were criticizing our demonstrations. They were calling us extremists. They were calling us law breakers and believers in anarchy and all of these things. And when I read it, I became so concerned and even upset and at points so righteously indignant that I decided to answer the letter.[46]

Indeed, this righteous indignation—this sense that his dignity and innate worth as a human being had been violated—that led King to write the Letter had also driven his original decision to join the movement for Black Civil Rights. This is apparent in his autobiographical writings, which show us that King had long had a strong sense of his own dignity. King came from a middle-class family and

---

[45] STF, 50.
[46] King, *Autobiography*, 187.

lived a comfortable early life. He grew up steeped in the tradition and sense of community offered by the Southern Black ministry, for both his father and maternal grandfather were Baptist preachers. He spent his childhood in the area known as "Black Wall Street" in Atlanta, which was home to some of the country's most prosperous Black businesses. It was only later that he personally experienced the full impacts of racial segregation, but, he says, the racist "incidents [that] happened in my late childhood and early adolescence [...] had a tremendous effect on my development."[47]

In his autobiography, he recounted one of these experiences. As a young boy, King had a white playmate who was the same age as him and lived across the street. When they started school—at separate schools—the friendship began to dissolve. Eventually, the boy told King that his father said that they couldn't play together any longer. King said that he would never "forget what a great shock this was to him."[48] King immediately asked his parents why the boy would say such a thing.

> We were at the dinner table when the situation was discussed, and here for the first time I was made aware of the existence of a race problem. I had never been conscious of it before. As my parents discussed some of the tragedies that had resulted from this problem and some of the insults they themselves had confronted on account of it, I was greatly shocked and from that moment on I was determined to hate every white person. As I grew older and older this feeling continued to grow.[49]

King was now aware of racial segregation and wondered how he ought to confront it. He spoke often of his father's insistence on his own dignity and refusal to accept poor treatment. He told of

---

[47] *Autobiography*, 6.
[48] Ibid., 7.
[49] Ibid., 7.

another formative encounter with racism, a trip to a downtown shoe store with his father. At the shoe store, the white clerk politely said,

> "I'll be happy to wait on you if you'll just move to those seats in the rear."
>
> Dad immediately retorted, "There's nothing wrong with these seats. We're quite comfortable here."
>
> "Sorry," said the clerk, "but you'll have to move."
>
> "We'll either buy shoes sitting here," my father retorted, "or we won't buy shoes at all."[50]

King's father took him by the hand and walked out of the store. This was the first time King had seen his father "so furious."[51] He walked down the street with King, muttering to himself, "I don't care how long I have to live with this system, I will never accept it." King said, "that experience revealed to me at a very early age that my father had not adjusted to the system, and he played a great part in shaping my conscience."[52]

Indeed, according to King, his father never did accept the system. He tells another story of when his father accidentally drove through a stop sign. According to King, the policeman who pulled them over said, "All right, boy, pull over and let me see your license."[53] King's father replied "indignantly," "I'm no 'boy.'" He pointed to King and said, "This is a boy. I'm a man, and until you call me one, I will not listen to you."[54] King's father's assertion of his dignity worked: "The policeman was so shocked that he wrote the ticket up nervously, and left the scene as quickly as possible."[55] King shows us

[50] Ibid., 8.
[51] Ibid., 8.
[52] Ibid., 8.
[53] Ibid., 8.
[54] Ibid., 8.
[55] Ibid., 8.

explicitly that his father's awareness of and insistence on his dignity caused him to act—to work to make the world conform to his ideas about human worth and dignity, rather than to the morally bankrupt practice of segregation.

According to King, his father was always aware of his own dignity and fought to have the dignity of all Black people recognized: "From before I was born, my father had refused to ride the city buses, after witnessing a brutal attack on a load of Negro passengers. He had led the fight in Atlanta to equalize teachers' salaries, and had been instrumental in the elimination of Jim Crow elevators in the courthouse."[56] As Rufus Burrows notes, King's father acted fearlessly and with dignity in these and other instances, even though it was dangerous to do so in a time when Black people were expected to know their place and to defer to whites.[57] Though racial segregation wounds Black dignity, as the example of King's father shows, there is a component of Black dignity that is inviolable, for it emanates from God. Though racial segregation can diminish self-respect, it cannot wipe it out entirely. This is why, even under Jim Crow, King's father is able to feel and express dignity. Witnessing these incidents of expressed dignity, King came to a profound sense that he too was a "somebody," precious in the eyes of God, and should not only respect himself but should be respected by others.[58] In these moments, King realizes that he was the son of a great Black man, of someone who expressed and acted on dignity, even when his life might be at stake. This only served to further confirm King's sense of worth. We see that for King, dignity is not only theological but can be deeply social and familial as well.

King's growing sense of dignity and self-respect was tested as he grew older. A few pages later, King tells us of a trip from Atlanta to Dublin, Georgia, that he took with his teacher, Mrs. Bradley, when

---

[56] Ibid., 5.
[57] Burrows, *God and Human Dignity*, 81.
[58] Ibid., 81.

he was fourteen years old. On the way home, the white bus driver ordered King and Mrs. Bradley to give up their seats to the white passengers that were boarding. When King did not immediately comply, the bus driver began cursing at them. King considered staying in his seat, but his teacher encouraged him to stand up and obey the law. King wrote, "that night will never leave my memory. It was the angriest I have ever been in my life."[59] He explains the impacts that the constant flow of perfectly legal and socially acceptable insults and oppressions had on his sense of self-worth and dignity, saying, "The first time that I was seated behind a curtain in a dining car, I felt as if the curtain had been dropped on my selfhood. I could never adjust to the separate waiting rooms, separate eating places, separate rest rooms, partly because the separate was always unequal, and partly because the very idea of separation did something to my sense of dignity and self-respect."[60]

For both King and his father, an affront to dignity produces justified anger—righteous indignation. The stories of these dignified men's anger at insults to their human worth—the police officer suggesting that King's father is a mere boy, the store clerk asking them to go to the back of the store to receive service, the bus driver forcing them to make room for white passengers—show a world trying to inculcate the lesson that Black men are not worthy of equal treatment because they are inferior to white Americans. As someone with a deep sense of dignity and self-respect, King's father knew—and King himself internalized—that these segregationist attitudes are not consistent with the inherent worth that all

---

[59] King, *Autobiography*, 9; my emphasis. He goes on to say: "I had grown up abhorring not only segregation but also the oppressive and barbarous acts that grew out of it. I had seen police brutality with my own eyes, and watched Negroes receive the most tragic injustice in the courts. I can remember the organization known as the Ku Klux Klan. It stands on white supremacy, and it was an organization that in those days even used violent methods to preserve segregation and to keep the Negro in his place, so to speak. I remember seeing the Klan actually beat a Negro. I had passed spots where Negroes had been savagely lynched. All of these things did something to my growing personality."

[60] Ibid., 10.

men truly possess, both in the eyes of God and under the American constitution. Affronts to his dignity caused righteous indignation, which in turn led King's father to defy the likely consequences and to challenge the store clerk and the police officer.

King tells us about these early experiences of racial segregation because of the role they played in moving him to participate in the Civil Rights Movement. As we can see, King was not moved to engage in political action immediately after his first experience of racial segregation. He didn't confront his best friend's racist parents. He didn't speak out in the store with his father. He didn't refuse to move on the bus with Mrs. Bradley. But these indignities and others piled up, and eventually, his anger overflowed, leading him to engage in political action. As King says, "there comes a time when people get tired of being trampled by oppression. There comes a time when people get tired of being plunged into the abyss of exploitation and nagging injustice."[61]

Through an accumulation of experience, King came to see that the humiliation and suffering that he and other Black Americans experienced because of racial segregation was not, as he initially thought, created solely by explicitly racist white Americans; it was more global and more systemic than any individual's personal beliefs about integration. Racial segregation meant that Black Americans were pervasively treated as legally inferior across a variety of social domains in multifarious ways. Through experience, King came to see that his particular experiences of racial segregation were manifestations of the larger systems of oppression, which King, like his father, could not accept. As with his father, it was this knowledge that produced in him a sense of "righteous indignation"—a form of anger that arises when the affront to one's dignity is experienced not only as a personal injury but also as an injustice.

Wyatt Tee Walker expressed a similar kind of anger toward the white clergymen whose "Call for Unity" called on Black people

---

[61] STF, 54.

to continue to submit to the system of racial segregation. He said, "I had anger toward them. I felt they were hypocrites. It's what I expected from white preachers."[62] For King, the impact of the clergymen's statement was different. King's righteous indignation did not turn inward, paralyzing him ("It's what I expected"). Like Walker, King perceived the statement as a call for the Black people of Birmingham to continue to patiently accept injustice. King refused. His righteous indignation overflowed into action: he responded with his own Letter, calling not for patience but for swift justice. King's righteous indignation at the clergymen's call for patience led him to instead take a dangerous, fearless political action: challenging these white men's implicit assertion that their moral and physical comfort was more important than justice for Black Americans. King wrote the Letter out of this spirit of righteous indignation, confronting these men's racism, as he had learned to do from his father.

King's sense of indignation is linked with his deep anguish at the injustice of being counseled to wait for justice. The experience of racial segregation itself was simply too painful to continue to endure. As he famously wrote in the Letter, in a passage that is very much worth quoting at length here:

> Perhaps it is easy for those who have never felt the stinging darts of segregation to say, "Wait." But when you have seen vicious mobs lynch your mothers and fathers at will and drown your sisters and brothers at whim; when you have seen hate filled policemen curse, kick and even kill your Black brothers and sisters; when you see the vast majority of your twenty million Negro brothers smothering in an airtight cage of poverty in the midst of an affluent society; when you suddenly find your tongue twisted and your speech stammering as you seek to explain to your six year old daughter why she can't go to the public amusement

---

[62] Rieder, *Gospel of Freedom*, 122.

park that has just been advertised on television, and see tears welling up in her eyes when she is told that Funtown is closed to colored children, and see ominous clouds of inferiority beginning to form in her little mental sky, and see her beginning to distort her personality by developing an unconscious bitterness toward white people; when you have to concoct an answer for a five year old son who is asking: "Daddy, why do white people treat colored people so mean?"; when you take a cross county drive and find it necessary to sleep night after night in the uncomfortable corners of your automobile because no motel will accept you; when you are humiliated day in and day out by nagging signs reading "white" and "colored"; when your first name becomes "n*****," your middle name becomes "boy" (however old you are) and your last name becomes "John," and your wife and mother are never given the respected title "Mrs."; when you are harried by day and haunted by night by the fact that you are a Negro, living constantly at tiptoe stance, never quite knowing what to expect next, and are plagued with inner fears and outer resentments; when you are forever fighting a degenerating sense of "nobodiness"—then you will understand why we find it difficult to wait. There comes a time when the cup of endurance runs over, and men are no longer willing to be plunged into the abyss of despair. I hope, sirs, you can understand our legitimate and unavoidable impatience.[63]

King is impatient for justice because of the suffering that the injustice of segregation caused him, personally, and other Black citizens, more generally. The Letter is a powerful expression of Black suffering. It shows that a central cause of Black suffering is the experience not only of fear, as discussed in the previous chapter, but of humiliation—the diminished self-respect that comes with the feeling of not counting, of being "nothing."

[63] WWCW, 92–93.

According to King, "righteous indignation" is the form of anger that arises in response to injustice; it says "this is not just."[64] Righteous indignation is, in part, cognitive. It is a way of apprehending one's situation in response to one's experiences. Multiple experiences of racism led King and his father to see rationally that racial segregation posed an unjust affront to their dignity, and their refusal to accept these indignities quietly was an appropriate response. Their situation was unjust and they were right to see it as such.

But indignation is not only cognitive, as we see in King's expression of the anguish and suffering of Black people in the Letter. Anger is not only a cognitive belief but also a feeling. As Myisha Cherry argues, the Letter is a "Black man's cry of pain, anger, and defiance"—the emotional consequence of living under systemic racism.[65] In a similar vein, Audre Lorde has famously argued that anger is not only a belief but also feeling of "grief," a "fire."[66] Cherry sees King's account of indignation as Lordean, but perhaps it is more appropriate to think of Lorde's account as being somewhat inspired by King! Ultimately, however, Cherry's and King's accounts of indignation diverge in important ways: dignity, which is central to King's view, plays almost no role in Cherry's account of Lordean rage, and Cherry suggests (based on empirical work in the social sciences) that Lordean rage motivates, in part, because it encourages positive emotions—a sense of eagerness, optimism, and self-belief. In contrast, discomfort and suffering play a more central role in King's view of righteous indignation; for King, eagerness, optimism, and self-belief are more likely to emerge as a *result* of manifesting one's dignity through political action than they are to motivate such action. And it is the desire to avoid continued suffering itself that motivates political action, in King's view.

---

[64] *Autobiography*, 340.
[65] Cherry, *The Case for Rage*, 89. Here, she is quoting Rieder, *Gospel of Freedom*.
[66] Audre Lorde, "The Uses of Anger," in Lorde, *Sister* Outsider (Berkeley, CA: Crossing Press, 2007), 124–134.

This makes sense. Indignation has powerful physiological effects. It is something that we feel in our chests, our heads, something that courses through our bodies. These feelings are intense and can be very uncomfortable. Anger is motivating, in part, precisely because it is uncomfortable. The more uncomfortable we are, the more we wish to act in order to eliminate the source of our discomfort, and the more impatient we may feel to have our suffering end. The unpleasant feeling of anger can create in us a sense of urgency, making our desires for justice "hotter" or more intense. When our desire for justice is inflamed by anger—when the cognitive belief in injustice is paired with a visceral affective negative feeling caused by that injustice—it may feel more intense and become more likely to motivate action.[67] Black Americans' intense suffering under segregation, so cavalierly dismissed by the "Call for Unity," motivated King and his supporters to act to end the source of that suffering: racism and the racial segregation that it produces, which impacts the personal, social, and public lives of Black Americans. As King wrote, the "sweltering summer of the Negro's legitimate discontent will not pass until there is an invigorating autumn of freedom and equality."[68]

King believed that activating anger—righteous indignation—was a key motivator for political action. Harry Belafonte, who was both an adviser and confidant of King's and a financial patron of the movement, once said that King "always felt that anger was a very important commodity, a necessary part of the Black movement in this country."[69] In his book, *My Song*, Belafonte writes, "I was angry when I met him. Anger had helped protect me. Martin

---

[67] Here, King combines rationality and affect, just as he does in his discussion of how sensible sermons operate: again we see that reason combined with feelings leads to action.

[68] Martin Luther King, Jr., "Read Martin Luther King Jr.'s 'I Have a Dream' Speech in Its Entirety,'" *Talk of the Nation*, National Public Radio, January 14, 2022. Available at: https://www.npr.org/2010/01/18/122601268/i-have-a-dream-speech-in-its-entirety.

[69] Edward Gilbreath, *Remembering Birmingham: Dr. Martin Luther King Jr's Letter to American 50 Years Later* (Downers Grove, IL: IVP Books, 2013), 12.

understood my anger and saw its value. But our cause showed me how to redirect it and to make it productive."[70] King echoes this sentiment in his tribute to W. E. B. Du Bois, writing, "History had taught him it is not enough for people to be angry—the supreme task is to organize and unite people so that their anger becomes a transforming force."[71]

King's sense of the importance of indignation and anger is too often overlooked, for people tend to focus only on his nonviolent tactics. For example, in *Anger and Forgiveness*, Martha Nussbaum argues that King rejected anger as a proper response to the wrongs that he and his followers had suffered. In a recent interview, Amia Sreenivasan offers a similar reading, saying, "King didn't believe the problems of Black America could be solved by a politics of anger. Anger couldn't generate the creative response to oppression that was required; only love could do that. Malcolm X's anger, King thought, was counterproductive, a 'great disservice to his people' and to the cause of Black liberation."[72]

However, some philosophers are starting to see the importance of anger in King's philosophy. In more recent work, Nussbaum revisits and revises her position on King, arguing that he did believe that anger could be an appropriate emotion.[73] She argues that, in his view, anger is appropriate when (i) it does not express a desire for retribution or payback; (ii) it does not stem from a status-injury; and (iii) when it is quickly transitioned out of. Although this is an evolution in Nussbaum's thinking about King, it still does

---

[70] Harry Belafonte, *My Song* (New York: Alfred A. Knopf, 2011), 442.

[71] Martin Luther King, Jr., "Honoring Du Bois," *Jacobin*, January 1, 2019. Available at: https://jacobinmag.com/2019/01/web-du-bois-martin-luther-king-speech.

[72] Amia Sreenivasan, "In Defense of Anger," aired on BBC Radio 4's Four Thought, August 27, 2014; Amia Sreenivasan, "The Aptness of Anger," *Journal of Political Philosophy*, 26.2 (2018): 123–144.

[73] Martha Nussbaum, "From Anger to Love: Self-Purification and Political Resistance," in Terry and Shelby (eds.), *To Shape a New World*, 105–126. Nussbaum's erroneous interpretation of King is taken up by Maxim LePourtre, "Rage Inside the Machine: Defending the Place of Anger in Demoratic Speech," *Politics, Philosophy, & Economics*, 17.4 (2018): 398–426.

not go far enough; King's view is actually quite different from what Nussbaum proposes here.

According to Nussbaum, King believed that anger was not an appropriate response to status-injury—a wrongful loss of one's relative status, as judged in comparison to that of other people. Nussbaum argues that this kind of anger is not morally appropriate because it is narcissistic. She writes, "[a]nger is not always, but very often, about status-injury. And status-injury has a narcissistic flavor: rather than focusing on the wrongfulness of the act as such, a focus that might lead to concern for wrongful acts of the same type more generally, the status-angry person focuses obsessively on herself and her standing vis-à-vis others."[74]

However, King's work on dignity and the effect that violation of dignity has on the psychology of those so violated suggests a different line of thought: for King, anger can indeed be an appropriate response to a status-based injury. Recall his father's anger at the shoe store clerk or at the policemen, both of whom violated his innate dignity and maligned his worth as a human being. These were forms of status-injury, because they sought to place him in a lower position relative to white people. King distinguishes between what we might call inappropriate anger—Nussbaum's narcissistic anger, felt in response to an *individual* status-injury—and what he calls righteous indignation. As discussed, righteous indignation is a kind of anger that arises when there is an affront to one's sense of dignity and this affront is viewed as an injustice—that is, as the result of an unjust system. It is King's understanding of the *injustice* of the personal indignities that Black Americans experience that produces in him the sense of righteous indignation. There is nothing selfish or self-centered about this emotion. King and his father see their injured sense of self-respect as emblematic of a more general phenomena that all Black Americans experience under the system of

---

[74] Martha C. Nussbaum, *Anger and Forgiveness: Resentment, Generosity, Justice* (New York: Oxford University Press, 2016), 21.

racial segregation. In King's view, righteous indignation is a form of appropriate anger that occurs in response to a status-based injury.

Nussbaum also misinterprets King's ideas about how anger could be weaponized to create political action. She argues that he thinks "anger may bring people to ... [the] movement; [but] once there it must undergo purification or change."[75] In Nussbaum's view, this means that anger must be "replaced" with "love".[76] It is true that King worried about the usefulness and value of anger. He acknowledged that anger, because of its potential for violence and other forms of reckless behavior, could be "a destructive passion."[77] He, for example, talked about anger and its potential role in the race riots of Watts and New York. Acts of violence may be committed in the name of dignity, but they are distinct from the kind of dignified conduct—which requires self-restraint, calmness—that King advocated. He cautioned us not to react with "internal violence of spirit"[78] or to "allow ourselves to become bitter."[79] In saying we ought not become bitter, King meant we must not allow ourselves to take our anger "out on other people" and that we must not be "mean" to them.[80]

King did worry about our tendency to direct our anger at specific individuals, for in his view, this type of anger was unlikely to lead to the kind of structural change that was needed for Black dignity. For example, King writes, "a group of ten thousand marching in anger against a police station and cussing out the chief of police will

---

[75] Nussbaum, "From Anger to Love," 116.
[76] Ibid., 122.
[77] King, "Interview by Martin Agronsky," 269.
[78] Martin Luther King, Jr. "Address at the Fourth Annual Institute on Nonviolence and Social Change at Bethel Baptist Church," in Carson et al. (eds.), *The Papers of Martin Luther King, Jr.*, Volume V, 333–343 at 342. Available at: https://kinginstitute.stanford.edu/king-papers/documents/address-fourth-annual-institute-nonviolence-and-social-change-bethel-baptist.
[79] King, *Autobiography*, 91; King, "Desegregation and the Future," in Carson et al. (eds.), *The Papers of Martin Luther King, Jr.*, Volume III, 474.
[80] King, "Unfulfilled Hopes, Sermon," in Carson et al. (eds.), *The Papers of Martin Luther King, Jr.*, Volume V, 361.

do very little to bring respect, dignity, and unbiased law enforcement. Such a demonstration will only produce fear and bring about an addition of forces to the station and more oppressive methods by the police."[81] In his view, if we wish to eliminate the source of our righteous indignation, our actions must be directed at the true cause of racial injustice: the racist social and political systems of the United States, not individuals. To prevent this sort of misdirection, King constantly encouraged his supporters to focus their attention and efforts on legal, political, and social institutions, not individuals.

King did not believe that anger needed to be purified or transformed into love to be useful; it could be "harnessed by directing that same passion into constructive channels."[82] He felt that righteous indignation was best expressed through good conduct, and he exhorted people to act on their anger in "calm" and useful ways: "as you press for justice be sure to move with dignity."[83] He argued that protest must be conducted in an "orderly" fashion and must exhibit "wise restraint and calm dignity," rather than angry and violent behavior that would turn protest into an insurrection, and wrote that, "for such discipline, generations yet unborn will commend you."[84] These future commendations would go to those who "avoided both external physical violence and internal violence of the spirit."[85]

---

[81] TOH, 59.

[82] King, "Advice for Living," 269.

[83] Martin Luther King, Jr., "The Most Durable Power," in Carson et al. (eds.), *The Papers of Martin Luther King, Jr.*, Volume VI, 302–303 at 302. Available at: https://kinginstitute.stanford.edu/king-papers/documents/most-durable-power-excerpt-sermon-dexter-avenue-baptist-church-6-november-1956.

[84] Martin Luther King, Jr., "Facing the Challenge of a New Age," in Carson et al. (eds.), *The Papers of Martin Luther King, Jr.*, Volume III, 73–89 at 86. Available at: https://kinginstitute.stanford.edu/king-papers/documents/facing-challenge-new-age-address-delivered-naacp-emancipation-day-rally.

[85] Martin Luther King, Jr., "Address at the Fiftieth Annual NAACP Convention," in Carson et al. (eds.), *The Papers of Martin Luther King, Jr.*, Volume V, 245–250 at 247. Available at: https://kinginstitute.stanford.edu/king-papers/documents/address-fiftieth-annual-naacp-convention.

Although her argument that anger must be *replaced by* love is mistaken, Nussbaum is right in her contention that King sees a connection between anger and love: King has linked dignified, calm nonviolent action with loving action. He writes, "this is the time that we must evince calm dignity and wise restraint. Emotions must not run wild. Violence must not come from any of us, for if we become victimized with violent intents, we will have walked in vain, and our twelve months of glorious dignity will be transformed into an eve of gloomy catastrophe. As we go back to the busses let us be loving enough to turn an enemy into a friend."[86] Anger must be constrained and by channeled through love, not dissolved or eliminated by it.

Nussbaum is also right in noting that for King, an appropriate sense of indignation requires an anger that does not desire retaliation. In contrast to Aristotle, who believed that the retributive wish was part and parcel of anger, King did not believe that anger inherently involves a desire for retribution. He believed that anger is a natural response to the frustrations and injustices experienced by Black Americans, and that this anger could express itself in two different ways: it could either lead to the development of a "wholesome social organization to resist with effective, firm measures any efforts to impede progress" or it could produce a "confused, anger-motivated drive to strike back violently, to inflict damage."[87] This second type, which "[p]rimarily ... seeks to cause injury to retaliate wrongful suffering," is the retributive type of anger, which King sees as simply "punitive—not radical or constructive."[88]

King is aware that anger can—and perhaps often does—produce a desire for retribution, which might lead to violent action. But, he

---

[86] Martin Luther King, Jr., "Statement on Ending the Bus Boycott," in Carson et al. (eds.), *The Papers of Martin Luther King, Jr.*, Volume III, 485–487 at 487. Available at: https://kinginstitute.stanford.edu/king-papers/documents/statement-ending-bus-boycott.
[87] TOH, 32.
[88] Ibid., 32.

believes that we cannot give in to this violent desire. He stipulated that "we must not flirt with retaliatory violence or drink the poisonous wine of hate. Our aim must not be to defeat the white man or pay him back for past injustices heaped upon us."[89] Of course, King was only human, and sometimes his anger got the best of him, but angry outbursts were not his goal. In *Stride Toward Freedom*, he apologizes for an incident in which he had loudly expressed his anger, saying, "I had spoken hastily and resentfully. Yet I knew that this was no way to solve a problem. 'You must not harbor anger,' I admonished myself. 'You must be willing to suffer the anger of the opponent, and yet not return anger. You must not become bitter. No matter how emotional your opponents are, you must be calm."[90] For King, righteous indignation should not express itself through bitterness, hatred, or resentment but through love, forgiveness, and a commitment to the beloved community.

To appropriately *express* our anger, then, we must cultivate a sense of indignation without a desire for retaliation. Its energy must be harnessed and channeled through love into dignified conduct. As I will discuss in Chapter 7, King believed that the skills required to appropriately channel our anger (and the other emotions) into nonviolent action could be learned. In preparation for direct action, King and his supporters organized and participated in a series of workshops on nonviolence, which involved practicing being ready to endure physical and verbal abuse, as well as being put in jail, without striking back in violence.[91] Each volunteer also signed a "Commitment Card" that pledged, among other things, to always seek justice, to never use violence, and to walk and talk in love. King thought that steps like these could help to prevent us

---

[89] Martin Luther King, Jr., "The Negro and the American Dream," in Carson et al. (eds.), *The Papers of Martin Luther King, Jr.*, Volume V, 508–511 at 510. Available at: https://kinginstitute.stanford.edu/king-papers/documents/negro-and-american-dream-excerpt-address-annual-freedom-mass-meeting-north.
[90] STF, 110.
[91] WWCW, 67.

from expressing the more destructive elements of indignation—retributive anger—and instead to channel it into dignified loving action.

In the end, King saw dignity as not only giving rise to action but also constraining the type of action that can and ought to arise from that indignation. As Derrick Darby argues, having dignity is, in part, about acting in accordance with standards of dignified conduct, particularly when confronting oppression—refusing violence and retaliation, refusing to stoop to the level of a Bull Connor.[92] According to King, these normative standards of dignified behavior grow out of the moral and religious imperative to unconditionally love others and act nonviolently. To act with dignity and treat others with dignity is to love them. This is likely why King does not use the language of "replacing" anger with love. In King's view, love is not a replacement for anger. As the next chapter shows, love (like dignity) operates as a moral constraint on anger and it directs anger down appropriate paths that are useful to the movement.

---

[92] Darby, "Vindication of Voting Rights," 171.

6
Love

Early in the Letter, King asks a question that was central to both his thought and his activism: "The question is not whether we will be extremists, but what kind of extremists we will be. Will we be extremists for hate or for love?"[1] As mentioned in Chapter 5, King believed that the correct answer—the answer that was both morally right and effective—lay in "the more excellent way of love and nonviolent protest."[2] For him, love was the "key to the solution of the world's problem."[3] Love was the middle path between the complacency that led to "donothingism" and the hatred and despair that led to violence.[4] To understand why King preferred the path of love, we must first understand what King meant by love, which is deeply connected with his views about living a complete life.

For King, a complete life involves three dimensions: self, society, and God. As King put it in his sermon on living a complete life,

> Love yourself, you are commanded to do that. (*Well*) That is the length of life. (*Well*) Love your neighbor as you love yourself (*Oh yeah*), you are commanded to do that. That's the breadth of life. (*Well, Oh yes*) But never forget that there is a first and even greater commandment: Love the Lord thy God with all thy *heart* (*Oh yes*), with all thy *soul* (*Yes*), and with all thy *mind*. (*Yes*) That

---

[1] WWCW, 102.
[2] Ibid., 102.
[3] Martin Luther King, Jr. "Loving Your Enemies," in Carson et al. (eds.), *The Papers of Martin Luther King, Jr.*, Volume VI, 126–128 at 127. Available at: https://kinginstitute.stanford.edu/king-papers/documents/loving-your-enemies.
[4] WWCW, 100.

is the height of life. And when you do this, you'll live the complete life.[5]

We have discussed in previous chapters the importance to King of self-love, which he believes is the first part of living a complete life. For him, self-love "is the push of a life forward to achieve its inner powers and ambitions. It is the ... inward concern for one's own welfare."[6] Self-love is necessarily a selfish dimension of life, but this form of selfishness is not morally wrong; in his view, there is such a thing as rational and moral self-interest. However, King's demand for self-love is about more than simple self-interest. King believes that loving ourselves is a moral demand—a precursor to the ability to love others: he says that we must love ourselves "properly" before we can love other people "adequately."[7]

Indeed, it is this moral form of self-concern that drives us from our early life to "discover" what we are made for—what specific abilities God has given us—and to use them well. Until we know this, we cannot fulfill God's purpose for us. Through this self-discovery, we may realize that we only have "have five talents, some two, some one, but the important thing is that you do the best with whatever you have."[8] In other words, self-love requires self-acceptance—acceptance of and love of ourselves just as God made us. King says, "no matter what it [the self's specific ability] is, never consider it insignificant because if it is for the upbuilding of humanity (*Yes*) it has cosmic significance."[9] As discussed in the previous chapter, King sees self-love as a part of dignity; loving

---

[5] Martin Luther King, Jr., "The Three Dimensions of a Complete Life," in Carson et al. (eds.), *The Papers of Martin Luther King, Jr.*, Volume VI, 395–405 at 405. Available at: https://kinginstitute.stanford.edu/king-papers/documents/three-dimensions-complete-life-sermon-delivered-friendship-baptist-church.
[6] Ibid., 397.
[7] Ibid., 398.
[8] Ibid., 398.
[9] Ibid., 398.

ourselves is a way of properly valuing ourselves as beings with inherent worth.

This individual and personal self-love is associated with the "length of life." The second dimension, the love of others, is linked to "the breadth of life"—"that dimension in which we are concerned about others."[10] To live the complete life, says King, we must eventually move beyond the narrow confines of our individualistic concerns and develop a concern for our fellow human beings. According to King, there are several different types of love that are essential to realizing the breadth of life: from least to most broad, these are utilitarian love, eros, motherly love, *philio*, humanitarian love, agape, and, finally, the love of God.

King defines "utilitarian love" as "love at the lowest level."[11] This is where a person loves someone that he or she can use: "they see other people as mere steps by which they can climb to their personal ends and ambitions."[12] Unlike self-love, which prepares the ground for self-acceptance and love of others, utilitarian love is truly selfish: the person who loves in this way is merely loving himself through someone else.[13] Utilitarian love also violates the dignity of the other person. Following Kant, King argues that when you use a person as a means, you depersonalize that person, turning them into a mere object or thing. Recalling Buber, he argues that the utilitarian love relationship is at the level of "I and It," rather than "I and Thou"—a dangerous and terrible relationship between two fully human children of God.[14] When we fail to treat people as "thous," we fail to treat them as persons. This is the "tragedy of this level of love"—which is ultimately, King says, "the tragedy of racial segregation."[15]

---

[10] Ibid., 399.
[11] Martin Luther King, Jr., "Levels of Love," in Carson et al., *The Papers of Martin Luther King, Jr.*, Volume VI, 437–445 at 438. Available at: https://kinginstitute.stanford.edu/king-papers/documents/levels-love-sermon-delivered-ebenezer-baptist-church.
[12] Ibid., 438.
[13] Ibid., 438.
[14] Ibid., 438–439.
[15] Ibid., 439.

The next level of love, "eros," is more meaningful. According to King, "Plato used to use that word a great deal in his dialogues as a sort of yearning of the soul for the realm of the divine. But now we see it as romantic love, and there is something beautiful about romantic love."[16] Romantic love rises above utilitarian love, since it is altruistic. A person who really loves with romantic love will die for the object of his love, and will do anything to satisfy the object of that love.[17] However, in King's view, this is not the highest form of love, "because it is basically selfish."[18] He continues, "you love your lover because there is something about that person that attracts you ... the way she looks ... the way she talks ... her glowing femininity ... her intellectual qualities ... other physical qualities—something about her . . . attracts you."[19] King doesn't explain why being attracted to someone is selfish, but perhaps it is because in eros, what draws you to the other person is the pleasure they give you, which makes romantic love inherently self-concerned or selfish, directed inward toward a single other person, rather than outward toward humanity or toward God.

The third type of love in King's taxonomy is motherly love, which he (perhaps surprisingly) places on the same level as romantic love. Motherly love is a great love, to be sure, but it is still not the highest level of love. One might wonder, how this could be? After all, a mother's love is ideally tender, patient, and boundless. But, King sees a kind of selfish impulse, similar to that which drives eros, at the root of motherly love: "a mother loves her child because it is her child."[20] In other words, this love stems from how it makes us feel—it is an inner-directed love, rather than a love that reaches outward.

The next level of love is what King calls *philio*, or "the sort of intimate affection between personal friends."[21] King suggests that

---

[16] Ibid., 439.
[17] Ibid., 439.
[18] Ibid., 440.
[19] Ibid., 440.
[20] Ibid., 440.
[21] Ibid., 440.

this type of love is of a higher level because it has a broader scope and is more inclusive. It is less about how the friend makes one feel than about the friend themselves; it is a more disinterested love. In King's rather conventional view, romantic love typically takes place between two individuals of the opposite sex in an exclusive partnership. He says, "In romantic love, the individuals in love sit face to face absorbed in each other,"[22] and jealousy arises (rightly, in King's view) when one individual moves "towards a love act with another individual."[23] In contrast, in friendship, jealousy rarely arises; *philio* leaves room for many friends, since it is not based on sex or physical attraction or familial relationship. Friendship rises to another level of love because friends come together and are united because of a common interest in something beyond themselves.[24] As King puts it, friends are absorbed not in each other but "in some great concern and some great cause and some great issue beyond themselves, something they like to do together. It may be going and swimming together. It may be discussing great ideas together. It may be in a great movement of freedom together."[25]

Yet *philio* is still not an ideal love, for King also finds something selfish about it too: it is "always based on an affection for somebody that you like," somebody whose company you enjoy, that you like to talk and deal with.[26] It is hard to be friends with people we don't like. To show what he means, King names two examples of people whom Black Americans might dislike and find hard to befriend (and thus hard to love as God commands):[27] James O. Eastland, a member of Congress from Mississippi in 1941 and from 1943 until 1978, who used his power as chair of the Senate Judiciary Committee to block civil rights legislation, and Marvin Griffin, the

[22] Ibid., 441.
[23] Ibid., 441.
[24] Ibid., 441.
[25] Ibid., 441.
[26] Ibid., 441.
[27] Ibid., 441.

governor of Georgia from 1955 to 1959, who King thought did not care much for democracy.

King argues that the next level of love is "humanitarian love," which is even yet broader and more inclusive than *philio*. In humanitarian love, "the individual rises to the point that he loves humanity. And he rises to the point of saying that within in every man there is a divine spark. He rises to the point of saying that within every man there is something sacred and so all humanity must be loved. And so when one rises to love at this point he does get a little higher because he is seriously attempting to love everybody."[28] Yet, even humanitarian love is not the highest and broadest type of love: "it has a danger point. It is impersonal; it says I love this abstract something called humanity, which is never quite concretized in an individual."[29] In other words, it is easy to say, "I love humanity," while not acting lovingly toward every individual human. King gives the example of the white Christian missionaries. They raise money to send to African countries because of humanitarian love, but as he points out, "if the Africans who got that money came into their churches to worship on Sunday morning they would kick them out. (*Yes they would*) They love humanity in general, but they don't love Africans in particular. [*laughter*] (*That's right*)."[30] This is why humanitarian love can't be the highest level of love: it is much easier to love an abstraction than an individual human being.

The next type of love that King discusses as part of a complete life is *agape*, which is a disinterested love for each individual human within humanity. This, he says, is the form of love that is closest to God's love for us: "*Agape* is higher than all of the things I have talked about."[31] Agape is love that is "understanding and creative, redemptive goodwill for all men."[32] It is not "motivated by some

[28] Ibid., 441.
[29] Ibid., 441.
[30] Ibid., 442.
[31] STL, 46.
[32] Martin Luther King, "Loving Your Enemies," in Clayborne Carson and Peter Holloran, *A Knock at Midnight* (Warner Books, 2000), 49.

quality in the object"; it is spontaneous, overflowing, and seeks nothing in return. When we love at this level, we love people not because we like them, or because they appeal to us, or because they are useful to us, but because God loves them: "you love every man, not for your sake but for his sake. And you love every man because God loves him.... And so it becomes all inclusive."[33]

For King, agapeic love is "the love of God operating in the human heart"—it is a distinctly Christian form of love. God loves us, regardless of our weaknesses, flaws, and failures. God's love is eternal, with no beginning or end.[34] God's love has breadth; it is a big, broad love that is all inclusive,[35] not limited to one race or any single nation.[36] God's love is self-giving and spontaneous: "God's gift to man was given not because God was asked to give it, but because he wanted to give it."[37] In King's view, "God's love is redemptive. God's love gives life and new light."[38] Agapeic love is a love that is indifferent to merit, bestowed out of pure generosity.[39] It requires that, like God, we love with "understanding, redemptive goodwill for all men"[40]—even those who oppose us or aim to defeat us.[41] With agapeic love, we "rise to the noble heights of loving

---

[33] King, "Levels of Love," 442.

[34] Martin Luther King, Jr. "God's Love" in Carson et al. (eds.), *The Papers of Martin Luther King, Jr.*, Volume VI, 179–181 at 180. Available at: https://kinginstitute.stanford.edu/king-papers/documents/gods-love-sermon-dexter-avenue-baptist-church

[35] Ibid., 180.

[36] Ibid., 180.

[37] Ibid., 181.

[38] Ibid., 181.

[39] Martin Luther King, Jr., "Contemporary Continental Theology," in Clayborne Carson, Ralph Luker, Penny A. Russell, and Peter Holloran (eds.), *The Papers of Martin Luther King, Jr.*, Volume II: *Rediscovering Precious Values, July 1951–November 1955* (Berkeley and Los Angeles: University of California Press, 1994), 113–139 at 127. Available at: https://kinginstitute.stanford.edu/king-papers/documents/contemporary-continental-theology.

[40] Martin Luther King, Jr., "Loving Your Enemies, Sermon (Detroit)," in Carson et al. (eds.), *The Papers of Martin Luther King, Jr.*, Volume VI, 421–429 at 424. Available at: https://kinginstitute.stanford.edu/king-papers/documents/loving-your-enemies-sermon-delivered-detroit-council-churches-noon-lenten.

[41] Ibid., 424.

the person who does the evil deed while hating the deed that the person does."[42]

King believes that, just as God loves even the faithless, Black American masses must love even those who may never love them back—a form of agapeic love, which "seeks nothing in return."[43] As Justin Rose notes, for King, this kind of love "is necessary in the struggle for justice because Black Americans, especially those among the masses, cannot depend on reciprocal sentimentality from white Americans"[44] or even from the Black elite. Agapeic love is crucial to the fight for justice precisely because it takes one outside the bounds of self-interest. It is self-interest, according to King, that has kept segregation in force: people (both white people and elite and middle-class Black people) are too focused on "their preferred economic positions, their political power, their so-called way of life"[45]—in other words, the matters of "the length of life"—to attend to higher questions of morality and justice. While King directly addresses his discussion of these matters to white people, this also applies to the Black middle and upper classes, who, in his view, too often maintain the status quo in order to protect their social and economic positions. Indeed, it perhaps especially applies to Black elites, for King believes that individuals who have been oppressed must focus not only on worldly things (the length of life) but also higher things (the breadth of life), for "those of us who have been on the oppressed end of the old order have as much responsibility to be concerned about breadth as anybody else."[46] King believes that, if Black and white Americans would "add breadth to length,

---

[42] Ibid., 425.
[43] Ibid., 425.
[44] Rose, *The Drum Major Instinct*, 26.
[45] Martin Luther King, Jr., "The Three Dimensions of a Complete Life [Unitarian]," in Carson et al. (eds.), *The Papers of Martin Luther King, Jr.*, Volume V, 571–579 at 575. Available at: https://kinginstitute.stanford.edu/king-papers/documents/three-dimensions-complete-life-sermon-delivered-unitarian-church-germantown.
[46] Ibid., 575.

the other-regarding dimension to the self-regarding dimension, we would be able to solve all of the problems ... in our nation today."[47]

This is why agapeic love "stands at the center of the movement."[48] King recognizes that it is difficult to like everyone. It is especially difficult to like those who are bombing our homes and threatening our children, or those who fight against civil rights legislation. But Jesus did not ask us to like them; he asked us to love them. In King's interpretation, Jesus's command to love our enemies was not "the pious injunction of a utopian dreamer" but the words of a "practical realist."[49] Jesus knew that the command was difficult.[50] But agapeic love is actually more attainable than a command to "like everybody" would be; it is easier to love those who oppose you than it is to like them.

The final type of love that is necessary to live a fully complete life is the human love of God. King says that we must reach up beyond ourselves, beyond humanity and the mundane world, high enough to discover and love God. Why would King make this request of his readers? After all, he was usually speaking to Christian audiences, who presumably already believed in and loved God. This is because for King, the "height of life" involves more than merely agreeing that God exists; it involves *action*. As King writes, "intellectual assent is merely agreeing that something is true, belief is *acting* like it is true"[51] [emphasis mine]. King worries that some within the Church pay "lip service" to God, saying they believe but living as if there is no God. As King puts it, these people are focused on creeds, not deeds. This is how he views the white moderate clergymen who wrote the "Call for Unity," and Birmingham's Black middle- and upper-class citizens who refused to show up to

---

[47] Ibid., 575.
[48] Martin Luther King, Jr., "Power of Nonviolence," in James Melvin Washington (ed.), *A Testament of Hope: The Essential Writings and Speeches of Martin Luther King Jr.* (New York: Harper One, 1986), 13.
[49] King, "Loving Your Enemies, Sermon (Detroit)," 422.
[50] King, "Loving Your Enemies," 128.
[51] King, "Three Dimensions," 402.

the protests. He worries that middle-class Black Americans have been so focused on the length of life—the material signs of progress in life, like "big cars" and "big bank accounts" and "beautiful homes"—that they forgot about the second and third dimensions of a complete life: the breadth of love for their fellow man and the height of their love for God, expressed through resolute action.

To reach the real height of a complete life, King says that his hearers and readers must accept, love, and emulate Christ. He exhorts them to see that "God's love stands before us. God's love is always ready. He's calling you now. Make the church the center of your life, for here, we come to the mercy seat."[52] In King's view, "God is love," and those who love God rise "to a knowledge of God."[53] Most importantly, to reach the heights of a complete life, they must put this love and knowledge into action. To be a Christian, in King's view, is to deliberately take up the cross—to make the deliberate choice to put ourselves "without reservation at the service of Christ and his kingdom; it is putting our whole being in the struggle against evil, whatever the cost."[54] To love God, then, is to engage in action to end evil and injustice—to do good deeds, not merely espouse creeds. By walking the path God has set for us, we realize our unique relationship with God and reach the full height of love.[55] By *walking and talking* in love, by loving our enemies, we are "able to be children of our father who is in heaven."[56]

We might ask, as King does, "why should we love our enemies?"[57] He gives us many reasons for doing so. The first reason is pragmatic. King believed that returning hate for hate would only multiply hate; in the modern world, with its nuclear weapons and global

---

[52] King, "Levels of Love," 445.
[53] King, "Levels of Love," 444.
[54] Martin Luther King, Jr., "It's Hard to be a Christian," in Carson et al. (eds.), *The Papers of Martin Luther King, Jr.*, Volume VI, 251–252 at 252. Available at: https://kinginstitute.stanford.edu/king-papers/documents/its-hard-be-christian.
[55] STL, 50.
[56] Ibid., 47.
[57] Ibid., 47.

tensions, refusing to love our enemies could end in the annihilation of all. For King, hate gives rise to and is embodied in violence, and Jesus's commandment to love our enemies was an "inescapable admonition," for, in King's words, "the chain reaction of evil—hate begetting hate, wars producing more wars—must be broken."[58]

To illustrate this point, King tells the story of driving with his brother from Atlanta, Georgia, to Chattanooga, Tennessee. His brother was driving the car, and for some reason oncoming drivers did not dim their headlights, as is customary when passing others in the night. King reports that his brother became angry and said that he would no longer dim his headlights for cars that came along on the highway. King replied: "'Wait a minute. Don't you do that. For if you refuse to dim your lights, there will be a little too much light on this highway . . . , and [it] may end up in destruction for all of us. Somebody will have to have sense enough on this highway to dim their lights.'"[59] King made explicit the connection between this story and the dangers of returning anger for anger, hate for hate, saying "maybe here we find an analogy to the whole struggle of life. Somebody must have sense enough to dim their lights."[60] Someone must be the first to dim their lights—to take action to end the cycle of racial violence—in order to avert the potential destruction of everyone on the road.

The second reason that we should love rather than hate our enemies is that hate harms ourselves as much as it does the other: "hate scars the soul and distorts the personality."[61] It is obvious how hate can harm the person who is hated; according to King, it was the force behind the brutal lynchings of Black Americans in the South, which inspired fear in Black men and women and thwarted their freedom.[62] But as King emphasized,

---

[58] Ibid., 47.
[59] King, "Loving Your Enemies, Sermon (Detroit)," 426.
[60] Ibid., 426.
[61] STL, 47.
[62] King, "Loving Your Enemies, Sermon (Detroit)," 426.

"hate damages a white man, in many instances, more than it damages the Negro, for it does something to the personality; it does something to the soul."[63] King argues that many overlook this fact: hate is "as damaging to the subject of hate as it is to the object of hate."[64] In his view, the individual who hates loses his sense of values, rationality, and objectivity; he "can't see right," and as a result, he is unable to "walk right."[65] According to King, people who are filled with hate (like those filled with fear) act with "irrational and abnormal unbalance."[66] Hate distorts the whole personality and is a barrier to right action.

The third reason that we should love our enemies is that "love has within [it] a redemptive power."[67] While "hate destroys and tears down . . . love creates and builds up."[68] Why is that? King believes that agapeic love requires forgiveness of those who inflict evil and injury upon us.[69] This forgiveness does not mean the wronged person ignores what has been done; "it means, rather, that the evil act no longer remains as a barrier to the relationship."[70] "It is a pardon. It is a fresh start, another chance, a new beginning."[71] According to King, forgiveness is the catalyst to a new relationship; it creates the grounds for reconciliation and, in turn, for community. Because of its connection to forgiveness, King believes, "love is the only force capable for transforming an enemy into a friend."[72] We never get rid of an enemy by meeting hate with hate; we get rid of an enemy by getting rid of enmity. By its very nature, hate destroys, tears down; by its very nature, love creates and builds up,

---

[63] Ibid., 426.
[64] Ibid., 426.
[65] Ibid., 427.
[66] STL, 48.
[67] King, "Loving Your Enemies, Sermon (Detroit)" 425.
[68] STL, 48.
[69] Ibid., 44.
[70] Ibid., 45.
[71] Martin Luther King, Jr., "The Meaning of Forgiveness," in Carson et al. (eds.), *The Papers of Martin Luther King, Jr.*, Volume VI, 580–581 at 580. Available at: https://kinginstitute.stanford.edu/king-papers/documents/meaning-forgiveness.
[72] STL, 48.

transforms with redemptive power.[73] Love gives rise to forgiveness; forgiveness makes reconciliation possible;[74] reconciliation makes friendship possible; and friendship makes moral progress more likely.

As an example of the transformative power of love, King discussed the relationship between President Lincoln and Edwin M. Stanton. Stanton was a lawyer who eventually served as Secretary of War in the Lincoln administration during the American Civil War. When Lincoln was campaigning for the presidency, Stanton was Lincoln's archenemy. Stanton used his powers and efforts to tarnish Lincoln's reputation publicly, saying things like, "You don't want this tall, lanky, ignorant man as your president."[75] Yet, despite this, when it came to choose his Secretary of War, Lincoln chose Stanton. Many of Lincoln's supporters believed this choice was a mistake. Lincoln responded, "Yes, I know Mr. Stanton. I am aware of all the terrible things he has said about me. But after looking over the nation, I find he is the best man for the job."[76] As King tells it, Stanton later reported that Lincoln was one of the greatest men that ever lived. King wrote, "if Lincoln had hated Stanton both men would have gone to their graves as bitter enemies. But through the power of love Lincoln transformed an enemy into a friend."[77] Love and friendship made Lincoln and Stanton's shared fight against the Confederacy possible—the fight that led to the abolition of the injustice of slavery. This, says King, is the power of agapeic love.

---

[73] Ibid., 48. In contrast, King claims that hate produces three outcomes. First, it multiplies hate; second, it harms the person who hates, distorting their personality and soul by making them irrational and imbalanced; third, it harms the person who is hated, often leading to violence. King doesn't give a developed argument for these claims. He thinks it is obvious that hate has the tendency to bring about bad consequences in these ways. On these points, see STL, 47–49.

[74] One might wonder, are there not conditions that the other side must meet to merit forgiveness and make reconciliation possible? In King's view, the answer is no. This is largely because he believes that moderates should not be blamed for their actions. On this see, STL, ch. 5 ("Loving your enemies") and Chapter 2 ("self-reliance") of this book.

[75] "Loving Your Enemies, Sermon (Detroit)," 427.

[76] STL, 49.

[77] Ibid., 49.

King has thus explained *why* we should love our enemies. Next, he turns to the practical question of *how* we go about it. First, he says, we must engage in self-analysis. King notes that while some people do hate others for no reason, this is not always true. He says, "there might be causes on your end. You might have done something in the past" to mistreat or hurt the other person.[78] As an example, King asks us to "notice the international situation[.] Communism is our enemy because of many of our blunders."[79] It is important, he says, that we first take a square look at ourselves, notice our own part in the conflict, and attempt to repair what we are responsible for.

Second, we must forgive our enemies. An enemy is someone who has done something to hurt us—someone who "has mistreated us or has mistreated our group," drawing us into conflict.[80] The only way to move through the conflict is for the mistreated person to develop the capacity to forgive—to dim one's headlights even when others do not. It "is through this method that we are able to restore the moral balance of society or individual relationships, for in the final analysis, forgiveness means a willingness to go any length to restore a broken relationship."[81] Forgiveness does not mean forgetting that the hurt or mistreatment occurred (perhaps this is why King often referred to "enemy-neighbors" or "enemy-friends"), "but it means that you erase it from your mind in the sense that it no longer serves as a determining factor in the future relationship."[82] It no longer remains a barrier to forming a new relationship. To begin loving your enemies, you must develop the capacity to forgive.

Third, to love our enemies, we must always be willing to see their good points: "We must recognize that the negative deed of the enemy does not represent all that the individual is."[83] King believes

---

[78] King, "Loving Your Enemies," 127.
[79] Ibid., 127.
[80] "Loving Your Enemies, Sermon (Detroit)," 423.
[81] Ibid., 423.
[82] Ibid., 423.
[83] Ibid., 423.

that we can find an element of goodness in even our worst enemies, for we are all divided against ourselves. If we look at ourselves and others hard enough, we see a strange and disturbing dichotomy—that while we believe we ought to do one thing, we very often do another. King believed, "there is something within all of us which causes us to cry out with Ovid the Latin poet, 'I see and approve the better things of life, but the evil things I do.'"[84] For King, this means that even in the worst of us, there is some good, and even in the best of us, there is some evil. When we realize this, we can first forgive and then love everyone, even our enemies, for we can find some good even in those who hate us most and who seek to defeat us. We can see our enemies in a new light, recognizing that the evilness of their acts is not all that they are, and that even in the face of fear, pride, ignorance, prejudice, and misunderstanding, "God's image is ineffably etched in his being."[85] Our enemies too are God's children, created with inherent worth and dignity, and deserving of love and respect.

Finally, to love our enemy we must let go of the desire for revenge. We must "seek at all times to win his friendship and understanding rather than to defeat him or humiliate him"[86] or to "pay him back" for injustices that he has heaped upon us.[87] Love requires instead that we seek "to lift or rather to change the opponent, to redeem him."[88] King's commitment to loving our enemies is part of his commitment to recognizing the inherent dignity of all. This recognition is incompatible with seeking to humiliate or undermine another person, even an enemy. To recognize the worth of everyone is

---

[84] Ibid., 423.
[85] STL, 45–46.
[86] King, "Loving Your Enemies, Sermon (Detroit)," 424; cf. STL, 46.
[87] King, "The Most Durable Power," in Carson et al. (eds.), *The Papers of Martin Luther King, Jr.*, Volume VI, 302.
[88] Martin Luther King, Jr., "Non-Aggression Procedures to Interracial Harmony," in Carson et al. (eds.), *The Papers of Martin Luther King, Jr.*, Volume III, 321–328 at 326. Available at: https://kinginstitute.stanford.edu/king-papers/documents/non-aggress ion-procedures-interracial-harmony-address-delivered-american.

to see the possibility of goodness in even the worst of people. This is why, even as we work to do away with an unjust system, we must engage in "an active love" for the individuals who may be caught up in that system.[89] We must aim to defeat segregation, not the segregationist. King believes "it is this type of spirit and this type of love that can transform opposers into friends. It is this type of understanding goodwill that will transform the deep gloom of the old age into the exuberant gladness of the new age. It is this love which will bring about miracles in the hearts of men."[90]

To put this kind of love into action, we will have to make sacrifices. As King sees it, this is an "inescapable" truth: we cannot accomplish anything in this life without sacrificing ourselves for one thing or another.[91] Agape, as a divine form of love, demands our all, and King believes that giving our all involves self-sacrifice. This sacrifice is redemptive, for it is through loving self-sacrifice that we transform the world and those around us. King famously said:

> My friends, we must keep on believing that unearned suffering is redemptive. We must say to our white brothers all over the South who would try to keep us down: We will match your capacity to inflict suffering with our capacity to endure suffering. We will meet your physical force with soul force. We will not hate you, and yet we cannot in all good conscience obey your evil laws. (Yes) Do to us what you will. Threaten our children, and we will still love you. (Yeah) Come into our homes at the midnight hours of life and take us out on some desolate highway and beat us and leave us there, and we will still love you. (Yeah) Run all around the country and send your literature, and say that we

---

[89] King, "Loving Your Enemies, Sermon (Detroit)," 424.
[90] Martin Luther King, Jr., "Facing the Challenge of a New Age," in Carson et al. (eds.), *The Papers of Martin Luther King, Jr.*, Volume III, 458.
[91] Martin Luther King, Jr., "Facing Life's Inescapables," in Carson et al. (eds.), *The Papers of Martin Luther King, Jr.*, Volume VI, 88–90 at 89. Available at: https://kinginstitute.stanford.edu/king-papers/documents/facing-lifes-inescapables.

aren't worthy of integration, that we are too immoral, that we are too low, that we are too degraded, yet we will still love you. (Yeah) Bomb our homes and go by our churches early in the morning and bomb them if you please (Well), and we will still love you. (Yeah) But we will wear you down by our capacity to suffer. (All right) And in winning the victory, we will not only win our freedom, we will so appeal to your heart and your conscience, that we will win you in the process. (Oh yeah) And our victory will be a double victory. (Yeah) We will win our freedom, and we will win the individuals who have been the perpetrators of the evil system that existed so long. (Yes sir) This is the thing that we must say; this is the thing that we must do. (Yes) If we do this, we will be able to bring into being, by the grace of God, this new world. (Yes).[92]

King believed that the leaders of the Civil Rights Movement exemplified this willingness to sacrifice themselves on the altar of love and justice.[93] In his view, there is nothing more "majestic and sublime" than the courage of individuals willing to suffer and sacrifice for their collective freedom.[94]

As an example of the kind of sacrifice that is demanded of us, King reminds us of Jesus's Good Samaritan parable. A man is robbed and left for dead on the side of a dangerous road between Jerusalem and Jericho. Two different men, a Levite and a priest, passed him by without stopping to help. Later, the Samaritan—a man of another race—came by, stopped, and helped the man.[95] King first

---

[92] Martin Luther King, Jr., "Some Things We Must Do," in Carson et al. (eds.), *The Papers of Martin Luther King, Jr.*, Volume IV, 341.

[93] Martin Luther King, Jr. "Address at Public Meeting of the Southern Christian Ministers Conference of Mississippi," in Carson et al. (eds.), *The Papers of Martin Luther King, Jr.*, Volume V, 281–290 at 282. Available at: https://kinginstitute.stanford.edu/king-papers/documents/address-public-meeting-southern-christian-ministers-conference-mississippi.

[94] Ibid., 282.

[95] Martin Luther King, Jr., "The Three Dimensions of a Complete Life (Germantown)," in Carson et al. (eds.), *The Papers of Martin Luther King, Jr.*, Volume

considers why the Levite and priest did not stop—perhaps they were busy with other commitments and priorities. But the possibility he returns to is that those men were simply afraid.[96] After all, as King writes, "the Jericho road is a dangerous road."[97] It is a mountainous road, wandering and curving, conducive to robbery. The two men may have been afraid to stop because they were afraid of a trap—afraid that they themselves would be robbed. The Levite and the priest may have wondered, "If I stop to help this man, what will happen to me?"[98] The Samaritan, in contrast, arrived with the question reversed, asking, "If I do not stop to help this man, what will happen to him?"[99]

King suggests that the Samaritan had the capacity for "a dangerous altruism."[100] Altruism is a "regard for, and devotion to, the interest of others"; dangerous altruism adds the element of self-denial—"saying 'no' to" the self's own desires.[101] Dangerous altruism requires us to subordinate our egos to the pressing concerns of God's Kingdom and racial justice.[102] It is difficult to carry out, for it requires that the "I" be immersed in the "thou."[103] The Samaritan risked his own life to save a brother,[104] without considering what would happen to his job, prestige, or status. King likens the Samaritan to Lincoln: "Abraham Lincoln did not ask 'What will happen to me if I issue the Emancipation Proclamation and bring

---

V, 571–579 at 574. Available at: https://kinginstitute.stanford.edu/king-papers/documents/three-dimensions-complete-life-sermon-delivered-unitarian-church-germantown.

[96] Ibid., 574.
[97] Ibid., 574.
[98] Ibid., 574.
[99] Ibid., 574.
[100] Ibid., 574.
[101] King, "It's Hard to be a Christian," 252.
[102] Ibid., 252.
[103] Ibid., 252.
[104] Martin Luther King, Jr., "On Being a Good Neighbor," in Carson et al. (eds.), *The Papers of Martin Luther King, Jr.*, Volume VI, 478–486 at 481. Available at: https://kinginstitute.stanford.edu/king-papers/documents/draft-chapter-iii-being-good-neighbor; STL, 25.

an end to chattel slavery.'"[105] He then exhorts his audience to take the same kinds of risks. He says, the Black professional should not ask, "'What will happen to my secure position, my middle-class status, or my personal safety, if I participate in the movement to end the system of racial segregation?' but 'What will happen to the cause of justice and the masses of Negro people who have never experienced the warmth of economic security, if I do not participate actively and courageously in the movement.'"[106] Like the Samaritan, King believes, Black Americans should focus not on the things they might be called on to give up, but on the cause of justice that their sacrifices will serve.[107]

According to King, the Samaritan's act was not only dangerous altruism but also "excessive altruism"[108]—he went above and beyond what he was morally required to do—and "universal altruism."[109] The Samaritan did not limit his compassion to his own race, tribe, or class.[110] He bandaged the man's wounds with his own hands and carried him to town on his horse; he gave an innkeeper two silver coins to pay for his food, lodging, and care and offered to meet any further financial needs that arose (Luke 10.35); and although he was a wealthy man, he did not feel himself above the poor traveler. As King says, the Samaritan "was a great man because he not only ascended to the heights of economic security but because he could condescend to the depths of human need."[111] The Samaritan prioritized not self-preservation but other-preservation.[112]

In King's view, universal compassion (which is agapeic love put into action) is both a fundamental religious value and a fundamental American value. Universal altruism stands "at the center

---

[105] STL, 26.
[106] Ibid., 26.
[107] Ibid., 26.
[108] Ibid., 27.
[109] Ibid., 23.
[110] King, "On Being a Good Neighbor," 479.
[111] King, "The Three Dimensions (Germantown)," 574.
[112] King, "On Being a Good Neighbor," 479.

of the Declaration of Independence," but it "has been shamefully negated by America's appalling tendency to substitute some for all."[113] What has negated it? King points to "[o]ur unswerving devotion to monopoly capitalism," which sets up the economy as a "tribal god" and produces "a tribal ethic"—one that benefits only the "security of the captains of industry, and not the laboring men whose sweat and skills keep the wheels of industry rolling."[114] The narrow tribal ethic of capitalism means that we are not concerned with what happens to people outside our group. King claims that manufacturers, acting in self-interest, will pass by thousands of working people left on some Jericho road, stripped of their jobs by automation. The owners reject attempts to ensure a more equitable distribution of wealth and a better life for working people, just as a white man who is concerned only with his own group's safety might pass by a Black man on the side of the road.[115]

According to King, the priest and the Levite saw the injured man as an entity or mere thing, a bleeding body rather than a person like themselves.[116] In contrast, the Samaritan saw the man as a person first. King argues that if the Samaritan had considered the injured man as a Jew rather than a person first, then he would not have stopped, since, at the time, Jews and Samaritans did not interact with one another. As King puts it, "Jesus implied that this Samaritan was good, that he was great, because he had the capacity to project the I into the Thou."[117] In other words, he had the capacity to fully respect the injured man as an individual possessing inherent and equal worth.

Ultimately, the Samaritan makes a voluntary choice to engage in his dangerous, excessive, universalist altruism. The story of the Samaritan reminds us that "taking up the cross is the voluntary or

---

[113] Ibid., 480.
[114] Ibid., 480;STL, 23.
[115] STL, 24.
[116] Ibid., 24.
[117] King, "The Three Dimensions of a Complete Life (Germantown)," 574.

deliberate choice of putting ourselves without reservation at the service of Christ and his kingdom; it is putting our whole being in the struggle against evil, whatever the cost."[118] But the story of the Samaritan does not encompass the whole of our moral responsibilities to one another and to the cause of justice.[119] In some of his earlier writings, King had presented some criticisms of the Samaritan, arguing that Jesus shared the story of the Samaritan not to show us the ideal version of love for our fellow man but to show us what initial steps to take as we work to reach that ideal. The weakness of the good Samaritan is that he "was concerned [*merely*] with temporary relief, not with thorough reconstruction. He sought to sooth the effects of evil, without going back to uproot the causes."[120] In other words, the Samaritan had not yet reached the full height of the complete life; despite his kindness and altruism, he does not display truly agapeic love.

Of course, these beginning steps are crucial; like the Samaritan, King believes, we must first help the injured man on the road. We should give charitably to the Red Cross and United Way. Amidst suffering, we should not simply pass by. But we should also do more than this. We must also "tear down unjust conditions and build anew instead of patching things up."[121] We must not only care for the victims of robbery but also ensure that the road is clear of robbers. The Jericho Road represents the structures and processes of a state that all of its citizens participate in and are subject to. As Justin Rose notes, these structures allow some to flourish while making others—the marginalized—more vulnerable to harm and deprivation.[122] King's point is that while we must help the individuals

---

[118] King, "It's Hard to be a Christian," 252.
[119] Martin Luther King, Jr., "The One-Sided Approach of the Samaritan," in Carson et al. (eds.), *The Papers of Martin Luther King, Jr.*, Volume VI, 239–240 at 239. Available at: https://kinginstitute.stanford.edu/king-papers/documents/one-sided-approach-good-samaritan.
[120] Ibid., 240.
[121] Ibid., 240.
[122] Rose, *The Drum Major Instinct*, 20.

who are harmed by unjust structures, we must also change the structures that harmed them in the first place—and we must voluntarily choose to make the sacrifices that are needed to make this change. We must choose to work determinedly to achieve freedom and human dignity, whatever the cost. This is how we fully realize agapeic love for our neighbors and our enemies.

Ultimately, in King's view, "love is always the regulating ideal" in the struggle for dignity and freedom.[123] This means that love must guide and govern all political action, including "the technique" for overcoming racial segregation.[124] To emphasize love as the regulating ideal requires that we channel our other emotions—fear, fearlessness, dignity, and indignation—through love and into action. King says:

> we have refused in our struggle to succumb to the temptation of becoming bitter and indulging in a hate campaign. We are not out to defeat or to humiliate ... [our enemy]. We are out to help him as well as ourselves. . . . The festering sore of segregation debilitates the white man as well as the Negro . . . and so we are not out to win a victory over the white man. And I assure you that the basic struggle in Montgomery after all is not between Negroes and white people. The struggle is at bottom a tension between justice and injustice. . . . It is a tension between the forces of light and the forces of darkness. And if there is a victory in Montgomery, it will not be a victory merely for fifty thousand Negroes, but it will be a victory for justice . . . a victory for democracy . . . and a victory for good will. This is at bottom the meaning of Christian love, and we are trying to follow that. It is that high type of love that I have talked about so often . . . we are talking about agape. We are talking about understanding good will. We are talking about a love which seeks nothing in return. We are talking about a love

---

[123] King, "Non-Aggression Procedures to Interracial Harmony," 326.
[124] Ibid., 328.

that loves the person who does the evil deed, while hating the deed that the person does. That is a higher type of love.[125]

For King, love is the reigning ideal. It should govern relations between people, even those who have long been enemies. This is, in his view, the only way to ensure true liberty for all.

King writes, freedom—"that vital, intrinsic value which determines one's selfhood"—is worth any sacrifice: "It is worth suffering for: it is worth losing a job for: it is worth going to jail for. I would rather be a poor free man than a rich slave. I would rather live in a humble dwelling by the side of the road with my freedom and a sense of dignity than to live on some palatial hillside a mental slave. Once more every Negro must be able to cry out with his forefathers: 'Before I'll be a slave, I'll be buried in my grave and go home to my Father and be saved.'"[126] Freedom for all will require significant sacrifice, even from those who are already suffering from oppression, but especially from those who are benefiting from it.

King recognizes that when the willingness to sacrifice the self is present, it is not always completely altruistic: there is a "danger of developing a martyr complex and of making others feel that he is consciously seeking sympathy. It is possible for one to be self-centered in his self-denial and self-righteous in his self-sacrifice."[127] However, because Black Americans are bound to suffer in an unjust system, King believes that self-sacrifice can help them find

---

[125] Martin Luther King, Jr., "The Montgomery Story," in Carson et al. (eds.), *The Papers of Martin Luther King, Jr.*, Volume III, 299–310 at 305–306. Available at: https://kinginstitute.stanford.edu/king-papers/documents/montgomery-story-address-delivered-forty-seventh-annual-naacp-convention.

[126] King, "Address at the Fourth Annual Institute on Nonviolence and Social Change at Bethel Baptist Church," in Carson et al. (eds.), *The Papers of Martin Luther King, Jr.*, Volume V, 333–344 at 339. Available at: https://kinginstitute.stanford.edu/king-papers/documents/address-fourth-annual-institute-nonviolence-and-social-change-bethel-baptist.

[127] Martin Luther King, Jr., "Suffering and Faith," in Carson et al. (eds.), *The Papers of Martin Luther King, Jr.*, Volume V, 443–444 at 443. Available at: https://kinginstitute.stanford.edu/king-papers/documents/suffering-and-faith.

potential and power in this reality. King himself had made this choice, committing himself to the Christian virtue of self-sacrifice to transform the unjust world in which we live—and, as we know looking back, he would end up paying the ultimate sacrifice, his life. He described his decision this way:

> "As my sufferings mounted I soon realized that there are two ways that I could respond to my situation: either to react with bitterness or seek to transform the suffering into a creative force. I decided to follow the latter course. Recognizing the necessity for suffering I have tried to make of it a virtue. If only to save myself from bitterness, I have attempted to see my personal ordeals as an opportunity to transform myself and heal the people involved in the tragic situation which now obtains. I have lived these last few years with the conviction that unearned suffering is redemptive."[128]

As King sees things, it is simply a fact that Black Americans will continue to suffer under the system of Jim Crow. Why not turn that suffering into something productive—through nonviolence and the sacrifices it requires—that will ultimately reduce this suffering?

King places a heavy emphasis on the willingness to sacrifice the self for the larger cause of justice—a position that bell hooks found overly oriented toward the other and too little oriented toward Black self-love. As she points out, he "talked more about loving our enemies" and the sacrifices it required than about loving the self.[129] But, in King's view, loving others was in fact a way of loving the self.

---

[128] Ibid., 444. King further asserts, "If only to save ourselves from bitterness, we need the vision to see the ordeals of this generation as an opportunity to transfigure ourselves and American society. Let us not fear going to jail. If the officials threaten to arrest us for standing up for our rights, we must answer by saying that we are willing and prepared to fill up the jails of the South. Maybe it will take this willingness to stay in jail to arouse the dozing conscience of our nation" (see King, "A Creative Protest," in Carson et al. (eds.), *The Papers of Martin Luther King, Jr.*, Volume V, 369.

[129] bell hooks, *Outlaw Culture: Resisting Representation* (New York: Routledge, 2006), 245.

In order to save himself from falling into hatred or bitterness, which he believed would twist his own personality and poison his soul, he deliberately chose instead to transform those emotions into action. He chose to sacrifice the self in order to save the self: "Recognizing the necessity for suffering I have tried to make of it a virtue. If only to save myself from bitterness, I have attempted to see my personal ordeals as an opportunity to transform myself and heal the people involved in the tragic situation which now obtains."[130]

In choosing to see sacrifice as a virtue, King ultimately believed he expressed care for himself by seeking to avoid the corrosive emotion of bitterness, which leads to meanness and cynicism, a "hardness of attitude and a total mercilessness" that lead to "taking all of this out on other people."[131] Bitterness and meanness are painful emotions that make it harder to relate to other people. This is bad for the bitter person and for the success of collective movements, since, in King's view, people often tried to deal with the painful emotion of bitterness "by withdrawing completely into themselves" rather than engaging in creative political action to foster change.[132] In the end, King believed that the willingness to make sacrifices was not just part of showing love for others but was also part of showing love for oneself by showing the world that Black freedom and dignity are worth fighting for. As we will see in the final chapters, love, as King understands it, is also the foundation of nonviolence—a method of self and structural transformation that is aimed at securing freedom and justice for all.

---

[130] King, "Suffering and Faith," 444.
[131] King, "Unfulfilled Hopes," in Carson et al. (eds.), *The Papers of Martin Luther King, Jr.*, Volume VI, 359.
[132] Ibid., 359.

PART 3
NONVIOLENCE

7
Nonviolence

King believed that the campaign in Birmingham was one of the toughest fights of the Civil Rights Movement, but that, if it were successful, it would break the back of segregation all over the nation. The city was for him the country's chief symbol of racial intolerance. He later wrote in his *Autobiography*:

> In the entire country, there was no place to compare with Birmingham. The largest industrial city in the South, Birmingham had become, in the thirties, a symbol for bloodshed when trade unions sought to organize. It was a community in which human rights had been trampled on for so long that fear and oppression were as thick in its atmosphere as the smog from its factories. Its financial interests were interlocked with a power structure which spread throughout the South and radiated into the North. The challenge to nonviolent, direct action could not have been staged in a more appropriate arena.[1]

King believed that a victory in Birmingham would set in motion the forces that were needed to change the entire course of the national drive for desegregation.

The Birmingham campaign started small, limited to sit-ins. King knew it was going to be a long struggle, and it was best to pace things, letting the drama of the campaign slowly build. The first sit-ins took place at lunch counters at downtown department stores and pharmacies in Birmingham. Protesters sat at counters

---

[1] Autobiography, 170.

designated for white patrons only and refused to leave when they were asked. They were arrested under local "trespass after warning" ordinances.[2]

After the first day of the campaign, a mass meeting was held. These mass meetings, held in churches across Birmingham, were a regular feature of the campaign—sixty-five meetings were conducted throughout the campaign. The goal of the mass meetings was to galvanize the Black community and draw it into the movement—to inspire their political emotions and channel those emotions into political will and action. At the mass meetings, King evoked dignity and love in his discussions of the philosophy of nonviolence and its methods, Ralph Abernathy fed attendees' faith through his spirit-lifting preaching, Wyatt T. Walker fostered fearlessness and action by recounting the practical planning and action taking place in the "behind-the-scenes" organizing, and Fred Shuttlesworth awoke people's indignation with his fiery words of zealous commitment. Sometimes local speakers would join the meeting to share their experiences of being Black in Birmingham. Freedom songs were always an important part of the meetings, lifting the spirits of the attendees and giving them the strength and energy to participate in the movement. Toward the end of each mass meeting, Abernathy, Shuttlesworth, and King would ask for volunteers to join the next day's demonstrations. They made it clear that they would not send anyone to demonstrate who was not committed to nonviolence in theory and in practice; volunteers must be able to accept and endure violence without retaliating.

Nonviolence was the thread from which the campaign was woven. Before the Birmingham campaign began, volunteers attended a series of training workshops on the principles of nonviolence. Workshop participants read literature on nonviolence to guide their behavior. During these workshops, according to King, they repeatedly asked themselves questions like, "Are you able to

[2] WWCW, 63.

accept blows without retaliating?" and "Are you able to endure the ordeal of jail?"³ In Montgomery, the training sessions came with mimeographed instructions, which included the slogan, "If pushed, don't push back; if cursed, don't curse back."⁴ The training sessions, which were mostly about preparing one's mind for nonviolence, included sociodramas acted out by experienced nonviolent resistors, including Reverend James Bevel and his wife Dianne Nash Bevel, Reverend Andrew Cotton, and Dorothy Cotton.⁵ The dramas were designed to prepare demonstrators for some of the challenges they were likely to face: "The harsh language and physical abuse of the police and self-appointed guardians of the law were frankly presented, along with the nonviolent creed in action."⁶

King tells us that every volunteer signed a commitment card pledging themselves to nonviolence. There were ten commitments on the card. They included (1) meditating on the teachings and life of Jesus; (2) remembering that reconciliation, not victory, is the true end; (3) walking and talking in the manner of love; (4) praying daily; (5) sacrificing personal wishes so others can be free; (6) observing courtesy with both friends and foes; (7) seeking to perform regular service for others; (8) refraining from violence in "fist, tongue, or heart"; (9) striving to be in good health, spiritually and bodily; and (10) following the principles of the movement and the directions of the captain during demonstrations.⁷ While not everyone who attended these training sessions would find themselves ready for action on the streets, there were plenty of other ways to contribute—errands to be run, phone calls to be made, and typing to be done. *All* volunteers—both those on the streets and

---

³ Martin Luther King, Jr., "Revolt Without Violence—The Negroes' New Strategy," in Carson et al. (eds.), *The Papers of Martin Luther King, Jr.*, Volume V, 392–396 at 395. Available at: https://kinginstitute.stanford.edu/king-papers/documents/revolt-without-violence-negroes-new-strategy.
⁴ STF, 175.
⁵ WWCW, 67.
⁶ Ibid., 66.
⁷ Ibid., 68.

those behind the scenes—were required to sign the commitments, which guided all the wide variety of creative approaches to carrying out nonviolence: direct action expressed through mass demonstrations; jail-ins, sit-ins, wade-ins, and kneel-ins; voter registrations; economic boycotts and legal actions; and yes, even phone calls and errand-running.

Jailing was an important political tactic for King, for it would generate "concern ... around the nation and the world for the moral stand that we have taken."[8] As King saw it, willingly and fearlessly choosing to enter and stay in jail (to "choose jail rather than bail"), was one way of arousing the dozing conscience of Black and white moderates in the United States and around the world.[9] He believed that self-suffering on the part of Black Americans would undermine the moral defenses of the moderates and thereby awaken and move them to participate in the movement for desegregation.

However, the first three days of lunch counter sit-ins had resulted in only thirty-five arrests, and King decided it was time to take the next step. On Saturday, April 6, 1963, King and his supporters began with a march on City Hall. From then on, King reports, "the daily demonstrations grew stronger."[10] They decided that April 12, 1963—Good Friday—would be the day that Ralph Abernathy and King would join the protestors on the streets to take part in the mass arrests they anticipated. As we know, King was indeed arrested on this day and eventually placed in solitary confinement.

King's and Abernathy's jailing was just one part of a broader tactical strategy—and indeed, their jailing did not have the immediate

---

[8] Martin Luther King, Jr., "Press Release from Dr. King (Inside Fulton County Jail)," in Carson et al. (eds.), *The Papers of Martin Luther King, Jr.*, Volume V, 527. Available at: https://kinginstitute.stanford.edu/king-papers/documents/press-release-dr-king-inside-fulton-county-jail.

[9] Martin Luther King, Jr., "Draft, Statement to Judge James E. Webb after Arrest at Rich's Department Store," in Carson et al. (eds.), *The Papers of Martin Luther King, Jr.*, Volume V, 522. Available at: https://kinginstitute.stanford.edu/king-papers/documents/draft-statement-judge-james-e-webb-after-arrest-richs-department-store.

[10] *Autobiography*, ch. 18.

effect that they had hoped for. On April 13, the afternoon after Abernathy and King were arrested, three hundred people gathered for a mass meeting at the Sixteenth Street Baptist Church,[11] and on Sunday, April 14, 1963, there was a march to support those who were arrested,[12] with police clubbing Black bystanders with billysticks and police dogs waiting on the sidelines.[13] On Monday, April 15, 1963, Bull Connor, who had lost the election, refused to leave office, insisting on remaining in charge of the response to the demonstrations. Despite his refusal, Birmingham's newly elected government was installed: Albert Boutwell was sworn in as mayor and nine new city council members took their positions at City Hall.

With King and Abernathy languishing in jail, the campaign's momentum seemed to stall rather than accelerate. The economic boycott continued, but it was largely failing. A voter registration clinic, held on Wednesday, April 17, 1963 at Sixteenth Street Baptist Church, was attended by 150 people and triggered legal action, but again had little effect on the public at large. Police Chief Jamie Moore interrupted the voter registration clinic, saying, "I don't have anything against you registering to vote. You know that. But if you march out of here as a parade you will be in violation of a city ordinance and we will take the necessary action to keep you from violating the law."[14] When several of the attendees of the clinic were arrested for parading without a permit shortly after they left the building, the AMCHR-SCLC filed a suit in federal court seeking a temporary order prohibiting Bull Connor—who was still asserting his authority over the city of Birmingham even though he was officially out of office—and other city officials, including the police, from arresting demonstrators.[15] But this did not

---

[11] Glenn T. Eskew, *But for Birmingham: The Local and National Movements in the Civil Rights Struggle* (Chapel Hill: University of North Carolina Press, 1997), 242.
[12] Ibid., 246.
[13] Ibid., 246–247.
[14] Ibid., 249.
[15] Ibid., 249.

make the headlines the movement needed to bring Black and white moderates into the fight.

On Friday, April 19, 1963, after eight days of imprisonment, Abernathy and King accepted bond and came out of jail. Not much had changed while King remained behind bars. Though the Letter, written and published while King was jailed, would later have an enormous impact, it initially receded into the background; like the Birmingham campaign more broadly, it was largely ignored by the mainstream media. The injunctions maintained a stranglehold over the protests and demonstrations, and fewer and fewer people were willing to be jailed.

King and the other organizers were feeling the pressure. On April 22, 1963, King returned to the platform to preach an altered and fiery version of the Letter at the mass meeting held at the Sixteenth Street Baptist Church. He directly addressed his "Black brothers and sisters," encouraging them "to go forward."[16] He told them about his time in jail, emphasizing racial solidarity: "you meet a friend . . . and they have to bring you some dinner, and they have to bring you some breakfast, and they know what you represent, and they say to you, 'Reverend, tomorrow morning, I'll slip the paper to you.'"[17] However, King knew that he would need more than the Letter and his passionate preaching to set light to the fuel laid for the Birmingham campaign to catch fire.

May was drawing closer, and King was worrying: "You know we've got to get something going. The press is leaving, we've got to get something going."[18] Aware that the campaign's political position was weakening, white leaders stopped negotiating. Something had to be done. Wyatt T. Walker, James Bevel, Andrew Young, and Dorothy Cotton—SCLC staff members—believed the only solution was to bring children into the campaign. It would provide the

---

[16] Rieder, *Gospel of Freedom*, 104.
[17] Ibid., 105.
[18] Ibid., 113.

bodies and the momentum the campaign desperately needed, and media images of young people accepting violence peacefully would catalyze the nation. Though King was reluctant to bring in the children until all other options had been exhausted, the others had already been doing the groundwork that was needed to get young people involved.[19]

According to King, "Bevel had the inspiration of setting a "D" Day, Thursday, May 2, when the students would go to jail in historic numbers. When D-day arrived, young people converged on the Sixteenth Street Baptist Church in wave after wave."[20] Hundreds of youths bravely faced Connor and his men, who obligingly performed spectacular violence upon the children's bodies and hauled them off to prison. According to King, on "D" Day, more than a thousand young people demonstrated and went to jail; at the campaign's height, there were at least 2,500 demonstrators in jail at one time.[21] Thanks to the young people, the campaign was finally able to put into action the Gandhian principle of "Fill up the Jails."

King was inspired by the children's actions, and at the mass meeting that night, on May 2, 1963, he came out in full support of what would be later called the Children's Crusade. This, King felt, was the turning point in the Birmingham Campaign: hundreds of children and students on the streets, engaging in nonviolent direct action, facing down Bull Connor, the Birmingham Police Commissioner, who was using brutal force to halt the demonstrations. Local police and fire departments blasted the protestors with high-pressure hoses,[22] knocking children down in the street; police officers clubbed them, and they were savagely attacked by police dogs. The media captured devastating images of these clashes, which were printed in newspapers and broadcast on television to the rest of the nation, who viewed in shock. King came

---

[19] Ibid., 111.
[20] King, *Autobiography*, 208.
[21] Ibid., 208.
[22] WWCW, 118.

to believe "that the introduction of Birmingham's children into the campaign was one of the wisest moves we made. It brought a new impact to the crusade, and the impetus that we needed to win the struggle."[23] He observed that almost immediately, a change began to happen in Birmingham:

> strangely enough, the masses of white citizens in Birmingham were not fighting us. Only a year or so ago, had we begun such a campaign, Bull Connor would have had his job done for him by murderously angry white citizens. Now, however, the majority were maintaining a strictly hands-off policy.[24]

This was a significant shift: the children's courage seemed to be changing hearts and minds, for the majority of white citizens were no longer actively fighting against King and his supporters. According to King, even Connor's own men were affected by the demonstrations, refusing, at least in one case, to hose down Black children.[25]

As King saw it, in the face of the children's resolution and bravery, "the moral conscience of the nation was deeply stirred and, all over the country, our fight became the fight of decent Americans of all races and creeds."[26] "Moral indignation" spread and "sympathy" was created. As a result, the movement saw a "growing involvement of the Negro community."[27] King believed that all of these factors worked together to create an atmosphere of optimism within the movement—a feeling that the barriers to change were doomed, already beginning to crumble. In King's view, this was the beginning of the end. There was now continuous national attention and social pressure on Birmingham authorities, generated by the children's

---

[23] King, *Autobiography*, 206.
[24] WWCW, 119.
[25] Ibid., 120.
[26] King, *Autobiography*, 209.
[27] Ibid., 209.

confrontation with Connor. On May 4, 1963, Birmingham capitulated and came to the table for negotiations. Ultimately, the public sentiment behind the Birmingham campaign led President John F. Kennedy to propose a Civil Rights bill in June 1963. On July 2, 1964, this bill was signed into law as the Civil Rights Act by President Lyndon Johnson, with King and other civil rights activists present.

The Letter, then, was an intervention that took place within a broader field of action. It was not written in advance of action nor outside of it but within its midst: it took place alongside the mass meetings, marches, boycotts, and jailings that were all part of King's motivational apparatus—his democratic propaganda, designed to call the nation into right moral action on segregation. The goal of these tactics was to extend the fearlessness, dignity, indignation, faith, and love of the activists in the Birmingham campaign to a larger Black audience, who would then be moved to join the cause, putting their own bodies on the line in nonviolent direct action.

According to King, it is an axiom of social change that no revolution can take place without a methodology suited to the circumstances of the time.[28] For him, nonviolence was that methodology, but he was well-versed in all the methodologies that had been espoused by the civil rights activists who came before him. After Emancipation, many different paths toward greater freedom for Black Americans were offered, and King discusses many of these as he makes his case for why his plan—mass nonviolent demonstration to end legal segregation and pass civil rights legislation—was the best one for this particular historical moment.

King first examined Booker T. Washington's approach. Washington asked Black Americans to "be content" with what white Americans permitted them to accomplish and do well with their lot. According to King, this path had "too little freedom in

---

[28] WWCW, 27.

its present and too little promise in its future."[29] W. E. B. Du Bois suggested the exact opposite of Washington: he encouraged the "talented tenth" to rise and pull the Black masses up with them. In the end, though, King saw this as just another version of racial uplift ideology, offering no active role for the Black masses to play; to King, this philosophy was "a tactic for an aristocratic elite who would themselves be benefited" while leaving behind the so-called untalented.[30]

He also considered the approach of Marcus Garvey, who had called for a return to Africa and a reinvigoration of Black pride. King saw this plan as doomed from the start. People with centuries-old roots in the United States could not pack up their bags and leave behind everything they knew and loved—and the rights and privileges they deserved and were entitled to fight for. King saw echoes of Garveyism in the position of some Black Muslim groups, which advocated a permanent separation of the races within the United States. This movement did gain some support, which King saw as a produce of people's frustration with the lack of militancy in his freedom movement. But, in King's view, few Black Southerners had heard of the Black Muslim movement; it simply did not have the deep roots in the South that it required to be put into practice.[31]

He also discussed the approach of the National Association for the Advancement of Colored People (NAACP), which was predicated on seeking racial progress through the federal courts. Though the NAACP did win many legal battles, including securing the right of Black Americans to participate in national elections, King believed the limits of this approach were clear after the *Brown v. Board of Education* (1954) decision, which was openly defied across the South. This diminished the masses' faith in litigation as the best route to progress.

---

[29] Ibid., 25.
[30] Ibid., 25.
[31] Ibid., 29.

Some thinkers suggested that racial progress could best be secured by class solidarity between Black Americans and working-class white Americans, who had similar social, political, and economic needs; together, these groups would have the clout to advocate for economic equality in America. King acknowledged the rationale behind this idea, saying, "it is undeniable that great masses of southern whites exist in conditions scarcely better than those which afflict the Negro community."[32] But, he said, the need for immediate change "was more urgently felt and more bitterly realized by the Negro than the exploited white."[33] In addition, King did not believe that working class white Americans would be willing to join with Black Americans in this work, for (as discussed in Chapters 1 and 2), *all* white people benefited economically and psychologically from the system of racial segregation. Recall how surprised he was that white people in Birmingham were not joining the police in the streets to beat demonstrators; he knew that "the underprivileged southern whites saw the color that separated them from the Negroes more clearly than they saw the circumstances that bound them together in mutual interest."[34] Black Southerners, he believed, would find few helpful allies among the white working class.

After showing the problems with these previous approaches, King reminds us, "Fortunately, history does not pose problems without eventually producing solutions. The disenchanted, the disadvantaged and the disinherited seem, at times of deep crisis, to summon up some sort of genius that enables them to perceive and capture the appropriate weapons to carve out their destiny."[35] The "appropriate weapon," he felt, was nonviolent protest. Together, Black citizens would take to the streets, buses, stores, parks, and other public facilities and demand their rights. They would desegregate America.

---

[32] Ibid., 29.
[33] Ibid., 29.
[34] Ibid., 29.
[35] Ibid., 30.

How did King arrive at—or "perceive and capture"—the "appropriate weapon" of nonviolent resistance? King explained his own "Pilgrimage to Nonviolence" largely as a story of intellectual development. It began at Morehouse with his first encounter, as an undergraduate student, with Thoreau's philosophy of nonviolence; it continued with his studies in philosophy and political theory at Crozier Theological Seminary, where he read Reinhold Niebuhr's criticisms of nonviolence and heard lectures by A. J. Muste and Mordecai Johnson that inspired him to buy and read stacks of books on Gandhi's work. During his doctoral studies in philosophy at Boston University, King talked with many proponents of nonviolence: faculty members such as Dean Walter Muelder and Professor Allen Knight Chalmers, as well as other students and visitors to campus. During this time, he also deepened his knowledge of personalism—which, as we saw, was central to his understanding of nonviolence—in his work with Edgard S. Brightman and L. Harold DeWolf.

By 1954—the end of King's formal intellectual and philosophical training—he had arrived at "the conviction that nonviolent resistance was one of the most potent weapons available to oppressed people in their quest for social justice."[36] King first worked to put this philosophy into concrete action in Montgomery, where he and Bayard Rustin, who had traveled to India for seven weeks to study the Gandhian philosophy of nonviolence in 1948, designed the first large-scale campaign of Gandhian-style nonviolent resistance to segregation in the United States. The methods that he used in Montgomery formed the basis of the following Civil Rights Movement actions, including the Birmingham campaign.

In *Why We Can't Wait*, King gives a different account of the origin of nonviolence—a difference that has received little attention. In *Why We Can't Wait*, King aims his account of nonviolence to appeal to the Black masses specifically. As King tells it here,

---

[36] STF, 89.

nonviolent coercion was a set of tactics that emerged from the masses of oppressed people themselves and was therefore uniquely suited to their social conditions. Black Americans were not ready to engage in violent insurrection: they were "unarmed, unorganized, untrained, disunited, and, most important, psychologically and morally unprepared for the deliberate spilling of blood."[37] As he tells it here, after Rosa Parks refused to move to the back of the bus, the bus boycott of 1955–1956 emerged spontaneously—a nonviolent campaign that was based "in the churches of the community."[38] (In fact, Rosa Parks was a civil rights activist who was well trained in nonviolence, and the idea of using economic boycotts to force change had long been part of King's planning.) King's focus here on the role of the Black church is important, for churches were a key part of the South's social conditions, and the Black church played an important role in the Civil Rights Movement. It became a locus of nonviolent political action, and Black ministers often worked within other movement organizations, such as the NAACP.

Here, King writes that the eventual "acceptance of nonviolent direct action was proof of a certain sophistication on the part of the Negro masses; for it showed that they dared to break with the old, ingrained concepts of our society."[39] King suggests that to see the potential and power in nonviolence, the Black masses had to be open to nonviolence as a moral and political tactic—an openness that required a complex view of masculinity. Nonviolence was a break with the established norms of masculinity and manhood, which required physical self-defense, the willingness and ability to return a physical blow.[40] This norm of masculine violence was the ground of many other Black leaders' approaches: thinkers from Frederick Douglass to Malcolm X and Stokely Carmichael argued that violence and self-defense were the only way to assert Black

---

[37] WWCW, 27.
[38] Ibid., 28.
[39] Ibid., 31.
[40] Ibid., 31.

dignity and manhood in the face of attack. For example, Douglass asserted that it was a fistfight with William Covey the slave-breaker that awakened him to a sense of his own dignity and "revived a sense of [his] own manhood." As he tells it, "I was a changed being after that fight. I was nothing before; I was a man now.... A man without force is a man without dignity."[41] This conflation of masculinity with violence persisted through other strains of thought about Black liberation during the Civil Rights Era, and in 1968, after King's assassination, Stokely Carmichael predicted a "violent struggle in which black people would stand up on our feet and die like men. If that's our only act of manhood, then Goddammit we're going to die."[42]

As Brandon Terry and Shatema Threadcraft have noted, in order to bring the Black masses on board, King had to deliberately work to unlink masculinity from self-defense and violence and link it instead with nonviolence.[43] Traditional masculinity saw the refusal to embrace violence as being itself an undignified stance. King's concept of dignified nonviolence subverted this norm, eschewing violence and embracing "feminine" ideals such as love. King was therefore under great pressure to show that nonviolence was manly. According to Threadcraft and Terry, King demonstrated the masculinity of nonviolence in at least two ways. First, he flipped the norm on its head: he "inverted militaristic language usually reserved for the instruments and organization of violence to redescribe nonviolence, repeatedly referring to his 'nonviolent army' and to those 'who enlisted in an army that marches under the banner of nonviolence.'"[44] As James Collacut notes, King purposely distinguished between the "armies of violence" and "the nonviolent army."[45]

---

[41] Quoted in Threadcraft and Terry, "Gender Trouble," 217; cf. Frederick Douglass, *The Life and Times of Frederick Douglass* (Hartford, CT: Park, 1883), 177.

[42] Clayborne Carson, *In Struggle: SNCC and the Black Awakening of the 1960s* (Cambridge, MA: Harvard University Press, 1981), 288.

[43] Threadcraft and Terry, "Gender Trouble," 212.

[44] Ibid., 215.

[45] James Collacut, "Martin Luther King Jr.: The Rhetoric of Weaponized Nonviolence as Democratic Propaganda," unpublished Paper; cf. WWCW, 33.

While armies of violence use swords that wound, the nonviolent army uses only "the sword that heals"; while armies of violence have "a caste of rank," the nonviolent army marches in "democratic phalanx."[46]

Second, Threadcraft and Terry argue, King worked to disassociate violence from virtue and heroism—positive traits of masculinity. For example, King warned that the tendency to engage in violence was derived from white supremacy, an obvious vice: "One of the greatest paradoxes of the Black Power movement is that it talks unceasingly about not imitating the values of white society, but in advocating violence it is imitating the worst, the most brutal and the most uncivilizing value of American life."[47] Similarly, King unlinked violence from courage by arguing that violence was the result of *fear*, channeled through hate: "first, fear, then hate, then war, and finally deeper hatred."[48] He argued that the stockpiling of arms was motivated by a desire to reduce the fear of death and annihilation (though, he said, it only made it greater), and argued that courage, confidence, and manhood must come from within, not from the brandishing of a gun.[49]

---

[46] WWCW, 33. King often referred to nonviolence as the "sword that heals," even making it a chapter title in his book *Why We Can't Wait*. He borrowed the term from Gandhi, who wrote: "Passive resistance is an all-sided sword, it can be used anyhow; it blesses him who uses it and him against whom it is used. Without drawing a drop of blood it produces far-reaching results. It never rusts and cannot be stolen. Competition between passive resisters does not exhaust. The sword of passive resistance does not require a scabbard. It is strange indeed that you should consider such a weapon to be a weapon merely of the weak" (*Hind Swaraj*, Section 17, Passive Resistance). King describes the "sword that heals" in the chapter of that title, writing that "moral force has as much strength and virtue as the capacity to return a physical blow" (WWCW, 31). King explains, "nonviolence is a powerful and just weapon. It is a weapon unique in history, which cuts without wounding and ennobles the man who wields it. It is a sword that heals. Both a practical and a moral answer to the Negro's cry for justice, nonviolent direct action proved that it could win victories without losing wars, and so became the triumphant tactic of the Negro Revolution of 1963" (WWCW, 16).

[47] Quoted in Threadcraft and Terry, "Gender Trouble," 217; King, *Where Do We Go from Here*, 66.

[48] STL, 124.

[49] Threadcraft and Terry, "Gender Trouble," 217. Martin Luther King, Jr., "A Testament of Hope," in TOH, 322–323.

King believed that this subversive picture of dignified, nonviolent masculinity would be appealing to the Black masses, because the Black working classes had long been excluded from and emasculated by white concepts of masculinity. King gives an example of this emasculation in the Letter, pointing out that white men and women in the South had referred to Black men as "boy" (rather than men) since slavery. SCLC staffer Hosea Williams explains:

> White folks, and particularly white southerners, have addressed African-Americans as a "boy," and a boy is someone controlled by a parent. But a man is someone [that] makes his or her own decisions in relation to the conditions, so what they were saying to the city [was] "We are no longer your children. We are men, and men make decisions for themselves."[50]

According to Steve Estes, "boy" was a form of verbal emasculation that paralleled the physical emasculation dealt to Black men in slave beatings, post-reconstruction lynchings, and twentieth-century KKK retaliation against civil rights activists.[51] King argued that the best way to combat the verbal and physical emasculation constantly being inflicted on working-class Black men in the South was a dignified, nonviolent struggle against the paternalism of the city "fathers."

In King's view, then, the masses' willingness to participate in nonviolent coercion reflected their willingness to adopt innovative thinking around masculinity. This required courage and confidence, for it meant departing from the status quo, the traditional concept of masculinity, and seeing the strength and virtue in nonviolence—seeing the act of *refraining* from physical violence

---

[50] Steve Estes, "I AM A MAN!: Race, Masculinity, and the 1968 Memphis Sanitation Strike," *Labor History*, 41.2 (2000), 153–170 at 169.
[51] Ibid., 162.

as itself an expression of masculine courage and dignity. Because of their exclusion from white conceptions of manhood, the Black masses were ready to rethink masculinity. They were willing to see that subjecting themselves to violence—forcing the oppressor to commit his brutality openly, in front of the world—was an act not of cowardice but of dignity and courage. They recognized that nonviolence is a sword that ennobles the man who wields it. Nonviolence, in King's view, was thus an ideal tool for the masses, for they were more open-minded than the moderates.[52]

Across his various writings and speeches, King gives a clear and systematic picture of what nonviolent coercion is and what it ought to aim for. First, he emphasizes that nonviolence is neither passive submission nor surrender. While the method of nonviolence is physically nonaggressive, the nonviolent protestor is not passively accepting violence but actively opposing evil and injustice. King says, "the mind and the emotions are active, actively trying to persuade the opponent to change his ways and to convince him that he is mistaken and to lift him to a higher level of existence."[53] In nonviolent resistance, the oppressed channel their emotions— their sense of fear, fearlessness, dignity, righteous indignation, and love—toward just ends by pressuring those who have not

---

[52] King's concept of nonviolent masculinity is itself ordered by patriarchy. He believed that Black women's "true" role was within the home, as mothers, and framed the emasculation of Black men through low pay as masculinizing Black women—forcing "our wives and daughters to go out and work in the white lady's kitchen," taking them away from their proper sphere of their own homes and children. As Estes points out, King's concept of Black womanhood eschewed domestic servitude in white homes but accepted it for Black women in their own homes (Estes, "I AM A MAN!," 161). This traditional patriarchal concept of the family may have resonated with the religious ideals of the Black masses, and as Terry and Threadcraft note, bell hooks criticized King for "following the example of white male patriarchs" in being "obsessively concerned with asserting their masculinity" (Threadcraft and Terry, "Gender Trouble," 206). King, like other male civil rights thinkers of his time, was himself a product of patriarchy, and he did not seem to take entirely seriously the political role or needs of Black women, rarely mentioning or supporting the political actions of women such as Fannie Lou Hamer or Ella Baker, who were crucial to the civil rights movement and its impact.

[53] King, "Non-Aggression Procedures to Interracial Harmony," in Carson et al. (eds.), *The Papers of Martin Luther King, Jr.*, Volume III, 325.

yet realized or acted on the urgent importance of desegregation. The method is emotionally and intellectually active, for it seeks to change the situation.

Second, King says that nonviolence is fundamentally loving and connective, seeking to build a better world: the oppressed aim to lift and change the opponent, to redeem him through understanding and friendship rather than to defeat or humiliate him. The goal is not victory but reconciliation, in service of eventually creating the beloved community.

Third, the method of nonviolent resistance supports resisters' moral and spiritual development, for it "does not seek merely to avoid external physical violence, but it seeks to avoid internal violence of spirit."[54] Nonviolent resisters must refrain from external violence, which includes aggressive or retaliatory physical violence as well as violent "talk" or public expression.[55] They must also work against internal violence, actively seeking to forgive and to eradicate their own hate in favor of agapeic love. They must center their "attention" on the evil system rather than the evil actor, separating the evil from the evildoer; they are trying to eliminate the evil and to thereby save, rather than punish, the evildoer.[56] This method is aimed at taking down the forces of evil—the systems that create and allow the evil—rather than the persons who happen to be doing the evil.[57]

Fourth, nonviolence "is characterized by a willingness to accept sacrifice without retaliation."[58] This is a somewhat different principle than that of nonretaliation on its own, as discussed above; this principle focuses on sacrifice, which King sees as crucial to

---

[54] Ibid., 326.
[55] Martin Luther King, Jr., "Outline, The Philosophy of Nonviolence," in Carson et al. (eds.), *The Papers of Martin Luther King, Jr.*, Volume V, 520–521 at 521. Available at: https://kinginstitute.stanford.edu/king-papers/documents/outline-philosophy-nonviolence.
[56] Ibid., 521.
[57] STF, 91.
[58] Ibid., 91.

putting nonviolence into action. He says, "the non-violent resister is prepared to suffer even unto death. He believes that it is only by suffering that he can bridge the gulf between himself and his opponent and reach his heart."[59] According to King, sacrifice is the best expression of the commitment to nonviolence and, in turn, the highest expression of agapeic love.[60]

Fifth, nonviolent resistance "has a magnificent universal quality."[61] Anyone can participate. The movement included disabled people, and some of the most valued participants were youngsters such as those who carried out the Children's Crusade, ranging in age from elementary pupils to teenage high school and college students.[62] Related to this universal quality is its democratic quality: in nonviolent resistance, there should be no caste or rank in the movement. In Birmingham, King says, "Doctors marched with window cleaners. Lawyers demonstrated with laundresses. Ph.D.'s and no-D.'s were treated with perfect equality by the registrars of the nonviolence movement."[63] There is room for anyone who wants to join and work for justice, so long as they are committed to the principle of love and the basic method of nonviolence.

Ultimately, King views nonviolence as the "gold badge of heroism"—as masculinity properly demonstrated and expressed through active and genuine love.[64] King believes that if Black Americans are to achieve the goal of desegregation, they must organize themselves into a mass movement that is both moderate and militant—by which King means a movement that is "courageous and prepared for positive action"[65] while at the same time "devoid of hate and resentment."[66] All the above elements of nonviolence

---

[59] King, "Outline, The Philosophy of Nonviolence," 521.
[60] Ibid., 521.
[61] WWCW, 33.
[62] Ibid., 33.
[63] Ibid., 33.
[64] Ibid., 32.
[65] STF, 48.
[66] Ibid., 48.

are indispensable: "the movement for equality and justice can only be a success if it has both a mass and militant character; the barriers to be overcome require both. Nonviolence is an imperative to bring about ultimate community."[67]

In *Why We Can't Wait*, King is primarily targeting the Black masses, but (as always) he also seeks to speak to other audiences. After thoroughly establishing the appeal of nonviolence for the Black masses, he then gives a more general argument for nonviolence that will also appeal to the Black and white moderates. In this second part of the argument, we find a novel argument for nonviolence: King says here that nonviolence is the best method *because it properly expresses the emotions*.

In King's view, love—which stands in opposition to violence—is the center of any struggle to change the unjust conditions of society, and is "the regulating ideal in the technique, in the method of nonviolence."[68] Violence assumes that evil can overcome evil, but in fact it multiplies evil because it aims to defeat, injure, and humiliate an oppressor. As King writes, this is the wrong goal: "the true aim should be to convert him, to change his understanding and his sense of values."[69] Nonviolence, grounded in love, ensures that one tyranny is not substituted for another and that instead we seek the highest good for all humankind. Cautioning against a reactive push for "Black supremacy" to replace white supremacy, King asserts, "God is not interested merely in the freedom of black men, and brown men, and yellow men; God is interested in the freedom of the whole human race."[70] King believes that the inherent dignity of all humans, including our opponents, must always be "respected."[71] This is why King writes, "as you press on for justice, be sure to move

---

[67] Ibid., 210.
[68] King, "Non-Aggression Procedures to Interracial Harmony," 326.
[69] Martin Luther King, Jr., "The Peril of the Sword," in Carson et al. (eds.), *The Papers of Martin Luther King, Jr.*, Volume VI, 598–599 at 599. Available at: https://kinginstitute.stanford.edu/king-papers/documents/peril-sword.
[70] STF, 216–217.
[71] King, "The Peril of the Sword," 599.

with dignity and discipline, using only the weapon of love."[72] For him, the weapon of love is nonviolence, which realizes our commitment to respect our opponents by converting them to morally correct action—an action of love. When we act nonviolently, we express our commitment to awakening the oppressor through nonviolent coercion—a loving form of force and pressure—to reach reconciliation and redemption.

Nonviolence, which develops the best qualities in us ("Nonviolence is the way of humility and self-restraint"[73]), is an expression of faith in humanity and, ultimately, faith in God. It enacts "the belief that there is within human nature amazing potentialities for goodness"[74]—a potential that comes directly from God. King saw his faith in God as a shield that allowed him to endure violence without returning it. King discussed this in relation to an incident that happened after an SCLC annual convention, when American Nazi Party member Roy James ran up to the platform and hit King, almost knocking him down. King's aides separated him from the assailant, and King did not strike back. He said later of this episode that he had no need to retaliate, for he had God by his side: "I'm confident He's with me. He's been with me in New York, He's been with me in Alabama. He's been with me to India. He's been with me to Europe. I have a bodyguard, and I have faith in His character." This faith in God, who traveled everywhere with him, is expressed in King's nonviolent response to incidents such as the attack by James: "And even they can kill you, you don't mind it, for you know God's character tells you that He's with you even in death. I tell you this morning, I know about it because I've observed His conduct. 'Though He slay me, yet will I trust Him.'"[75]

---

[72] Martin Luther King, Jr., "Paul's Letter to American Christians," in Carson et al. (eds.), *The Papers of Martin Luther King, Jr.*, Volume VI, 338–346 at 344. Available at: https://kinginstitute.stanford.edu/king-papers/documents/pauls-letter-american-christians-sermon-delivered-commission-ecumenical.

[73] STF, 216.

[74] Ibid., 216.

[75] Martin Luther King, Jr., "The Perfect Faith," Available at: https://kinginstitute.stanford.edu/volume-viii-preview-perfect-faith.

Nonviolence is both an expression of love of God and love of self—of Black dignity, the commitment of the oppressed to love and respect themselves even as they suffer injustice. This commitment to self-love is realized and expressed through the fearless self-sacrifice of nonviolent resistance to violence. King tells us that "the nonviolent approach does not immediately change the heart of the oppressor. It first does something to the hearts and souls of those committed to it. It gives them new self-respect; it calls up resources of strength and courage that they did not know they had."[76] Nonviolent actors are characterized by a dynamic unity and an "amazing self-respect," expressed in the "willingness" to suffer and the "refusal to hit back."[77] As Alexander Livingston puts it, for King, "Black dignity is enacted through fearless resistance."[78] Courageously taking a stand—making sacrifices for one's own freedom and the freedom of other Black Americans—is the highest expression of self-love and of Black dignity. Through collective courageous sacrifice, fueled by dignity and indignation, King believed, "suffering may become a source of human and social force,"[79] for "[i]t reaches the opponent and so stirs his conscience that reconciliation becomes a reality."[80]

This commitment requires fearlessness and courage—in King's words, "it is not a method for cowards."[81] As he points out, the simple absence of violence is not the same as principled nonviolence: "if one uses this method because he is afraid or merely because he lacks the instruments of violence, he is not truly nonviolent."[82] Nonviolence is far from a "do-nothing" method in which the resister accepts evil. It requires the oppressed to actively resist,

[76] STF, 217.
[77] King, "Facing the Challenge of a New Age," in Carson et al. (eds.), *The Papers of Martin Luther King, Jr.*, Volume III, 462.
[78] Livingston, "Tough Love," 858.
[79] King, "Outline, The Philosophy of Nonviolence," 521.
[80] STF, 217.
[81] Ibid., 90.
[82] Ibid., 90.

to stand up for what is right and just, even in the face of what is feared, including violent retaliation. Nonviolence is thus a middle path, neither using violence yourself nor simply giving up and becoming resigned to the fate of oppression. Nonviolence is an active refusal to conform or acquiesce to unjust circumstances: "you stand up and resist strongly, but without violence."[83] In King's view, nonviolence is the only way for Black Americans to courageously take a stand for their own freedom and dignity with humility and restraint.

Indeed, as Karuna Mantena argues, restraint is central to King's notion of dignity, as is discipline.[84] These qualities are expressed in his campaigns of nonviolent coercion in a variety of ways. Discipline is visible in the careful planning, organization, and execution of campaigns and in the sensibly designed socio-dramas and training sessions. Restraint is evident in the use of prayers, songs, and silence during large-scale demonstrations, which, according to Mantena, created a slow and deliberate pace that conveyed the inner calm and resiliency—the dignity—of the protestors.[85] Dignity was also conveyed through the sheer diversity of participants in the marches, which expressed the movement's commitment to the universality of human dignity: as Mantena suggests, King "brought to the forefront of action those bodies assumed to be the weakest and most vulnerable"—women, children, the elderly, and the disabled.[86] Marches were thus a live staging of Black dignity.

In King's view, then, nonviolence is an active expression of dignified self-love, a self-assertive willingness to stand against injustice and endure, no matter the cost to oneself. However, some Black thinkers disagree with King's idea that self-sacrifice creates

---

[83] King, "Some Things We Must Do," in Carson et al. (eds.), *The Papers of Martin Luther King, Jr.*, Volume IV, 341.
[84] Karuna Mantena, "Showdown for Nonviolence," in Shelby and Terry (eds.), *To Shape a New World*, 78–101 at 97.
[85] Ibid., 97.
[86] Ibid., 100.

self-respect and a sense of one's own dignity. For example, bell hooks argues that King's form of nonviolence, with its emphasis on self-sacrifice, is so self-abnegating that it effaces self-respect. She aligns more with Malcolm X's position, noting that "while King had focused on loving our enemies, Malcolm called us back to ourselves, acknowledging that taking care of blackness was our central responsibility. Even though King talked about the importance of black self-love, he talked more about loving our enemies."[87] Alexander Livingston expands on hook's call to "tak[e] care of blackness" and attend to "the importance of black self-love." According to Livingston, "King figures sacrificial resistance as a kind of self-care but [. . .] the work of loving care may require turning away from the burdens of political action and sacrifice to nurture practices of liberation beyond resistance alone." As Livingston sees it, self-love entails tending to the boundaries of the self rather than relinquishing them. In other words, it requires radical self-care.

The concept of radical self-care was first discussed in the work of Black and Latinx feminists such as bell hooks, Audre Lorde, Gloria Anzaldua, and Patricia Hill Collins.[88] Radical self-care requires self-determination, self-preservation, and self-restoration, among other things. As Nicol and Yee recently describe it, radical self-care involves

> practices that keep us physically and psychologically healthy and fit, making time to reflect on what matters to us, challenging ourselves to grow and checking ourselves to ensure that what we are doing aligns with what matters to us. . . . Practiced faithfully,

---

[87] hooks, *Outlaw Culture*, 291.
[88] bell hooks, *Sisters of the Yam: Black Women and Self-Recovery* (Boston: South End Press, 1993); Gloria Anzaldúa, *Borderlands = La frontera: The new mestiza* (San Francisco: Spinsters/Aunt Lute Books, 1987); Audre Lorde, *A Burst of Light* (Ithaca: Firebrand Books, 1988); Patricia Hill Collins, *Black Feminist Thought: Knowledge, Consciousness, and the Politics of Empowerment* (New York: Routledge, 2000).

radical self-care involves owning and directing our lives and choosing with whom, how, and how often we engage in our nested, interconnected worlds so that we can be unapologetically ourselves in the face of unrelenting pressure and expectations to be otherwise.[89]

This concept of self-care puts limits on self-sacrifice: we should not sacrifice so much of ourselves that we fail to care for our own interests.

Considering this discussion, we might read King's emphasis on the necessity of self-sacrifice as implying that the Black self is not worth the same as the selves of those whom they are encouraged to love and sacrifice for—namely, white people. However, Myisha Cherry rebuts this reading, arguing that agapeic love and self-love are interconnected. First, she argues, agapeic love presupposes self-love: someone who has little regard for herself is not likely to have much regard for others.[90] In this she follows James Baldwin, who argued that the race problem would not be solved until white people began to love themselves. This is because white supremacy does not originate from extreme self-love but from deep self-hatred: in Baldwin's view, a person cannot engage in agapeic love until she first loves herself. These points can be extended to King's views about nonviolence: nonviolence—love in action—only becomes possible when a person has sense of self-love and of her own dignity and worth. Self-love plays a core role in moving people such as King's father to take a stand against white supremacy.

While hooks mentions Malcolm X as anticipating her concerns, Malcolm X offered a very different picture of what is required for love and dignity than hooks. He emphasized not radical self-care but self-defense as the highest expression of Black self-love and

---

[89] D. J. Nicol and J. A. Yee, "Reclaiming Our Time": Women of Color Faculty and Radical Self-Care in the Academy," *Feminist Teacher*, 27.2–3 (2017): 133–156 at 134.

[90] Cherry, "Love, Anger, and Racial Injustice."

self-respect. In Malcolm's view, all humans have a right to self-defense, and the exercise of this right is a basis for human dignity and self-respect. Like hooks, he does believe that begging for integration (which is how he saw nonviolent coercion) is self-abnegating, an act that is damaging to Black dignity. He argues that it takes power to garner respect, and like Douglass, he saw power as emanating from exercising one's right to (physical) self-defense. In an interview with Louis Lomax, Malcolm famously called King an Uncle Tom, someone who acquiesced rather than fought back against oppression, asking Black people to remain defenseless in the face of that cruel beast, the American white man.[91]

Is this an accurate characterization of King's view on nonviolence, dignity, and self-love? No. As Cherry explains, King believes that agapeic love, achieved through forgiveness and sacrifice, not only requires self-love (as a precondition) but actually gives rise to self-love. Love works in both directions. You must have self-love to practice agapeic love; and having agapeic love in turn fosters self-love. According to Cherry, by loving other people, we can foster better self-love; we can avoid the death trap of self-hatred on the one hand and of narcissistic self-love on the other. King believed that by engaging in nonviolent action—an expression and act of agapeic love—we cultivate better self-love. King believed that ultimately, nonviolence was the best way of preserving Black life. He believed that Black self-defense would lead to Black death, for striking back would lead to more violence; nonviolence, then, expresses the value of Black life and is an act of Black self-love, for King.

To love ourselves well, King believes, we must engage in agapeic love, thinking of others as much as ourselves, and believing that others have the same capacity for goodness that we do. This

---

[91] Louis E. Lomax, "A Summing Up: Louis Lomax Interviews Malcolm X," in *When the Word Is Given: A Report on Elijah Muhammad, Malcolm X, and the Black Muslim World*. Available at: https://teachingamericanhistory.org/document/a-summing-up-louis-lomax-interviews-malcolm-x/.

connects with nonviolence in several ways. First, King cautioned that those who supported violence were implicitly (if unintentionally) encouraging a superiority complex—"a sort of inner satisfaction and a sense of superiority by pulling everybody else down."[92] To advocate violence, one must believe that white people were incapable of transformation and that America was beyond hope. Second, to bring about the beloved community, one must act in community with *all* others, Black and white. He writes:

> the oppression of the Negroes by whites has left an understandable residue of suspicion. Some of this suspicion is a healthy and appropriate safeguard. An excess of skepticism, however, becomes a fetter. It denies there can be reliable white allies, even though some white allies have died heroically at the side of Negroes in our struggle and others have risked economic and political peril to support our cause.[93]

Working in community with others in nonviolent action allows us to better love both those we stand in community with and ourselves. King suggests that when Black people stand by the side of white people—not below them, not relying on white leadership or ideology, but standing side by side as allies—they are taking their place as equal partners in a common endeavor.[94] This alliance paves the way for organized strength and new independence, both of which foster great Black self-love. In these different ways, self-love and agapeic love reinforce each other. They are not as separate as hooks' arguments might suggest.

As hooks herself recognizes, the civil rights movement aimed at giving justice and freedom to all, not just those suffering from

---

[92] Martin Luther King, Jr., "Overcoming an Inferiority Complex," in Carson et al. (eds.), *The Papers of Martin Luther King, Jr.*, Volume VI, 305.
[93] WDWGH, 52.
[94] Ibid., 53.

oppression.[95] In asking Black people to engage in the self-sacrifice required for political transformation, as hooks explains, King was calling for communion with "a world beyond the self, the tribe, the race, the nation"—a "constant invitation for personal expansion and growth."[96] He was asking Black Americans to step away from thinking in "us versus them" terms, to work together to reject the white supremacist capitalist patriarchy that damaged everyone living under it. This was, as hooks sees it, King's way of "Facing the Challenge of a New Age" and ensuring "freedom and justice for all."[97] For reasons discussed in earlier chapters, King believed this change would come only through pressure collectively exercised by Black Americans. The change was primarily for the benefit of Black people, but it would ultimately secure justice for everyone, for as Maya Angelou and Angela Davis have said, "no one of us can be free until everybody is free." King encouraged Black Americans to identify with the broader American collective, and by taking care of this collective, Black people were also taking care of the self.

King's views about the connections between agapeic love and self-love are both practical and metaphysical. In his view, the self exists without boundaries—by its very nature, it is in connection with others. As King writes, "we are all tied in a single garment of destiny, and [. . .] if one black person suffers, if one black person is down, we are all down."[98] Nonviolence might require individual Black people to put themselves at risk, but they do so out of love, primarily for the sake of other Black individuals and the larger Black community. For King, taking care of the Black collective is a way of taking care of the Black self because the two are, by their nature, intimately intertwined.

---

[95] hooks, *Outlaw Culture*, 297.
[96] Ibid., 297.
[97] Ibid., 297.
[98] Quoted in "Memphis Sanitation Workers' Strike," in Carson (ed.), *Martin Luther King Jr. Encyclopedia*. Available at: https://kinginstitute.stanford.edu/memphis-sanitation-workers-strike.

8
Transformation

As we have seen, King believes the emotions of fear, fearlessness, faith, dignity, and indignation should be encouraged and appealed to. These emotions should not only be constrained by love (as we saw in Chapter 6) but must also be channeled through love into nonviolent action. How exactly does this channeling occur? And how does nonviolence lead to genuine racial progress? King believed that the answer was transformation: the personal transformation of the racially oppressed would, in turn, produce the social transformation of the oppressors, and together they would foster the structural transformation that was needed for genuine racial progress. This is King's strongest argument for nonviolence: it not only best expresses our emotions but works to encourage their continued expression through transformation—fear into fearlessness, dignity into indignation, and hate through and into love. Through this continuous loop, he thought, nonviolence has the potential to transform society and its structures.

For King, personal transformation begins by paying close and careful attention to ourselves. First, we must engage in self-analysis; we must identify our weaknesses—our hatred, despair, or rage.[1] This opens the door for self-improvement. Second, once we have identified our weaknesses, we must accept them, without rationalization—without convincing ourselves that our weaknesses are healthy or normal. This is how we give self-analysis meaning. Third, once we have identified and accepted our weaknesses, we

---

[1] King, "Mastering Our Evil Selves"/"Mastering Ourselves," in Carson et al. (eds.), *The Papers of Martin Luther King, Jr.*, Volume VI, 96.

must work to overcome them. To overcome them, King writes, "we must use the method of substitution": "we must find one good thing that we like to do as well as we like the evil thing, and every time we are persuaded to do the evil thing the good will overw[h]elm it."² The bad should be approached indirectly, in King's view — crowded out through the expulsive power of the good.

King describes this substitution process as a kind of "sublimation" or "transmutation," a way of mastering our "inadequacies" or "liabilities" by somehow transforming them into "something meaningful and constructive."³ In traditional psychoanalytic theories, sublimation is a subconscious way of redirecting energy away from an unacceptable emotion into a more socially acceptable one. King challenges this understanding of sublimation in two respects. First, what King advocates here is a kind of conscious or willing sublimation that occurs through the exercise of a dynamic will.⁴ As Brandon Terry and Shatema Threadcraft argue, King subscribed to a hierarchical concept of the self, seeing the mind and reason as distinct from and superior to the body and feeling.⁵ For King, the rational will acts as a guide, channeling disorderly feelings into right and good action. Second, he reminds us that we should not merely be "thermometers indicating and registering the temperature of the majority opinion" but "thermostats serving to transform and regulate the temperature of society," working to transform "the *is* into what *ought to be*."⁶ Here, King returns to the importance of holding a "minority idea," of being brave enough to have a revolution of

---

² Ibid., 96.
³ King, "Overcoming an Inferiority Complex," in Carson et al. (eds.), *The Papers of Martin Luther King, Jr.*, Volume VI, 309.
⁴ Martin Luther King, Jr., "Draft Chapter of 'Shattered Dreams,'" in Carson et al. (eds.), *The Papers of Martin Luther King, Jr.*, Volume VI, 514–527 at 521. Available at: https://kinginstitute.stanford.edu/king-papers/documents/draft-chapter-x-shatte red-dreams.
⁵ Threadcraft and Terry, "Gender Trouble," 217.
⁶ Emphasis mine; Martin Luther King, Jr., "Draft Chapter II: 'Transformed Nonconformist,'" in Carson et al. (eds.), *The Papers of Martin Luther King, Jr.*, Volume VI, 70.

values and to put those new values into action through nonconformity. We must transform our emotions and channel their energy through love toward what is right and what ought to be, not just what is considered socially acceptable.

For King, this revolution of values requires not only desegregation but the deconstruction of the capitalist economic structure that exploits both Black and white Americans, both men and women. As Andrew Douglas and Jared Loggins put it, King seeks a "wholesale transformation of the social form of domination, what King clearly recognized as the 'restructuring [of] the whole of American society."[7] King says that we must channel our emotive energy into action that will reconstruct society. In a world where people are considered as objects, morality is forgotten; to prevent the "thingification" of other humans through exploitation and domination—to truly bring about the beloved community—one must become what King called a "transformed nonconformist."

This transformation must begin at the individual level, by mastering ourselves and fostering transformation through "continuous prayer and social life." But what does social life have to do with individual transformation? To answer this question, King tells us a story that came down from Dr. George Truett of Texas.[8] A big fire broke out one day in a large hotel in a Southern city. Just when the firemen thought their work was done and the fire was out, they heard a little girl screaming. At the top of the hotel, fifteen stories above, they saw the face of a little white girl on the very top floor. The fire chief asked his youngest and bravest fireman to rescue her. The man bravely climbed up the ladder and rescued the little girl. Things were going well until he was about halfway down

---

[7] Andrew J. Douglas and Jared A. Loggins, *Prophet of Discontent : Martin Luther King, Jr. and the Critique of Racial Capitalism* (Atlanta,: University of Georgia Press, 2021), 30.

[8] Martin Luther King, Jr., "Garden of Gethsemane," in Carson et al. (eds.), *The Papers of Martin Luther King, Jr.*, Volume VI, 275–283 at 277. Available at: https://kinginstitute.stanford.edu/king-papers/documents/garden-gethsemane-sermon-delivered-dexter-avenue-baptist-church.

the ladder. At that moment flames began to leap at him from all sides and billows of smoke began to break forth. The young brave fireman lost his courage.

> The fire chief . . . called forth all of the firemen around and he cried out in terms that rang out all over the space that they stood in: "Cheer him on!" . . . . and finally the cheers from the ground reached the ladder, the middle, where the young man was with the little girl. The cheers reached his ears. And when he heard the cheers from below, something happened to him. And he began to brace up, he began to regain his courage. He began to regain his faith and he regained his strength. And when he heard those cheers and they came close to him, he started once more to descend the ladder. And as a result of the cheers, as a result of the support from below, he was able to come on down the ladder and bring the little girl safely to the end.[9]

King believed in the transformative power of community and friendship—he believed that the cheers and encouraging words of our friends and loved ones could help us regain our courage, strength, and power and move us to bravely charge forward.

If social life can transform and foster action, why do we need prayer? Although encouragement from friends was crucial, King believed, he also knew that we cannot always depend on other humans to be there for us in our quest for transformation: "this is the tragic picture of life, that at our darkest moments our friends often go to sleep."[10] Here, King is thinking of the Black and white moderates, who had abandoned the Black masses in the struggle for racial progress. According to King, the one friend that will never leave us is God: when our friends abandon us, we can move forward "simply through a positive and constructive and abiding faith

---

[9] Ibid., 278.
[10] Ibid., 278.

in God."[11] This is where prayer comes in. Through prayer, our souls become united with the life of God. King writes that when we pray, "Oh, God, help us to realize though that in the midst of this, there is a way out as we face life's central test," it will help us "to realize that God is the answer. In the midst of all of our trials and tribulations, God is the answer. In the midst of all of our disappointments, God is the answer."[12] King believed that prayer will "help us to live with that philosophy."[13] Through prayer, we can transform fear into fearlessness, dignity into indignation, hate into love. Through prayer, "our will will somehow become his will. . . . We will be just, because God is justice; we will love, because God is love; we will be good, because God is goodness; we will be wise, because God is wisdom."[14] King believes that man can transform through unity with God, and prayer is a way of connecting with God.

Prayer is "spiritually uplifting"; it can "break the spell of that which blinds our minds" and "purify our hearts," enabling us to break free of old ways of thinking and appropriately channel our emotions into political action.[15] Prayer allows us to channel our fear and overcome disappointment and doubt by giving us "broad visions, penetrating ey[e]s, and [the] power of endurance."[16] King believed that when we ask God to free us from our sins—of our weaknesses, of our unacceptable urges and feelings—and to set us free, we will be led "into fruitful effort."[17]

Through prayer, we recognize our weaknesses and accept them, validating ourselves and our feelings, and then we surrender to God; we can channel the energy of our negative urges and feelings into something constructive. Through prayer, we can confront, acknowledge, and release our weaknesses to God and move toward

---

[11] Ibid., 281.
[12] Ibid., 283.
[13] Ibid., 283.
[14] King, "Mastering Our Evil Selves"/"Mastering Ourselves," 97.
[15] King, "Garden of Gethsemane," 138.
[16] Ibid., 138.
[17] Ibid., 138–139.

right action. In this sense, prayer is a form of worship at its best. "Through worship one's worse self comes face to face with his better self, and the better self comes face to face with something still better."[18] In King's view, God is the source of moral transformation, and when we pray, we cooperate with God in promoting this transformation.

As we discussed earlier, worship at its best is a democratic social experience, with people of all walks of life—employer and employee, rich and poor, white-collar worker and common laborer come together in community to pray. King argued that the "fellowship and sense of oneness that we get in public worship cannot be surpassed."[19] Common prayer helps people to see that despite their different backgrounds, they are all children of a common father, who "are all caught in an inescapable network of mutuality, tied in a single garment of destiny." This sense of mutuality and oneness can be transformative, helping to channel emotional energy into right action—collective nonviolent action—that benefits the community as a whole. This is why King always started the mass meetings with a prayer. He well knew the power of prayer to stir the emotions and galvanize people—especially Black churchgoing people—into action: in Montgomery, at one of the Montgomery Improvement Association's (MIA) regular Monday night mass meetings, King delivered an emotional prayer to a rapt audience that was so powerful that he had to stop the meeting. He said later that he "decided it was time to stop the prayer because the audience had gone almost to pandemonium."[20] King's prayers at mass meetings were meant to rouse people's emotions and channel that energy into mass action.

---

[18] Martin Luther King, Jr., "Worship," in Carson et al. (eds.), *The Papers of Martin Luther King, Jr.*, Volume VI, 225.
[19] Ibid., 225.
[20] "Negro Minister Questions Plan for All-White Buses," *Montgomery Advertiser*, January 16, 1957. Also quoted in Martin Luther King, Jr., "Address to MIA Mass Meeting at Bethel Baptist Church," in Carson et al. (eds.), *The Papers of Martin Luther King, Jr.*, Volume IV, 109–110 at 109. Available at: https://kinginstitute.stanford.edu/king-papers/documents/outline-address-mia-mass-meeting-bethel-baptist-church.

To summarize: transformation requires that we honestly confront our inadequacies and liabilities by bringing them to the forefront of our minds and "daringly" staring at them.[21] Once we understand our inadequacies, we must "use them as the raw material out of which we mold and create something meaningful."[22] In King's view, transformation is ultimately a way of developing virtue:[23] transformation requires us to transform emotions such as anger and fear into a constructive force for democracy, freedom, racial justice, and reconciliation. We are only able to transform in this way through our acquaintance with goodness, which comes through prayer—our belief in, connection with, and surrender to God.

King suggests that personal transformation is the first step to nonviolence: "it is only through an inner spiritual transformation that we find the strength to revolt vigorously against the evils of the world and yet remain humble and loving."[24] Prayer, self-acceptance, and most importantly, the cultivation of love are key to this transformation. Here, he echoed the ideas of Gandhi and of Richard Gregg, an American social philosopher who developed a theory of nonviolence based on Gandhi's work.[25] Gandhi, like King, had a hierarchical concept of self: he believed that the transformative power of nonviolence comes from self-discipline—from channeling the "heat" of anger through the will, harnessing its

---

[21] Martin Luther King, Jr., "When Your String Breaks," in Carson et al. (eds.), *The Papers of Martin Luther King, Jr.*, Volume VI, 354–355 at 354. Available at: https://kingin stitute.stanford.edu/kingpapers/when-your-string-breaks.
[22] Ibid., 355.
[23] Martin Luther King, Jr., "Six Talks Based on Beliefs That Matter by William Adams Brown," in Clayborne Carson, Ralph Luker, and Penny A. Russell (eds.), *The Papers of Martin Luther King, Jr.*, Volume I: *Called to Serve, January 1929–June 1951* (Berkeley and Los Angeles: University of California Press, 1992), 280–289 at 285. Available at: https://kinginstitute.stanford.edu/king-papers/documents/six-talks-based-beliefs-matter-william-adams-brown.
[24] King, "Draft Chapter II: 'Transformed Nonconformist,'" 474.
[25] King's views were deeply influenced by Gregg. He corresponded with Gregg about the application of nonviolence in Montgomery, and King wrote the foreword to the second edition of Gregg's book, *The Power of Nonviolence* (Nyack, NY: Fellowship Publications, 1959).

energy "into a power which can move the world."[26] Similarly, Gregg believed that our emotions create an uprush of energy—a surge of power—that can lead us to immediate action, which discharges our emotional energy. The goal of nonviolence, then, is to harness this energy and to channel it toward a good end. This is the function of love, which, Gregg argued, is the great and central emotion in nonviolence.

Like King, Gregg held that fear and anger were often barriers to appropriate political action. Gregg argued that, on its own, fear often expresses itself in flight and anger in fight, or "pugnacity"—responses meant to separate oneself from threat.[27] But Gregg argues that "love is stronger than fear and anger [...] because it is able to manipulate and guide their energy."[28] This concept of energy flow is central to his view of the workings of love. He says:

> In so far as life is made up of a flow of energy, any principle is sound which increases the flow of energy, and makes possible the joining and mutual reinforcement of two or more channels of energy. An increase of life energy gives power and joy.... So love is a great principle in moral dynamics. It does not suppress or thwart the energy behind fear and anger but uses it, and finds ways to steer it into channels desirable to both parties to the conflict.[29]

Gregg defines love as expansive; it is:

> an interest in people so deep, and determined, and lasting as to be creative; a profound knowledge of or faith in the ultimate possibilities of human nature; a courage based upon a conscious or subconscious realization of the underlying unity of all life

---

[26] M. K. Gandhi, K. Gandhi, and A. Surabati (eds.), *Young India: A Weekly Journal.* 6. Pub: Sept 15, 1920.
[27] Gregg, *Power of Nonviolence*, 67.
[28] Ibid., 62.
[29] Ibid., 63.

and eternal values or eternal life of the human spirit; a strong and deep desire for and love of truth; and a humility that is not cringing or self-deprecatory or timid but is rather a true sense of proportion in regard to people, things, qualities and ultimate values.[30]

According to Gregg, love is a form of "courage," for it involves the desire to take risks and face one's fears. As the catalyst that transmutes emotions into action, love takes conflict to a morally "higher plane" by using sublimation to appropriately channel the energy of opposing emotions.[31] Indeed, love is an "intelligent" emotion that does not allow any energy to go to waste through suppression or denial but channels it all into right action: like a dam, love regulates and channels the productive energy of the other emotions into directions that are desirable to both parties of the conflict, redirecting them in a more "inclusive synthesis in which they can be reconciled with the ideals of human association."[32]

Like Gregg, King also believed that nonviolent coercive action, which is driven by love, was itself a way of sublimating or transforming emotions like anger and fear into productive action. He writes:

> the discontent is so deep, the anger so ingrained, the despair, the restlessness so wide, that something has to be brought into being to serve as a channel through which these deep emotional feelings, these deep angry feelings, can be funneled. There has to be an outlet, and I see this campaign as a way to transmute the inchoate rage of the ghetto into a constructive and creative channel. It becomes an outlet for anger.[33]

---

[30] Ibid., 49.
[31] Ibid., 59.
[32] Ibid., 57.
[33] Martin Luther King, Jr., "Showdown for Nonviolence," in James M. Washington (ed.), *A Testament of Hope* (New York: Harper Collins, 1986), 64–72 at 69.

Through love, faith, and dignity, nonviolent action channels the energy of very legitimate fear and rage into good—prayer, songs, jokes, satire, marches, demonstrations, and economic boycotts. Nonviolent action becomes an outlet, allowing us to face, express, and deal with our negative emotions constructively through action, without causing harm. In finding constructive and healthy ways of coping with our emotions, and of expressing ourselves and our emotions authentically, we avoid shame and foster self-confidence, dignity, and courage. When we act in ways that are calm, confident, and dignified, we engage in the kind of good conduct that King believed that love, as a regulative ideal, demands.

According to King, campaigns of communal nonviolent action create "basic psychological and motivational transformation" in Black Americans.[34] As Black people participate together in nonviolent action—songs, sermons, prayers, meetings, and marches—they undergo a slow and steady transformation. These activities generate and then lovingly transform the emotions, channeling their energy constructively through love into right action.[35] But the campaigns did even more than this. As King argues, this "change in human psychology is normally a slow process," but participation in the campaigns would produce faster effects: "it is safe to predict that, when a people is ready for change as the Negro has shown himself ready today, the response is bound to be rapid and constructive."[36] Participation had a deeply and rapidly transformative effect: according to King, participation in the campaign led Black people to rapidly shake off three hundred years of psychological

---

[34] WWCW, 170.

[35] King writes about music's unique ability to express love: "But if I struck four chords of music everyone of the could could understand the emotion which I am attempting to convey. As we set out in life we must strick the chord of God's eternal sound which is love and it will be understood by all people" (Martin Luther King, Jr., "Sermon Notes and Outlines I," in Carson et al. (eds.), *The Papers of Martin Luther King, Jr.*, Volume VI, 561–566 at 562. Available at: https://kinginstitute.stanford.edu/king-papers/documents/sermon-notes-and-outlines-i.

[36] WWCW, 170.

slavery, saying, "We can make ourselves free."[37] Participation in the nonviolent campaign caused "an impulse" for liberty and equality to "burst through."[38]

In King's view, participation created an almost instant sense of pride and self-love among Black protestors, and it inspired some onlookers to want to feel the same, spreading the transformative power of loving nonviolence across the country. King said of the Montgomery campaigns: "I know that the Negroes of Montgomery are already walking straighter because of the protest. And I expect that this generation of Negro children throughout the United States will grow up stronger and better because of the courage, the dignity, and the suffering of the nine children of Little Rock, and their counterparts in Nashville, Clinton, and Sturges."[39] King believed the psychological impact of nonviolence was long-lasting and crossed generational boundaries, fostering a greater sense of self-respect and dignity in all Black Americans.[40] This kind of victory built on itself, for it further enhanced the sense of Black dignity and self-love. Even in the face of a "white backlash" that "declared true equality could never be a reality in the United States," mass civil disobedience transmuted the intense fear and smoldering rage and frustration of Black Americans into a constructive and creative force through the power of their participation in "an effective, militant, and nonviolent movement of massive proportions."[41]

As we saw in the previous chapter, nonviolence properly expresses the emotions of fear, fearlessness, dignity, indignation,

---

[37] Ibid., 134.
[38] Ibid., 134.
[39] STF, 215.
[40] Nonviolence also encouraged King's own sense of self-love and dignity. In Birmingham, King felt that "he had to win and to vindicate his dignity in order to merit and enjoy his self-esteem. He had to let white men know that the picture of him as a clown—irresponsible, resigned and believing in his own inferiority—was a stereotype with no validity. This method was grasped by the Negro masses because it embodied the dignity of struggle, of moral conviction and self-sacrifice. The Negro was able to face his adversary, to concede to him a physical advantage and to defeat him because the superior force of the oppressor had become powerless" (WWCW, 35).
[41] King, *Autobiography*, 37.

faith, courage, and love; as we can now see, nonviolence also enhances these very emotions, inducing and strengthening them, and encouraging the right expression of those emotions in further nonviolent action. This cycle is important, for nonviolent action is difficult work, and it is hard to maintain the appropriate and constructive motivation to continue to participate in it. Participants always face significant costs, setbacks, and suffering—emotionally, economically, and politically—and this can leave them feeling despair, frustration, exhaustion, and hopelessness. If not properly channeled, these feelings can lead to apathy or to unconstructive actions, such as violence: violence, says King, is often produced by hopelessness combined with despair. After a visit to Watts, Los Angeles, in 1965, King came to believe "that the riots grew out of the depths of despair which afflict a people who see no way out of their economic dilemma."[42] It is especially important, then, that nonviolent action continuously generate and regenerate the energy it needs to sustain itself—to operate in what we might call a feedback loop of emotion transformed into right action. Sermon, songs, and prayer are the flint that starts a fire; boycotts, marches, and demonstrations are the fuel that fan and feed the flame. All forms of nonviolence work together to start the movement and to keep it going.

In King's view, nonviolence had the potential to transform not only the racially oppressed person—especially among the Black masses—who was already doing the work of personal transformation described above, but also the oppressor, who was not likely to be doing this work. King writes that nonviolent action enabled the participant "to transmute hatred into constructive energy, to seek not only to free himself but to free his oppressor from his sins. This transformation, in turn, had the marvelous effect of changing the face of the enemy. The enemy the Negro faced became not the individual who had oppressed him but the evil system that permitted

[42] Ibid., 291.

that individual to do so."[43] In other words, nonviolence created more love and more forgiveness, which could then create the possibility of more transformation, ad infinitum.

King explains how nonviolence changes the (white) oppressor. During his negotiations with the businessmen of Birmingham, he said, the businessmen stopped for lunch and were immediately confronted with a mass demonstration full of Black faces. The businessmen were astounded, suddenly realizing the movement could not be stopped. When they returned to the negotiations, one of the men who had been most staunch in his opposition said, "You know, I've been thinking this thing through. We ought to be able to work something out."[44] According to King, this change marked the beginning of the end of the negotiations.[45] Exposure to the nonviolent demonstrations brought this man to change his views, which in turn transformed Birmingham—and, eventually, the country.

King believed that nonviolence was the key to all of these types of transformation. Recall that nonviolence is, in part, love for one's enemy, expressed in action. King reminds us that "when Jesus says, 'love the enemy,' he's saying love the enemy because there is something about love that can transform, that can change, that can arouse the conscience of the enemy. And only by doing this are you able to transform the jangling discords of society into a beautiful symphony of brotherhood and understanding."[46] In King's view, love expressed through nonviolent action stimulates the conscience of the oppressor and thereby has the potential to transform him.

King believed nonviolence was effective in the South, since bloodthirsty segregationists facing nonviolent Black protestors were forced to either engage nonviolently or to show themselves as monstrous to the world. Nonviolent direct action, King argued, "muzzled the guns of the oppressor because even he could not

---

[43] WWCW, 32.
[44] Ibid., 125.
[45] Ibid., 125.
[46] Martin Luther King, Jr., "Loving Your Enemies, [Sermon Detroit]," 427.

shoot down in daylight unarmed men, women, and children."[47] According to King, over time, as protestors repeatedly turned the other cheek, the oppressors would realize their moral wrong and feel shame: "This dynamic unity, this amazing self-respect, this willingness to suffer, and this refusal to hit back will soon cause the oppressor to become ashamed of his own method. He will be forced to stand before the world and his God splattered with the blood and reeking with the stench of his Negro brother."[48]

In King's view, shame is key to this transformation of the oppressors. King explains how nonviolence engenders shame in the oppressors. According to King, when the nonviolent resister says,

"Punish me. I do not deserve it. But because I do not deserve it, I will accept it so that the world will know that I am right and you are wrong," you [the oppressor] hardly know what to do. You feel defeated and secretly ashamed. You know that this man is as good a man as you are; that from some mysterious source he has found the courage and the conviction to meet physical force with soul force.[49]

This explanation echoes Gregg's account of the power of nonviolence to transform the oppressor. As Gregg tells it, in the face of nonviolence, the oppressor senses a lessening respect and support from the crowd. The oppressor loses some of his prestige, some of his inner sense of self-respect, and instead feels a growing sense of inferiority.[50] Similarly, King writes that nonviolence "arouses a sense of shame within" the oppressors; this shame "does something

---

[47] King, *Autobiography*, 348.
[48] Martin Luther King, Jr., "Remarks in Acceptance of the Forty-Second Spingarn Medal at the Forty-Eighth Annual NAACP Convention," in Carson et al. (eds.), *The Papers of Martin Luther King, Jr.*, Volume IV, 228–233 at 233. Available at: https://kinginstitute.stanford.edu/king-papers/documents/remarks-acceptance-forty-second-spingarn-medal-forty-eighth-annual-naacp.
[49] WWCW, 21.
[50] Gregg, *Power of Nonviolence*, 29.

to touch the conscience" and "disturbs this sense of commitment he's had."[51] When confronted with the nonviolent action of the oppressed, he says, the oppressor's sense of shame lowers his own concept of himself, bringing him down in his own eyes to the level of the oppressed. This creates a growing sense of equality with the oppressed, and thus despite himself—against his own will—he becomes hesitant, less and less firm in his own position.

In contrast, when someone who has been physically attacked hits back, the violent response gives the attacker reassurance and moral support for her own violence. It confirms that the attacker and the victim are operating on the same scale of moral values—a scale that treats violence as the right way to settle the conflict between the two. This vindicates the attacker's approach, giving her confidence and energizing her. Nonviolence has the opposite effect. According to Gregg, nonviolence inverts the energy of the attack, using it against the attacker in a kind of "moral jiu-jitsu": it uses the energy of the initial attack to put the oppressor morally off balance.[52] When the victim does not hit back but accepts the attack with calmness, fearlessness, and loving self-control, she expresses confidence in her own worth and in her belief that racial desegregation is an urgent matter requiring immediate remedy. The nonviolent response to violence challenges the oppressor's worldview and exposes her to a new world of moral values. She is surprised and moved into an uncertainty of her own values and methods.[53] Because of the novelty of the situation, she is uncertain about how to handle it, and loses her poise and self-confidence. The oppressor becomes increasingly aware of the nonviolent resister's courage and dignity. She experiences a sense of wonder and curiosity, which draws her attention to the victim and her expressed beliefs. All this cumulatively puts the oppressor in a vulnerable state—a more

---

[51] TOH, 304.
[52] Gregg, *Power of Nonviolence*, 44.
[53] Ibid., 44.

suggestible and receptive position. This, Gregg says, is how nonviolence can produce a change in the oppressor's moral perspective. Even though this is not what the oppressor initially wanted, she can become newly aware of the oppression she is participating in and its injustice. This process of moral transformation, says King, indicates the coercive or forceful power of nonviolence.[54]

When Black Americans took to the streets, King tells us, the "blanket of fear was lifted."[55] The issue of desegregation was brought to the forefront of the nation's conscience, and there was a moral awakening, as some of the moderates and even a few of the segregationists began to recognize the moral wrongness of segregation—an intellectual and affective awakening, wrought by nonviolence, which touched the minds and hearts of the oppressors. As Black participants in the movement expressed and cultivated dignity, indignation, courage, faith, and love, these emotions spread to the oppressors who witnessed them, ultimately compelling at least some of them—those whom King calls "the best of America"—to join the movement.

King was not naïve. He did not believe that moral shame was the only or even the most effective way to motivate the oppressor. While King may have remained somewhat hopeful about its power among Black moderates, especially by the end of his life, he recognized that Black Americans could not reliably expect most white moderates to feel shame.[56] However, King believed that until this affective motivation was achieved, self-interest could act as a substitute to drive people to act in moral ways. Recall that King used economic boycotts, such as the Montgomery Bus Boycott, to make it uncomfortable for the oppressors to continue as they were. In the face of an economic boycott, the costs of inaction became higher than action and the buses were eventually desegregated. However, appeals

---

[54] This is King's language; Gregg never refers to nonviolence as coercive.
[55] TOH, 645.
[56] On King's views on shame, see Krishnamurthy, "Democratic Propaganda."

to self-interest were not the best way to motivate the oppressors; King preferred affective paths to moral progress over appeals to self-interest. King had both pragmatic and moral reasons for this: most importantly, he was in search of what he called a "permanent peace,"[57] not a temporary end to racial segregation, and he felt that actions aimed merely at the self-interest of the oppressors were unlikely to lead to permanent peace and justice.

King's worries parallel John Rawls's worries about what he calls a *modus vivendi*, in which people cooperate because of shared material interests. As Rawls noted, this type of agreement may be unstable and unlikely to last over the long run.[58] When one party's material interests are no longer being satisfied, they may lose motivation to participate in the arrangement, and it will be likely to fall apart. If cooperative action to end racial segregation were based on material self-interest—a Rawlsian *modus vivendi*—then the threat of dissolution would always loom, and as soon as the arrangement failed to satisfy their material self-interest, the oppressors would revert to the status quo.

Even if a Rawlsian *modus vivendi* (achieved by imposing costs on the oppressors) did secure a permanent peace, it would not necessarily be (to use another phrase from Rawls) a permanent peace "for the right reasons." The oppressors would be acting out of material self-interest—an interest in protecting themselves—rather than out of a moral recognition that racial segregation is wrong. King, like Rawls, wished to ensure a just and stable society for the morally right reasons—a society where citizens were completely sincere in their belief in the wrongness of racial segregation and fully committed to ensuring true integration by conscientiously transforming their own minds and fully embracing Black people as their true brothers and sisters.

---

[57] Martin Luther King, Jr., "The Quest for Peace and Justice," Nobel Lecture, December 11, 1964.
[58] John Rawls, *Political Liberalism* (New York: Columbia University Press, 2005), 147.

In King's view, then, stability for the right reasons would be achieved not merely through appeals to self-interest but through moral transformation, wrought in part by the experience of shame. Experiences of shame—when they are possible—have the power to open minds and hearts, genuinely changing people's (self-interested) desires and behavior. In at least the "best of America," King believed, the experience of shame could be a "creative force," spurring consistent work to end racial segregation now and to establish the foundation for genuine integration in the future.

Let us return to the question of how to sustain people's political motivation to continue to engage in the difficult work of nonviolent protest. In King's view, the sharing of the political emotions was a crucial part of the cycle of political motivation. As Danielle Allen has argued, before we engage in risky collective political action, we need assurance that other people are also willing to do their part.[59] This is only rational: we cannot succeed in ending racial segregation if other people do not also take action to end it. Nobody wants to be first, and given the effort and risk involved, it seems right to seek reassurance that other people are also willing to do their part before we do ours. King's view of the emotions suggests that we gain this reassurance when we know that our emotions are shared by others. We know that to abolish racial segregation, many people must do their part; we are willing to do our part so long as we know others are willing to do so too. If we both know that we are experiencing the same emotions—sharing the emotions of fear, dignity, indignation, courage, faith, and love—we are both more likely act on those emotions. When we know each other's desire to end racial segregation and share the emotions that prompt us to action, we have reassurance that others will do their part, which in turn motivates us to do our part.

---

[59] Danielle Allen, *Talking to Strangers: Anxieties of Citizenship Since Brown v. Board of Education* (Chicago: University of Chicago Press, 2009).

Collective social movements such as the Civil Rights Movement work in part because they create the conditions under which the emotions of nonviolence can be seen to be shared. Social movements begin when people are brought together, whether in the basements of churches or in public courtyards, and learn of one another's shared sentiments. Out of shared feeling, cooperative action arises, and this cooperative action slowly and progressively gains force through repeated shared experiences of success and failure. These shared experiences assure us further that we have the emotions of nonviolence in common and give us confidence in the future regularity of each other's conduct. Secure in the conviction that others are just as indignant, courageous, faithful, and loving as we are, we continue to be moved to do our part. Within the context of a collective social movement, the emotions of nonviolence make us more likely to engage in the sort of long-term action that is necessary to overcome racial segregation. Participating in practices such as praying, signing commitment cards, and demonstrating are all ways of properly and continuously stimulating the emotions of nonviolence, which are then channeled into collective sustained nonviolent action.

In the end, King believed that "nonviolence is the only way to reestablish the broken community. It is the method which seeks to implement just law by appealing to the conscience of . . . [those] who through blindness, fear, pride or irrationality have allowed their conscience to sleep."[60] This is the power of love in action: by refusing hate and physical aggression, we can end the chain of violence in the world, and through dignity, indignation, courage, faith, and love, we can begin to form "a community where men can live together without fear."[61] Nonviolence, which has the power to forcefully persuade and motivate the best of the oppressors, clears the ground for reconciliation and political friendship.

[60] TOH, 110.
[61] TOH, 58.

After the demonstrations in Birmingham began, King tells us, the movement grew spectacularly: "the number of SCLC affiliates jumped from 85 to 110,"[62] as both Black and white Americans were "stirred into action and formed an alliance that aroused the conscience of the nation."[63] King believed that the alliance between Black and white Americans, between Northerners and Southerners, was crucial to the movement's success: "It is extremely significant that in many places the Negro students have found white allies to join in their actions. It is equally significant that on a mass scale students and adults in the North and elsewhere have organized supporting actions, many of which are still only in their early stages."[64] According to King, "more than one million Americans attended solidarity demonstrations in Washington, DC, New York, Los Angeles, San Francisco, Cleveland, Chicago and Detroit."[65] As word of Birmingham spread, other organizations—civic, religious, labor, and professional—went on record as supporting the movement. Slowly, both Black and white clergy—Presbyterian, Catholic, Jewish—trickled in, taking their places beside King and the other demonstrators on the streets.

Nonviolence, or love in action, is about transformation: individual transformation produces community or collective transformation, which in turn leads to structural transformation. Individual transformation, which takes place at a psychological level, is about stimulating, expressing, and channeling the right emotions. This individual transformation is the basis for collective or community transformation, which creates the conditions for political action aimed at institutional change. We can see this progression in King's

---

[62] WWCW, 144.
[63] Martin Luther King, Jr., *The Trumpet of Conscience: Dr King's Final Testament on Racism, Poverty and War* (Boston, MA: Beacon, 1967), 46.
[64] Martin Luther King, Jr., "The Burning Truth in the South," in Carson et al. (eds.), *The Papers of Martin Luther King, Jr.*, Volume V, 447–451 at 450. Available at: https://kinginstitute.stanford.edu/king-papers/documents/burning-truth-south
[65] WWCW, 144.

description of how Birmingham led to the end of segregation. As he tells it, America was

> profoundly aroused by Birmingham because it witnessed the whole community of Negroes facing terror and brutality with majestic scorn and heroic courage. And from the wells of this democratic spirit, the nation finally forced Congress (*Well*) to write legislation (*Yes, sir*) in the hope that it would eradicate the stain of Birmingham. The Civil Rights Act of 1964 gave Negroes some part of their rightful dignity (*Speak, sir*)."[66]

Note the progression in this passage: it shows how the nation's emotional response (they were "profoundly aroused") was prompted by seeing and sharing in the emotions of nonviolence being expressed by demonstrators (they "witnessed" the demonstrators' "majestic scorn and heroic courage"), which led to moral transformation and then action ("from the wells of this democratic spirit, the nation finally forced Congress to write legislation"). The Letter, as a sensible sermon or a piece of democratic propaganda, is an attempt to stimulate this same process: to produce political action by arousing the emotions of nonviolence—fear, dignity, indignation, courage, faith, and love. The Letter itself did not lead directly to legislation. It could not do this work on its own. What it could do is motivate people to take action, which could in turn lead to a change in legislation.

The direct political action that happens on the streets is crucial, for it actively transforms the political structure within which the emotions of nonviolence arise. When racial segregation (which produces fear, indignity, frustration, and despair) is deconstructed, it clears the ground for a better environment for love, friendship, and forgiveness—it makes way for the beloved community to

---

[66] King, "Our God Is Marching On!"

emerge. We see that love in action, with its capacity to transform the enemy, is not only a regulative ideal but a revolution in values. At its core, it is a refusal to see other people as objects; it is a call to live life differently—creatively and in true community with one another. Through the practice of nonviolence, love reconfigures relationships. People come together through the value they place on "dethingification"—on democracy, equality, and racial justice. Ultimately, by changing the environment and reconstituting relations of friendship, love channels the emotions into and creates the basis for sustained political action.

How to sum up all of these arguments for nonviolence to arrive at King's views? According to King, if you are properly motivated by the political emotions of dignity, righteous indignation, fear, fearlessness, faith, and, most of all, love, then nonviolence is the philosophy and tactic that will eventually end racial segregation. It is the only path by which all the emotions can be appropriately expressed and channeled through love into political action. Nonviolence is able to sustain these emotions, because it can foster transformation—individual, collective, and structural. In the end, King believes, nonviolence properly expresses and sustains emotions to power the collective social movement toward equality that will, one day, create the beloved community.

Postscript

Situating King: A Beginning

The animating question behind both this book and King's theory of the emotions is this: how can and ought we motivate racially oppressed people to engage in the nonviolent direct action that is required to desegregate the South? King's answer is that we can and must appeal to a wide range of emotions—primarily fear, fearlessness, faith, dignity, indignation, and love.

King saw his own views about political motivation as a middle ground between two opposing positions in the Black church: the intellectualists and emotionalists. Intellectualists hold that all that is needed for motivation is knowledge. Emotionalists hold that something more than knowledge—for example, emotions or desires—is needed for motivation. King believed that a combination of facts and feelings was the most effective way to move people. For example, it is important for people to believe that racial segregation is wrong and to know the arguments that prove this claim to be true. Without this kind of propositional knowledge, King worried that people could be led by their emotions toward the wrong ends. But he also believed that having propositional knowledge is often not enough to be moved to act. After all, as King highlights, many people already knew that racial segregation was wrong, but few took to the streets to change things. This is why King held that it was equally important to activate the emotions. When properly guided by reason and argument, the emotions of fear, fearlessness, faith, indignation, and love have the potential to move people toward the right ends—toward ending segregation through nonviolent coercion.

The Church wasn't the only source of inspiration for King's views on how to motivate political action; both abolitionists and civil rights activists had long been considering this problem. Years before King, Ida B. Wells had faced a similar motivational issue. In the decades following the Civil War, lynching had become widespread in the South, and, like King, she wondered why Black people weren't working together to act to end the horrible practice. In her view, it was because many Black Americans lacked the propositional knowledge needed for action. She wrote, "the Afro American himself did not know as he should have known," because "the press contains unreliable, doctored reports of lynchings."[1] They didn't always know exactly what it involved, how prevalent it was, or the sort of fallacious reasoning that was typically used to justify it. Therefore, Black Americans were not "in a position to [...] act."[2] Wells believed that "one of the most necessary things for the [Black] race to do is get these facts before the public."[3] Therefore, she engaged in an educational campaign, using facts and rational arguments to "arouse the conscience" of the American people, especially Black Americans, to demand for justice for every citizen.[4] Wells strongly believed that Black people must act on their

---

[1] Ida B. Wells, *Southern Horrors: Lynch Law in All its Phases (1892)* in Ida B. Wells, *The Light of Truth: Writings of an Anti-Lynching Crusader* (New York: Penguin, 2014), 57–82 at 80.

[2] Ibid., 82.

[3] Ibid., 80. Here I offer the standard view—offered for example by Frederick Douglass—that Wells does not prioritize affect in her mode of presentation. Instead, Wells follows dispassionate journalistic standards, centering the facts—i.e., statistical data about lynching and first-person testimony from whites about their justifications for lynching. As Douglass saw it, Wells "dealt with the facts with cool, painstaking fidelity" leaving the "naked" facts "to speak for themselves" (Frederick Douglass in his prefatory letter to *Southern Horrors*, quoted in Juliet Hooker, *Black Grief/White Grievance: The Politics of Loss* (Princeton, NJ: Princeton, 2023), 156). For a different interpretation of Ida B. Wells's appeal to facts, see Hooker, *Black Grief*, especially chapter 3. In her attempt to present a capacious account of Black loss, Hooker suggests that Wells appeals not only to facts but also affect. Perhaps, both Hooker and the standard view are right. Wells certainly prioritizes facts and data in her *Red Record: Tabulated Statistics and Alleged Causes of Lynching in the United States, 1892–1893–1894* (Chicago: Donohue & Henneberry, 1895); but, in other works, perhaps she takes another more affectively laden approach to discussing lynching.

[4] Ibid., 58.

own behalf, employing "the boycott, emigration, and the press" to stamp out the lynch law.[5]

King combined Wells's emphasis on disseminating facts with Frederick Douglass's goal of inspiring righteous indignation in order to end legalized racism. Douglass believed that most Americans—perhaps especially Black Americans—already knew the rational moral arguments that slavery and lynching were morally wrong. In his Fourth of July speech, he pointed out that the rational moral case for the wrongness of slavery was already well established, and that he need not make further argument on that ground:

> Would you have me argue that man is entitled to liberty? that he is the rightful owner of his own body? You have already declared it. Must I argue the wrongfulness of slavery? Is that a question for Republicans? Is it to be settled by the rules of logic and argumentation, as a matter beset with great difficulty, involving a doubtful application of the principle of justice, hard to be understood? [...] There is not a man beneath the canopy of heaven, that does not know that slavery is wrong *for him*.[6]

In Douglass's view, most Americans already know, by inference based on true premises, that slavery is wrong: denying people their liberty is obviously a "revolting barbarity" and a "shameless hypocrisy." Yet, people still lacked the motivation to act to end slavery.

As Douglass saw it, knowing the major and minor premises of a moral argument and drawing from them the moral conclusion that slavery is wrong is not enough to motivate people to act. Recall, from our earlier discussion, according to Douglass, what is needed to rouse Americans to action is overwhelming emotion: "It is not light that is

---

[5] Ibid., 82.
[6] Frederick Douglass, "What to the Slave Is the Fourth of July?" July 5, 1852. Available at: https://www.pbs.org/wgbh/aia/part4/4h2927t.html.

needed, but fire; it is not the gentle shower, but thunder. We need the storm, the whirlwind, and the earthquake. The feeling of the nation must be quickened; the conscience of the nation must be roused; the propriety of the nation must be startled."[7] Douglass is here drawing a distinction between what we have called "motivational intellectualism"—Wells's view that all that is needed for moral motivation is moral knowledge—and "motivational non-intellectualism"—the view that moral motivation also requires emotions or desires. Douglass favored the latter approach, holding that intellectualism ignored or overlooked—or at least vastly underestimated the importance of—other motivational forces such as emotions and desires.

Douglass spent almost three weeks writing his Fourth of July speech. His motivation for doing so was clear. Leading up to that Independence Day, Douglass saw two Americas: one America still in chains, with 3 million enslaved Black Americans, and another, free America, where white Americans celebrated their freedom from colonial bondage with "joyous enthusiasm." Douglass saw the hypocrisy of these white Americans and was disgusted. Like King when he wrote the Letter, Douglass was furious when he wrote the speech. A similar motivation drove Douglass to write his autobiography, the *Narrative of the Life of Frederick Douglass an American Slave*. He documented in the preface to the book his motivation for his speaking tours around the country, addressing "the multitudes, in various parts of our republic, whose minds he has enlightened on the subject of slavery, and who have been melted to tears by his pathos, or roused to virtuous indignation by his stirring eloquence against the enslavers of men!" Like his lectures, the *Narrative* was designed to "enlighten" (impart rational moral knowledge to), move "to tears" (inspire emotions in), and "rouse to virtuous indignation" (galvanize into political action) his readers.

Wells had emphasized the dissemination of facts through education, and Douglass had believed that people knew the facts and

---

[7] Ibid.

needed to be inspired to action through emotion. King found the final piece of the puzzle of how to inspire political action in W. E. B. Du Bois's work about the aesthetics of democratic propaganda. Du Bois, like the Black thinkers who had gone before him, believed that "the black world must fight for freedom [...] with the weapons of Truth [and] with the sword of the intrepid, uncompromising Spirit"—facts and emotions. Du Bois, however, added another dimension, saying that Black Americans must channel the combination of facts and emotion into direct political action: they must fight "with organization in *boycott,* propaganda and mob frenzy."[8]

Like Wells, Du Bois believed that facts were important to this fight. He felt that it was key that Black Americans have a deep understanding of the race problem within the United States, and he worked hard to document and disseminate facts about how employment, economic inequality, and household value were racialized in the United States. Where Du Bois differed from Wells was in how he believed these facts should be best transmitted. While Wells took an educational approach, Du Bois did not think that dry pedagogy would move people to fight for their freedom. He believed that the facts—and the lived experiences of what those facts represented in real lives—must be conveyed in an emotional register, through propaganda.

As we discussed near the beginning of this book, Du Bois saw his own writing as art, and as he argued, "all art is propaganda."[9] As Melvin Rogers writes, Du Bois "weds truth and goodness to the work of the artist and art to propaganda."[10] For Du Bois, art is always a form of moral propaganda, designed to spread "truth and goodness."[11] Du Bois thus encourages Black artists to resist merely satisfying white audiences with distorted literary and pictorial

---

[8] W. E. B. Du Bois, *Dusk of Dawn*, in Nathan Huggins (ed.), *Writings* (New York: Library of America, 1940), 549–802 at 557.
[9] W. E. B. Du Bois, *Criteria of Negro Art* (New York: Crisis, 1926), para. 29.
[10] Rogers, "The People, Rhetoric, and Affect," 194.
[11] Du Bois, *Criteria of Negro Art*, para. 11.

depictions of Blackness. According to him, his own "writing has always been used [as] propaganda for gaining the right of black folk to love and enjoy."[12] Du Bois thus sought to stir the "souls of Black folk" through song, story, personal narrative, and pictures, rather than mere dissemination of facts and data. He believed that these alternative mediums were necessary to rouse people's emotions—particularly sympathy and shame—and, in turn, lead them to action.[13]

The debate about how best to encourage political motivation to work for civil rights continued during the Civil Rights Movement, when it was especially important to encourage Black political action. During this period, activists and thinkers again divided themselves along intellectualist and emotionalist lines. Stokely Carmichael, an early member of SNCC and later a leader of the Black Nationalist movement, subscribed to an intellectualist view. Carmichael believed that white Americans were incapable of fixing legal segregation and racial prejudice on their own. As he explains in a speech titled "Black Power," Carmichael concerned himself primarily with the question of how Black people ought to "move" within the United States, asking: how do we Black Americans "begin to clear away the obstacles that we have in this society, to make us live like human beings?" Carmichael saw Black America as "engaged in a psychological struggle in this country," and argued that in order to escape oppression, Black Americans must act collectively—"must wield the group power" that they had.[14] How could Black Americans be moved to engage in this kind of collective political action? Carmichael gives us some indication in this speech, in which he uses the structures of logic to debunk white people's

---

[12] Ibid., para. 29.
[13] Rogers, "The People, Rhetoric, and Affect"; Gooding-Williams, "Beauty as Propaganda."
[14] BlackPast, B. (2010, July 13). (1966) Stokely Carmichael, "Black Power". BlackPast.org. Available at: https://www.blackpast.org/african-american-history/speeches-african-american-history/1966-stokely-carmichael-black-power/.

assumption that an all-Black movement like the Black power movement cannot succeed. As he writes, "it is the word 'black' that bothers people in this country, and that's their problem, not mine. That's the lie that says anything black is bad."[15] He continues:

> You're all a college and university crowd. You've taken your basic logic course. You know about major premise, minor premise. People have been telling you anything all black is bad. Let's make that our major premise.
> Major premise: Anything all black is bad.
> Minor premise or particular premise: I am all black.
> Therefore . . . I'm never going to be put in that bag; I'm all black and I'm all good. Anything all black is not necessarily bad. Anything all black is only bad when you use force to keep whites out. Now that's what white people have done in this country, and they're projecting their same fears and guilt on us, and we won't have it. Let them handle their own affairs and their own guilt. Let them find their own psychologists. We refuse to be the therapy for white society any longer. We have gone stark, raving mad trying to do it.[16]

In many ways, perhaps because of his time as a philosophy major at Howard University, Carmichael followed the intellectualist tradition, emphasizing logic and reason in his writings and speeches. Carmichael used these logical appeals in an attempt to cognitively undo the fear and guilt that grows out of internalized racism, for these emotions are barriers to collective action toward racial progress and justice.

Malcolm X, one of the most visible and vocal advocates of Black nationalism, also emphasized Black empowerment. He believed that, for Black Americans, the "objective is complete freedom,

---

[15] Ibid.
[16] Ibid.

complete justice, complete equality, by any means necessary."[17] This complete equality required "complete and immediate recognition and respect as human beings."[18] At least initially, Malcolm rejected King's message of nonviolence, but he respected King as a "fellow-leader of our people."[19] Malcolm sent King articles on the Nation of Islam as early as 1957 and invited him to participate in mass meetings throughout the early 1960s.[20] Malcolm wanted King in particular to hear Elijah Muhammad's message, but he also worked to establish an open forum in which Black leaders could work together to explore solutions to the "race problem."[21]

Malcolm and King often aired their philosophical and methodological differences in public. Malcolm castigated King in speeches, magazine articles, newspapers, and radio and television interviews, calling him a "fool," a "chump," a "clown," a "traitor," a "false shepherd," "reverend chickenwing," a "twentieth century Uncle Tom."[22] King never accepted Malcolm's invitations and left it to his secretary, Maude Ballou, to handle all communication with Malcolm.[23] He described Malcolm using terms such as "crazy," "tragic," "irresponsible," and "demagogic."[24] However, after Malcolm was assassinated in 1965, King wrote to his widow, Betty Shabazz, saying, "While we did not always see eye to eye on methods to solve the race problem, I always had a deep affection for Malcolm and

---

[17] Malcolm X, "At the Audubon," in George Breitman (ed.), *Malcolm X Speaks: Selected Speeches and Statements* (New York: Grove Press, 1965), 115–136. Available at: https://teachingamericanhistory.org/document/at-the-audubon/.

[18] Ibid.

[19] "Malcolm X," in Clayborne Carson, Tenisha Armstrong, Susan Carson, Erin Cook, Susan Englander (eds.), *The Martin Luther King, Jr., Encyclopedia* (Westport, CT: Green Wood, 2008). Available at: https://kinginstitute.stanford.edu/encyclopedia/malcolm-x.

[20] Malcolm X, "From Malcolm X," in Carson et al. (eds.), *The Papers of Martin Luther King, Jr.*, Volume V, 491. Available at: https://kinginstitute.stanford.edu/king-papers/documents/malcolm-x-0.

[21] "Malcolm X," in *Martin Luther King, Jr., Encyclopedia*.

[22] Lewis V. Baldwin, "A Reassessment of the Relationship Between Malcolm X and Martin Luther King, Jr.," *The Western Journal of Black Studies*, 13.2 (1989): 103–113 at 104.

[23] "Malcolm X," in *Martin Luther King, Jr., Encyclopedia*.

[24] Baldwin, "Malcolm X and Martin Luther King, Jr.," 104.

felt that he had the great ability to put his finger on the existence and root of the problem."[25]

In 1966, King elaborated further on the personal and philosophical differences between the two men, writing:

> I met Malcolm X once in Washington, but circumstances didn't enable me to talk with him for more than a minute.
>
> He is very articulate, but I totally disagree with many of his political and philosophical views—at least insofar as I understand where he now stands.... I know that I have often wished that he would talk less of violence, because violence is not going to solve our problem.
>
> And, in his litany of articulating the despair of the Negro without offering any positive, creative alternative, I feel that Malcolm has done himself and our people a great disservice. Fiery, demagogic oratory in the black ghettos, urging Negroes to arm themselves and prepare to engage in violence, as he has done, can reap nothing but grief.[26]

King here expresses his disagreement not only with Malcolm's political tactics but also about which emotions the movement ought to foster and appeal to. In his view, Malcolm X placed too much emphasis on the negative emotions—despair, grief, frustration, and hate. King worried that without a concomitant appeal to love, which imposes constraints upon these powerful emotions, they would produce retaliatory violence and, inevitably, more anger and hate, only entrenching racial injustice and inequality more deeply.

However, King may have misunderstood or oversimplified here Malcolm's actual views about Black political motivation, and particularly his view of despair. At a roundtable in October 1961,

---

[25] "Malcolm X," in *Martin Luther King, Jr., Encyclopedia*.
[26] King, *Autobiography*, 265–266.

Kenneth B. Clark asked Malcolm about the role of despair in his political thinking and philosophy: "Mr. X, you sound to me as if you are preaching a doctrine of complete and utter despair. Are you?" Malcolm coolly replied:

> No, I'm facing facts. If you try and swim the Atlantic Ocean and after several attempts you find you don't make it, well, if your objective is the other side, what are you going to do? It's not a case of having utter despair. You have to go back to shore and try and find another method of getting across if that's where you want to go.[27]

King believed that Malcolm had suffered terribly at the hands of white racism and, in King's view, his hatred, bitterness, and despair were an expression of this suffering.[28] But according to Malcolm himself, he was not articulating despair; he was sharing facts and articulating a program for action.

Malcolm's views about Black political action are, like Carmichael's, very much in the intellectualist tradition. Malcolm felt that there were two important barriers to Black political action. First was a lack of access to true facts. In his 1964 speech at the Audubon, he said:

> We have always thought that we were struggling by ourselves, and most Afro-Americans will tell you just that—that we're a minority. By thinking we're a minority, we struggle like a minority. We struggle like we're an underdog. We struggle like all of the odds are against us. This type of struggle takes place only because

---

[27] Malcolm X, "Malcolm X at Open Mind Roundtable," October 15, 1961. Available at: https://www.icit-digital.org/articles/malcolm-x-at-open-mind-roundtable-october-15-1961.

[28] This forced sterilization was so common in the state that it was known as the "Mississippi appendectomy." Hamer said later, "In the North Sunflower County Hospital, I would say about six out of the 10 Negro women that go to the hospital are sterilized with the tubes tied." (Coretta Scott King, *My Life with Martin Luther King, Jr.* (New York: Henry Holt & Co, 2017), 259–260).

we don't yet know where we fit in the scheme of things. We've been maneuvered out of a position where we could rightly know and understand where we fit into the scheme of things.[29]

In Malcolm's view, Black people erroneously saw themselves as a minority who would lose the struggle for Black freedom and equality. He sought to correct this false belief by encouraging Black Americans to learn the facts of their history and place in the world—to see that they were not a minority but a very powerful global majority.

The second barrier was the lack of an effective new program of action. He wrote that people would not be ready to act "until they realize they need one [a program of action], and until they realize that all existing programs aren't programs that are going to produce productive results."[30] He thought that an effective program would emerge when the problem was fully and correctly understood: "I, for one, believe that if you give people a thorough understanding of what it is that confronts them, and the basic causes that produce it, they'll create their own program; and when the people create a program, you get action."[31] In Malcolm's view, once Black Americans fully understood the American race problem and what gave rise to it, they would understand how best to resolve it. This new understanding, coupled with a recognition of their collective power, would, in his view, lead Black Americans to take action.

Avid voting and women's rights activist and community organizer Fannie Lou Hamer had a different approach from Malcolm and Carmichael. Like Douglass in his narratives, she focused on stirring emotion by talking about her life and what had led her to advocacy. Hamer was one of twenty children born to a family of sharecroppers in the Mississippi Delta who grew up picking

---

[29] Malcolm X, "Malcolm X at the Audubon Ballroom."
[30] Ibid.
[31] Ibid.

cotton and cutting corn. In August 1962, Hamer showed up for a "mass meeting" organized by Student Nonviolent Coordinating Committee (SNCC), where she was told something she had never heard before: Black people had the right to vote. Hamer realized that while she had the right to vote, she did not know why she should exercise that right. She asked herself, "What did she really have? Not even security." She had endured much at the hands of white supremacy: a lynching in a nearby town had terrorized Black residents since the early 1900s, and the KKK was ever-present; in 1961, she went to a local hospital for minor surgery to remove a tumor and was sterilized without her consent; and she was brutalized by police on multiple occasions. During her testimony before the Credentials Committee at the Democratic National Convention (on August 22, 1964), Hamer told the story of how in June 1963, on the way home from a voter registration workshop in Mississippi, she and several other workshop participants were arrested.[32] In prison, the white policemen sexually assaulted her and ordered other Black prisoners (on threat of death) to brutally beat her. She suffered from permanent damage to her kidneys and other injuries.

These experiences showed her how important the right to vote was, for she believed that once this right was secured, voting would be able to protect human rights, especially the rights of Black women. She believed, like King, that many white Americans were "caught up" in maintaining the segregationist status quo and would not work for political change, and that Black Americans therefore should take things in their own hands. Hamer traveled around the country telling her story. Like Douglass, she hoped her story would rouse feelings of dignity and indignation in her listeners and lead Black voters to the polling office.

---

[32] Fannie Lou Hamer, "Testimony Before the Credentials Committee, Democratic National Convention," August 22, 1964. Available at: https://americanradioworks.publ icradio.org/features/sayitplain/flhamer.html.

While King respected Hamer's approach, he was also somewhat skeptical that her personal testimony would be enough to encourage Black Americans to register and vote in high enough numbers to create change through the polls. In his discussion of the political challenges of Mississippi, he wrote:

> We will never forget Aaron Henry and Fannie Lou Hamer. Their testimony educated a nation and brought the political powers to their knees in repentance, for the convention voted never again to seat a delegation that was racially segregated. But the true test of their message would be whether or not Negroes in Northern cities heard them and would register and vote.[33]

King was not convinced that Hamer's personal testimony, which primarily drew on creating sympathy and outrage in her audiences, was enough to draw Black people to the polling offices in the face of resistance, nor that voting rights alone would be enough to create change. There was still something missing: the transformative power of the broader emotions of nonviolence, which could create and sustain the momentum of a mass movement of direct political protest.

In trying to carve out his own answer to the question of political motivation, King followed in Du Bois's footsteps, taking a position between the intellectualism of Wells and the emotionalism of Douglass with his sensible sermons. These sermons were meant not only to help Black people understand why racial segregation was wrong, but also to motivate them to act. Like Hamer and Douglass, he appealed to personal stories from his own history and the history of other people he knew, but he framed those stories with facts about the moral, social, and economic ills of racial segregation. For example, he began *Why We Can't Wait* with a moving

---

[33] King, *Autobiography*, 253.

story of a little boy and girl experiencing the ills of racial segregation, then in the first chapter turned to the economic impacts of racial segregation, then made logical arguments for the dignity of Black people and the moral wrongness of racial segregation. Like Wells, he thought that empirically understanding racial segregation was important to motivation; like Douglass, he thought that viscerally understanding the emotional experience of Black life was motivating; like Du Bois, he believed that the facts and the emotion needed to be framed as propaganda, calling people to action. But he added something all his own: in the Letter, King conveyed his own emotions of nonviolence—fear, courage, dignity, righteous indignation, and love—in order to inspire similar emotions in his readers. King believed that these emotions, shaped by reason, would move people to the streets.

In King's view, Black churches had long known how to motivate people to act and how to keep this motivation going for the long run: "the Negroes, many years ago, discovered something great and they were great psychologists."[34] King built on the traditions of Black theology by reading broadly in (the largely white field of) social psychology. His ideas on white ignorance and on fear were influenced by his readings of Freud, to whom he said "we owe a great debt [...] for opening to us the uncharted regions of the subconscious."[35] His reflections on love, forgiveness, and faith were influenced by Jung's work, especially *Modern Man in Search of a Soul* (1933).[36] Here, Jung argued that "[m]odern man has heard enough about guilt and sin. He is sorely beset by his own bad conscience and wants rather to learn how he is to reconcile himself with his own nature, how he is to love the enemy in his own heart

---

[34] King, "Some Things We Must Do," in Carson et al. (eds.), *The Papers of Martin Luther King, Jr.*, Volume IV, 330.

[35] Martin Luther King, Jr., "Accepting Responsibility for Your Actions," in Carson et al. (eds.), *The Papers of Martin Luther King, Jr.*, Volume VI, 139–142 at 139. Available at: https://kinginstitute.stanford.edu/king-papers/documents/accepting-responsibility-your-actions.

[36] C. G. Jung, *Modern Man in Search of a Soul* (San Diego, CA: Harcourt, Brace, 1933).

and call the wolf his brother."[37] Jung, like King, felt that religious faith could help people heal their psychological damage: "of all of the hundreds and thousands of patients that have come to me for treatment and counsel over the past few years, I think I can truly say that all of them past the middle of life had conditions which could be cured by the proper religious faith."[38] Jung's desire to de-emphasize the guilt and moral wrongdoing of our enemies resonates with King's emphasis on friendship, reconciliation, and faith. However, King goes beyond Jung by thinking about the political (rather than therapeutic) role of the emotions, and by seeing the role of faith in the ability to transcend one's own nature through nonviolent action.

As we can see, King's views on the political emotions were influenced by the Black thinkers who came before him and some of the most important psychologists of his time. By engaging with these two traditions, he developed a unique, detailed, and coherent theory of the political emotions that can be used to motivate democratic political action. Ultimately, the main conclusion to draw from King's philosophy of the political emotions is that abstract theorizing must be accompanied by action: we cannot separate questions about the nature and existence of racial injustice from questions about how we can overcome that injustice. Racial segregation is an injustice in need of urgent remedy. In King's view, we can overcome racial injustice if the oppressed who suffer from

---

[37] Quoted in Martin Luther King, Jr., "Beyond Condemnation," in Carson et al. (eds.), *The Papers of Martin Luther King, Jr.*, Volume VI, 199–201 at 201. Available at: https://kinginstitute.stanford.edu/king-papers/documents/beyond-condemnation-sermon-dexter-avenue-baptist-church.

[38] Quoted in King, "Overcoming and Inferiority Complex," in Carson et al. (eds.), *The Papers of Martin Luther King, Jr.*, Volume VI, 315. See also, Jung, *Modern Man in Search of a Soul*, 264; Fosdick, *On Being a Real Person*, 74. In addition to Freud and Jung, other social psychologists influenced King's thinking. For example, his views on the inferiority complex produced by racial segregation, and his belief in the importance of dignity and self-respect, were influenced by the work of "Dr. Kenneth Clark and other social psychologists who came to see, through long study, that segregation does something to the personality" (King, "Overcoming and Inferiority Complex," in Carson et al. (eds.), *The Papers of Martin Luther King, Jr.*, Volume VI, 315).

this injustice are motivated through reason and emotion to take to the streets and, through loving, dignified nonviolent action, put pressure on the agents and institutions that keep the unjust system in place. In King's view, the key question is not why white people choose to continue in a state of inaction or ignorance (though King did think that understanding this was useful). The actual key question is this: how can and ought we move oppressed people to the streets to practice nonviolent coercion with dignity and love and thus transform the oppressors and, eventually, the systems they uphold in order to enter into the beloved community?

Bibliography

Abernathy, Ralph. *And the Walls Came Tumbling Down: An Autobiography* (New York: Harper & Row, 1990).
Adams, Noah. "The Inspiring Force of 'We Shall Overcome.'" *All Things Considered*, NPR, August 28, 2013. Available at: https://www.npr.org/2013/08/28/216482943/the-inspiring-force-of-we-shall-overcome.
Allen, Danielle. "Integration, Affirmation, and the Freedom of Life." In Tommie Shelby and Brandon Terry (Eds.), *To Shape a New World: Essays on the Political Philosophy of Martin Luther King Jr.* (Cambridge, MA: Harvard University Press, 2018), 146–169.
Allen, Danielle. *Talking to Strangers: Anxieties of Citizenship Since Brown v. Board of Education* (Chicago: University of Chicago Press, 2009).
Anzaldúa, Gloria. *Borderlands = La frontera: The new mestiza* (San Francisco, CA: Spinsters/Aunt Lute Books, 1987).
Baldwin, Lewis V. "A Reassessment of the Relationship Between Malcolm X and Martin Luther King, Jr." *The Western Journal of Black Studies*, 13.2 (1989): 103–113.
Balfour, Lawrie. "Darkwater's Democratic Vision." *Political Theory*, 38.4 (2010): 537–563.
Bass, Jonathan. *Blessed Are the Peacemakers* (Baton Rouge: Louisiana State University Press, 2001).
Belafonte, Harry. *My Song* (New York: Alfred A. Knopf, 2011).
Bernstein, David. "The Longest March." *Chicago Magazine*, July 25, 2016. Available at: http://www.chicagomag.com/Chicago-Magazine/August-2016/Martin-Luther-King-Chicago-Freedom-Movement/.
"Birmingham Campaign." In Clayborne Carson, Tenisha Armstrong, Susan Carson, Erin Cook, Susan Englander (Eds.), *The Martin Luther King, Jr. Encyclopedia*. (Westport, CT: Greenwood Press). Available at: https://kinginstitute.stanford.edu/encyclopedia/birmingham-campaign.
BlackPast, B. Stokely Carmichael, "Black Power," 2010, July 13 (1966). BlackPast.org. Available at: https://www.blackpast.org/african-american-history/speeches-african-american-history/1966-stokely-carmichael-black-power/.
Boggs, Grace Lee. "Grace Lee Boggs in Conversation with Angela Davis." *Making Contact, Radio Stories and Voices to Take Action*, February 20, 2012. Available at: https://www.radioproject.org/2012/02/grace-lee-boggs-berkeley/.

Boxill, Bernard R. "Self-Respect and Protest." In *Philosophy Born of Struggle*, ed. Leonard Harris, 2nd ed. (Dubuque, IA: Kendall/Hunt, 2000), 312–322.

Branch, Taylor. *Parting the Waters* (New York: Simon & Schuster, 1988).

Bromell, Nick. *The Time Is Always Now: Black Thought and the Transformation of US Democracy* (Oxford: Oxford University Press, 2013).

Burrows, Rufus. *God and Human Dignity: The Personalism, Theology, and Ethics of Martin Luther King, Jr.* (South Bend, IN: University of Notre Dame, 2006).

Carmichael, Stokley. "Black Power." 1966. Available at: https://www.blackpast.org/african-american-history/speeches-african-american-history/1966-stokely-carmichael-black-power/.

Carson, Clayborne (ed.). *The Autobiography of Martin Luther King, Jr.* (New York: Grand Central Publishing, 1998).

Carson, Clayborne. *In Struggle: SNCC and the Black Awakening of the 1960s* (Cambridge, MA: Harvard University Press, 1981).

Carson, Clayborne, and Peter Holloran (eds.). *A Knock at Midnight: Inspiration from the Great Sermons of Reverend Martin Luther King, Jr.* (New York: IPM, 2000), 79–100.

Carson, Clayborne, and Kris Shepard. *A Call to Conscience: The Landmark Speeches of Martin Luther King, Jr.* (New York: IPM/Warner Books, 2001), 171–199.

Carson, Clayborne, and Tenisha Armstrong (eds.). *The Papers of Martin Luther King, Jr.* Volume VII: *To Save the Soul of America, January 1961–August 1962* (Oakland: University of California Press, 2014).

Carson, Clayborne, Tenisha Armstrong, Susan Carson, Adrienne Clay, and Kieran Taylor (eds.). *The Papers of Martin Luther King, Jr.* Volume V: *Threshold for a New Decade, January 1959–December 1960* (Berkeley and Los Angeles: University of California Press, 2005).

Carson, Clayborne, Tenisha Armstrong, Susan Carson, Erin Cook, and Susan Englander (eds.). *The Martin Luther King, Jr. Encyclopedia* (Westport, CT: Greenwood, 2008).

Carson, Clayborne, Stewart Burns, Susan Carson, Dana Powell, and Peter Holloran (eds.). *The Papers of Martin Luther King, Jr.* Volume III: *Birth of a New Age, December 1955–December 1956* (Berkeley and Los Angeles, CA: University of California Press, 1997).

Carson, Clayborne, Susan Carson, Adrienne Clay, Virginia Shadron, and Kieran Taylor (eds.). *The Papers of Martin Luther King, Jr.* Volume IV: *Symbol of the Movement, January 1957–December 1958* (Berkeley and Los Angeles: University of California Press, 2000).

Carson, Clayborne, Susan Carson, Susan Englander, Troy Jackson, and Gerald L. Smith (eds.). *The Papers of Martin Luther King, Jr.* Volume VI: *Advocate of the Social Gospel, September 1948–March 1963* (Berkeley and Los Angeles: University of California Press, 2007).

BIBLIOGRAPHY 245

Carson, Clayborne, Ralph Luker, and Penny A. Russell (eds.). *The Papers of Martin Luther King, Jr.* Volume I: *Called to Serve, January 1929–June 1951* (Berkeley and Los Angeles: University of California Press, 1992).
Clayborne Carson, Ralph Luker, Penny A. Russell, and Peter Holloran (eds.), *The Papers of Martin Luther King, Jr.*, Volume II: *Rediscovering Precious Values, July 1951–November 1955* (Berkeley and Los Angeles: University of California Press, 1994)
Cherry, Myisha. *The Case for Rage* (New York: Oxford, 2021).
Cherry, Myisha. "Love, Anger, and Racial Injustice." In Adrienne M. Martin (ed), *The Routledge Handbook on Love in Philosophy* (New York: Routledge, 2018).
"Connor, Theophilus Eugene 'Bull,'" In Clayborne Carson, Tenisha Armstrong, Susan Carson, Erin Cook, Susan Englander (eds.). *The Martin Luther King, Jr., Encyclopedia* (Westport, CT: Greenwood Press). Available at: https://kinginstitute.stanford.edu/encyclopedia/connor-theophilus-eugene-bull.
Collacut, James. "Martin Luther King Jr.: The Rhetoric of Weaponized Nonviolence as Democratic Propaganda." Unpublished paper.
Collins, Patricia Hill. *Black Feminist Thought: Knowledge, Consciousness, and the Politics of Empowerment* (New York: Routledge, 2000).
Cowper, William. "The Negro's Complaint" (London: Harvey and Darton, 1788).
Darby, Derrick. "A Vindication of Voting Rights." In Brandon M. Terry and Tommie Shelby (eds.), *To Shape a New World* (Cambridge, MA: Harvard University Press, 2018), 161–183.
Day, J. P. "Hope." *American Philosophical Quarterly*, 6.2 (1969): 89–102.
Douglass, Andrew J., and Jared A. Loggins. *Prophet of Discontent: Martin Luther King, Jr. and the Critique of Racial Capitalism* (Atlanta: University of Georgia Press, 2021).
Du Bois, W. E. B. *Criteria of Negro Art* (New York: Crisis, 1926).
Du Bois, W. E .B. *Dusk of Dawn*. In *Writings*, Nathan Huggins (ed.) (New York: Library of America, 1940), 770–771.
Douglass, Frederick. *The Life and Times of Frederick Douglass* (Hartford, CT: Park, 1883).
Douglass, Frederick. "Oration in Memory of Abraham Lincoln," April 14, 1876. Available at: http://teachingamericanhistory.org/library/document/oration-in-memory-of-abraham-lincoln/.
Douglass, Frederick. "What to the Slave Is the Fourth of July?" July 5, 1852. Available at: https://www.pbs.org/wgbh/aia/part4/4h2927t.html.
Downie, R. S. "Hope." *Philosophy and Phenomenological Research*, 24.2 (1963): 248–251.
"Editorial." *New York Times*, April 17, 1963, A40.

Eskew, Glenn T., *But for Birmingham: The Local and National Movements in the Civil Rights Struggle* (Chapel Hill: University of North Carolina Press, 1997).
Estes, Steve. "I AM A MAN!: Race, Masculinity, and the 1968 Memphis Sanitation Strike." *Labor History*, 41.2 (2000): 153–170.
Fosdick, Harry. *On Being a Real Person* (New York: Harper & Brothers, 1943).
Gaines, Kevin. *Uplifting the Race* (Chapel Hill: University of North Carolina Press, 1996).
Gandhi, M. K. *Hind Swaraj and Other Writings*, Anthony Parel (ed.) (Cambridge: Cambridge University Press, 2009).
Gandhi, M. K., K. Gandhi, and A. Surabati (eds.). *Young India: A Weekly Journal*: Pub: September 15, 1920.
Garvey, Marcus. "Universal Negro Improvement Association." In Robert A. Hill (ed.), *The Marcus Garvey and University Negro Improvement Association Papers*, Volume 1 (Berkeley: University of California Press, 1982).
Gilbreath, Edward. *Remembering Birmingham: Dr. Martin Luther King Jr's Letter to America—50 Years Later* (Downers Grove, IL: IVP Books, 2013).
Gooding-Williams, Robert. "Beauty as Propaganda: On the Political Aesthetics of W. E. B. Du Bois." The 2021 Dewey Lecture in Law and Philosophy, University of Chicago Law School, Chicago, Illinois, February 10, 2021.
Gooding-Williams, Robert. "Du Bois, Politics, Aesthetics: An Introduction." *Public Culture*, 17 (Spring 2005): 203–215.
Gooding-Williams, Robert. "The Du Bois–Washington Debate and the Idea of Dignity." In Brandon M. Terry and Tommie Shelby (eds.), *To Shape a New World* (Cambridge, MA: Harvard University Press, 2018), 19–34.
Gregg, Richard. *The Power of Nonviolence* (Nyack, NY: Fellowship Publications, 1959).
Hamer, Fannie Lou. "Testimony Before the Credentials Committee, Democratic National Convention." August 22, 1964. Available at: https://americanradioworks.publicradio.org/features/sayitplain/flhamer.html.
Harding, Vincent. "Foreword." In Howard Thurman, *Jesus and the Disinherited* (Boston, MA: Beacon Press, 1996), vii–xviii.
Higginbotham, Evelyn Brooks. *Righteous Discontent* (Cambridge, MA: Harvard University Press, 1993).
Hooker, Juliet. *Black Grief/White Grievance: The Politics of Loss* (Princeton, NJ: Princeton, 2023).
hooks, bell. *Outlaw Culture: Resisting Representation* (New York: Routledge, 2006).
hooks, bell. *Sisters of the Yam: Black Women and Self-Recovery* (Boston, MA: South End Press, 1993).
Jung, C. G. *Modern Man in Search of a Soul* (San Diego, CA: Harcourt, Brace, 1933).

King, Martin Luther, Jr. "Accepting Responsibility for Your Actions." In Carson et al. (eds.), *The Papers of Martin Luther King, Jr.*, Volume VI, 139–142. Available at: https://kinginstitute.stanford.edu/king-papers/documents/accepting-responsibility-your-actions.
King, Martin Luther, Jr. "Address at Albany." In Carson and Armstrong (eds.), *The Papers of Martin Luther King, Jr.*, Volume VII. Available at: https://kinginstitute.stanford.edu/king-papers/documents/address-delivered-albany-movement-mass-meeting-shiloh-baptist-church.
King, Martin Luther, Jr, "Address at the Fiftieth Annual NAACP Convention." In Carson et al. (eds.), *The Papers of Martin Luther King, Jr.*, Volume V, 245–250. Available at: https://kinginstitute.stanford.edu/king-papers/documents/address-fiftieth-annual-naacp-convention.
King, Martin Luther, Jr. "Address at the Fourth Annual Institute on Nonviolence and Social Change at Bethel Baptist Church." In Carson et al. (eds.), *The Papers of Martin Luther King, Jr.*, Volume V, 333–343. Available at: https://kinginstitute.stanford.edu/king-papers/documents/address-fourth-annual-institute-nonviolence-and-social-change-bethel-baptist.
King, Martin Luther, Jr. "Address at Public Meeting of the Southern Christian Ministers Conference of Mississippi." In Carson et al. (eds.), *The Papers of Martin Luther King, Jr.*, Volume V, 281–290. Available at: https://kinginstitute.stanford.edu/king-papers/documents/address-public-meeting-southern-christian-ministers-conference-mississippi.
King, Martin Luther, Jr. "Address to MIA Mass Meeting at Bethel Baptist Church." In Carson et al. (eds.), *The Papers of Martin Luther King, Jr.*, Volume IV, 109–110. Available at: https://kinginstitute.stanford.edu/king-papers/documents/outline-address-mia-mass-meeting-bethel-baptist-church.
King, Martin Luther, Jr. "Advice for Living." In Carson et al. (eds.), *The Papers of Martin Luther King, Jr.*, Volume IV, 375. Available at: .https://kinginstitute.stanford.edu/king-papers/documents/advice-living-6
King, Martin Luther, Jr. *All Labor Has Dignity* (Boston, MA: Beacon Press, 1963).
King, Martin Luther, Jr. "The American Dream." In Clayborne Carson and Peter Holloran (eds.), *A Knock at Midnight: Inspiration from the Great Sermons of Reverend Martin Luther King, Jr.* (New York: IPM, 2000), 79–100.
King, Martin Luther, Jr. "Beyond Condemnation." In Carson et al. (eds.), *The Papers of Martin Luther King, Jr.*, Volume VI, 199–201. Available at: https://kinginstitute.stanford.edu/king-papers/documents/beyond-condemnation-sermon-dexter-avenue-baptist-church.
King, Martin Luther, Jr. "The Birth of a New Age." In Carson et al. (eds.), *The Papers of Martin Luther King, Jr.*, Volume III, 344. Available at: https://kinginstitute.stanford.edu/king-papers/documents/birth-new-age-address-delivered-11-august-1956-fiftieth-anniversary-alpha-phi.

King, Martin Luther, Jr. "The Birth of a New Nation." In Carson et al. (eds.), *The Papers of Martin Luther King, Jr.*, Volume IV, 155–167. Available at: https://kinginstitute.stanford.edu/king-papers/documents/birth-new-nation-sermon-delivered-dexter-avenue-baptist-church.

King, Martin Luther, Jr. "The Burning Truth in the South." In Carson et al. (eds.), *The Papers of Martin Luther King, Jr.*, Volume V, 447–451. Available at: https://kinginstitute.stanford.edu/king-papers/documents/burning-truth-south.

King, Martin Luther, Jr. "Challenge to the Churches and Synagogues." In MLKPP, Martin Luther King, Jr. Papers Project, Stanford University, Stanford, CA.

King, Martin Luther, Jr. "The Chief Characteristics and Doctrines of Mahayana Buddhism." in Carson et al. (eds.), *The Papers of Martin Luther King, Jr.*, Volume I, 314–315. Available at: https://kinginstitute.stanford.edu/king-papers/documents/chief-characteristics-and-doctrines-mahayana-buddhism.

King, Martin Luther, Jr. "Christ, the Center of Our Faith." In Carson et al. (eds.), *The Papers of Martin Luther King, Jr.*, Volume V, 201–202. Available at: https://kinginstitute.stanford.edu/king-papers/documents/christ-center-our-faith.

King, Martin Luther, Jr. "Conquering Self-Centeredness." In Carson et al. (eds.), *The Papers of Martin Luther King, Jr.*, Volume IV, 248–259. Available at: https://kinginstitute.stanford.edu/king-papers/documents/conquering-self-centeredness-sermon-delivered-dexter-avenue-baptist-church.

King, Martin Luther, Jr. "Contemporary Continental Theology." In Carson et al. (eds.), *The Papers of Martin Luther King, Jr.*, Volume II, 113–139. Available at: https://kinginstitute.stanford.edu/king-papers/documents/contemporary-continental-theology.

King, Martin Luther, Jr. "A Creative Protest." In Carson et al. (eds.), *The Papers of Martin Luther King, Jr.*, Volume V, 367–370. Available at: https://kinginstitute.stanford.edu/king-papers/documents/creative-protest.

King, Martin Luther, Jr. "The Crisis of the Modern Family." In Carson et al. (eds.), *The Papers of Martin Luther King, Jr.*, Volume VI, 209–213. Available at: https://kinginstitute.stanford.edu/king-papers/documents/crisis-modern-family-sermon-dexter-avenue-baptist-church.

King, Martin Luther, Jr. "Desegregation and the Future." In Carson et al. (eds.), *The Papers of Martin Luther King, Jr.*, Volume III, 471–479. Available at: https://kinginstitute.stanford.edu/king-papers/documents/desegregation-and-future-address-delivered-annual-luncheon-national-committee.

King, Martin Luther, Jr. "Does Segregation Equal Integration?: Interview with Mike Wallace," June 25, 1958. In *Martin Luther King, Jr.: The Last Interview and Other Conversations* (Brooklyn, NY: Melville, 2017), 23–42.

King, Martin Luther, Jr. "Draft of Chapter II: Transformed Nonconformist." In Carson et al. (eds.), *The Papers of Martin Luther King, Jr.*, Volume VI,

BIBLIOGRAPHY 249

466–476. Available at: https://kinginstitute.stanford.edu/king-papers/documents/draft-chapter-ii-transformed-nonconformist.

King, Martin Luther, Jr. "Draft of Chapter III: On Being a Good Neighbor." In Carson et al. (eds.), *The Papers of Martin Luther King, Jr.*, Volume VI, 478–486. Available at: https://kinginstitute.stanford.edu/king-papers/documents/draft-chapter-iii-being-good-neighbor.

King, Martin Luther, Jr. "Draft of Chapter VIII, 'The Death of Evil Upon the Seashore.'" In Carson et al. (eds.), *The Papers of Martin Luther King, Jr.*, Volume VI, 504–514. Available at: https://kinginstitute.stanford.edu/king-papers/documents/draft-chapter-viii-death-evil-upon-seashore.

King, Martin Luther, Jr. "Draft of Chapter XIV, 'The Mastery of Fear or Antidotes for Fear.'" In Carson et al. (eds.), *The Papers of Martin Luther King, Jr.*, Volume VI, 535–545. Available at: https://kinginstitute.stanford.edu/king-papers/documents/draft-chapter-xiv-mastery-fear-or-antidotes-fear#:~:text = We%20can%20master%20fear%20not,affirmation%20of%20one%27s%20essential%20nature.

King, Martin Luther, Jr. "Draft of Chapter 'Shattered Dreams.'" In Carson et al. (eds.), *The Papers of Martin Luther King, Jr.*, Volume VI, 514–527. Available at https://kinginstitute.stanford.edu/king-papers/documents/draft-chapter-x-shattered-dreams.

King, Martin Luther, Jr. "Draft, Statement to Judge James E. Webb after Arrest at Rich's Department Store." In Carson et al. (eds.), *The Papers of Martin Luther King, Jr.*, Volume V, 522. Available at: https://kinginstitute.stanford.edu/king-papers/documents/draft-statement-judge-james-e-webb-after-arrest-richs-department-store.

King, Martin Luther, Jr. "Drum Major Instinct." In Clayborne Carson and Peter Holloran (eds.), *A Knock at Midnight: Inspiration from the Great Sermons of Reverend Martin Luther King, Jr.* (New York: IPM, 2000), 165–186.

King, Martin Luther, Jr. "The Ethical Demands of Integration." In James M. Washington (ed.), *A Testament of Hope* (New York: Harper Collins, 1986), 117–125.

King, Martin Luther, Jr. "Facing the Challenge of a New Age." In Carson et al. (eds.), *The Papers of Martin Luther King, Jr.*, Volume III, 73–89. Available at: https://kinginstitute.stanford.edu/king-papers/documents/facing-challenge-new-age-address-delivered-naacp-emancipation-day-rally.

King, Martin Luther, Jr. "Facing Life's Inescapables." In Carson et al. (eds.), *The Papers of Martin Luther King, Jr.*, Volume VI, 88–90. Available at: https://kinginstitute.stanford.edu/king-papers/documents/facing-lifes-inescapables.

King, Martin Luther, Jr. "Faith in Man." In Clayborne Carson, Susan Carson, Susan Englander, Troy Jackson, and Gerald L. Smith (eds.), In Carson et al. (eds.), *The Papers of Martin Luther King, Jr.*, Volume VI, 253–255. Available at: https://kinginstitute.stanford.edu/king-papers/documents/faith-man.

King, Martin Luther, Jr. "The Future of Integration." State University of Iowa, November 11, 1959, 1–13. Available at: http://natedsanders.com/lot-36943.aspx.
King, Martin Luther, Jr. "Garden of Gethsemane." In Carson et al. (eds.), *The Papers of Martin Luther King, Jr.*, Volume VI, 275–283. Available at: https://kinginstitute.stanford.edu/king-papers/documents/garden-gethsemane-sermon-delivered-dexter-avenue-baptist-church.
King, Martin Luther, Jr. "God's Love." In Carson et al. (eds.), *The Papers of Martin Luther King, Jr.*, Volume VI, 179–181. Available at: https://kinginstitute.stanford.edu/king-papers/documents/gods-love-sermon-dexter-avenue-baptist-church.
King, Martin Luther, Jr. "Guidelines for a Constructive Church." In Clayborne Carson and Peter Holloran (eds.), *A Knock at Midnight: Inspiration from the Great Sermons of Reverend Martin Luther King, Jr.* (New York: IPM, 2000), 105–115.
King, Martin Luther, Jr. "Honoring Du Bois." *Jacobin*, January 1, 2019.
King, Martin Luther, Jr. "I Have a Dream." In James M. Washington (ed.), *Testament of Hope: The Essential Writings and Speeches of Martin Luther King Jr.* (New York: Harper Collins, 1986), 217–220.
King, Martin Luther, Jr. "Interview on 'Front Page Challenge.'" In Carson et al. (eds.), *The Papers of Martin Luther King, Jr.*, Volume V, 191–194. Available at: https://kinginstitute.stanford.edu/king-papers/documents/interview-front-page-challenge.
King, Martin Luther, Jr. "Interview by Martin Agronsky for 'Look Here.'" In Carson et al. (eds.), *The Papers of Martin Luther King, Jr.*, Volume IV, 292–299. Available at: https://kinginstitute.stanford.edu/king-papers/documents/interview-martin-agronsky-look-here.
King, Martin Luther, Jr. "Interview by Richard D. Heffner for 'The Open Mind.'" In Carson et al. (eds.), *The Papers of Martin Luther King, Jr.*, Volume IV, 126–131. Available at: https://kinginstitute.stanford.edu/king-papers/documents/interview-richard-d-heffner-open-mind.
King, Martin Luther, Jr. "It's Hard to be a Christian." In Carson et al. (eds.), *The Papers of Martin Luther King, Jr.*, Volume VI, 251–252. Available at: https://kinginstitute.stanford.edu/king-papers/documents/its-hard-be-christian.
King, Martin Luther, Jr. "Letter from Albany Jail." In Christopher C. Meyers (ed.), *The Empire State of the South: Georgia History in Documents and Essays* (Macon, GA: Mercer University Press, 2008), 307–308.
King, Martin Luther, Jr. "Levels of Love." In Carson et al. (eds.), *The Papers of Martin Luther King, Jr.*, Volume VI, 437–445. Available at: https://kinginstitute.stanford.edu/king-papers/documents/levels-love-sermon-delivered-ebenezer-baptist-church.
King, Martin Luther, Jr. "A Look to the Future." In Carson et al. (eds.), *The Papers of Martin Luther King, Jr.*, Volume IV, 269–276. Available at: https://

kinginstitute.stanford.edu/king-papers/documents/look-future-address-delivered-highlander-folk-schools-twenty-fifth-anniversary.
King, Martin Luther, Jr. "Love, Law, Civil Disobedience." In Bill Blaisdell (ed.), *Essays on Civil Disobedience* (Minneapolis, MN: Dover, 2016), 120–131.
King, Martin Luther, Jr. "Loving Your Enemies." In Carson et al. (eds.), *The Papers of Martin Luther King, Jr.*, Volume VI, 126–128. Available at: https://kinginstitute.stanford.edu/king-papers/documents/loving-your-enemies.
King, Martin Luther, Jr. "Loving Your Enemies." In Clayborne Carson and Peter Holloran (eds.), *A Knock at Midnight: Inspiration from the Great Sermons of Reverend Martin Luther King, Jr.* (New York: IPM, 2000), 41.
King, Martin Luther, Jr. "Loving Your Enemies, Sermon (Detroit)." In Carson et al. (eds.), *The Papers of Martin Luther King, Jr.*, Volume VI, 421–429. Available at: https://kinginstitute.stanford.edu/king-papers/documents/loving-your-enemies-sermon-delivered-detroit-council-churches-noon-lenten
King, Martin Luther, Jr. "Mastering Our Fears." In Carson et al. (eds.), *The Papers of Martin Luther King, Jr.*, Volume VI, 319–321.
King, Martin Luther, Jr. "Mastering Our Evil Selves"/"Mastering Ourselves." In Carson et al. (eds.), *The Papers of Martin Luther King, Jr.*, Volume VI, 94–97. Available at: https://kinginstitute.stanford.edu/king-papers/documents/mastering-our-evil-selves-mastering-ourselves.
King, Martin Luther, Jr. "The Mastery of Fear, Sermon Outlines." In Carson et al. (eds.), *The Papers of Martin Luther King, Jr.*, Volume VI, 318–319. Available at: https://kinginstitute.stanford.edu/king-papers/documents/mastery-fear.
King, Martin Luther, Jr. "The Mastery of Fear, Sermon Notes." In Carson et al. (eds.), *The Papers of Martin Luther King, Jr.*, Volume VI, 317–318.
King, Martin Luther, Jr. "The Meaning of Forgiveness." In Carson et al. (eds.), *The Papers of Martin Luther King, Jr.*, Volume VI, 580–581. Available at: https://kinginstitute.stanford.edu/king-papers/documents/meaning-forgiveness.
King, Martin Luther, Jr. "MIA Mass Meeting at Holt Street Baptist Church." In Clayborne Carson and Kris Shepard (eds.), *A Call to Conscience: The Landmark Speeches of Martin Luther King, Jr.* (New York: IPM/Warner Books, 2001), 7–12. Available at: https://kinginstitute.stanford.edu/king-papers/documents/mia-mass-meeting-holt-street-baptist-church.
King, Martin Luther, Jr. "Montgomery Bus Boycott." In Josh Gottheimer (ed.), *Ripples of Hope: Great American Civil Rights Speeches* (New York: Basic Civitas Books, 2003), 210–216.
King, Martin Luther, Jr. "The Montgomery Story." In Carson et al. (eds.), *The Papers of Martin Luther King, Jr.*, Volume III, 299–310. Available at: https://kinginstitute.stanford.edu/king-papers/documents/montgomery-story-address-delivered-forty-seventh-annual-naacp-convention.

King, Martin Luther, Jr. "The Most Durable Power." In Carson et al. (eds.), *The Papers of Martin Luther King, Jr.*, Volume VI, 302–303. Available at: https://kinginstitute.stanford.edu/king-papers/documents/most-durable-power-excerpt-sermon-dexter-avenue-baptist-church-6-november-1956.

King, Martin Luther, Jr. "My Trip to the Land of Gandhi." In Carson et al. (eds.), *The Papers of Martin Luther King, Jr.*, Volume V, 231–238. Available at: https://kinginstitute.stanford.edu/king-papers/documents/my-trip-land-gandhi.

King, Martin Luther, Jr. "The Negro and the American Dream." In Carson et al. (eds.), *The Papers of Martin Luther King, Jr.*, Volume V, 508–511. Available at: https://kinginstitute.stanford.edu/king-papers/documents/negro-and-american-dream-excerpt-address-annual-freedom-mass-meeting-north.

King, Martin Luther, Jr. "Non-Aggression Procedures to Interracial Harmony." In Carson et al. (eds.), *The Papers of Martin Luther King, Jr.*, Volume III, 321–328. Available at: https://kinginstitute.stanford.edu/king-papers/documents/non-aggression-procedures-interracial-harmony-address-delivered-american.

King, Martin Luther, Jr. "Nonviolence and Racial Justice." In Carson et al. (eds.), *The Papers of Martin Luther King, Jr.*, Volume IV, 118–119. Available at: https://kinginstitute.stanford.edu/king-papers/documents/nonviolence-and-racial-justice.

King, Martin Luther, Jr. "Nonviolence and Social Change." In Cornel West (ed.), *Radical King* (Boston, MA: Beacon Press, 2015), 147–154.

King, Martin Luther, Jr. "On Being a Good Neighbor." In Carson et al. (eds.), *The Papers of Martin Luther King, Jr.*, Volume VI, 478–486. Available at: https://kinginstitute.stanford.edu/king-papers/documents/draft-chapter-iii-being-good-neighbor.

King, Martin Luther, Jr. "The One-Sided Approach of the Samaritan." In Carson et al. (eds.), *The Papers of Martin Luther King, Jr.*, Volume VI, 239–240. Available at: https://kinginstitute.stanford.edu/king-papers/documents/one-sided-approach-good-samaritan.

King, Martin Luther, Jr. "Our God Is Marching On." Available at: https://kinginstitute.stanford.edu/our-god-marching.

King, Martin Luther, Jr. "Our Struggle." In Carson et al. (eds.), *The Papers of Martin Luther King, Jr.*, Volume III, 236–241. Available at: https://okra.stanford.edu/transcription/document_images/Vol03Scans/236_Apr-1956_Our%20Struggle.pdf.

King, Martin Luther, Jr. "Overcoming an Inferiority Complex." In Carson et al. (eds.), *The Papers of Martin Luther King, Jr.*, Volume VI, 303–316. Available at: https://kinginstitute.stanford.edu/king-papers/documents/overcoming-inferiority-complex-sermon-delivered-dexter-avenue-baptist-church#:~:text=Now%20it%20seems%20to%20me,my%20inherited%20abilities%20and%20handicaps.

BIBLIOGRAPHY 253

King, Martin Luther, Jr. "Paul's Letter to American Christians." In Carson et al. (eds.), *The Papers of Martin Luther King, Jr.*, Volume VI, 338-346. Available at: https://kinginstitute.stanford.edu/king-papers/documents/pauls-letter-american-christians-sermon-delivered-commission-ecumenical.

King, Martin Luther, Jr. "The Perfect Faith." Available at: https://kinginstitute.stanford.edu/volume-viii-preview-perfect-faith.

King, Martin Luther, Jr. "The Peril of Superficial Optimism in the Area of Race Relations." In Carson et al. (eds.), *The Papers of Martin Luther King, Jr.*, Volume VI, 214-215. Available at: https://kinginstitute.stanford.edu/king-papers/documents/peril-superficial-optimism-area-race-relations.

King, Martin Luther, Jr. "The Peril of the Sword." In Carson et al. (eds.), *The Papers of Martin Luther King, Jr.*, Volume VI, 598-599. Available at: https://kinginstitute.stanford.edu/king-papers/documents/peril-sword.

King, Martin Luther, Jr. "Playboy: Interview: Martin Luther King, Jr." In James M. Washington (ed.), *Testament of Hope: The Essential Writings and Speeches of Martin Luther King Jr.* (New York: Harper One, 1986), 340-377.

King, Martin Luther, Jr. "Power of Nonviolence." In James Melvin Washington (ed.), *A Testament of Hope: The Essential Writings and Speeches of Martin Luther King Jr.* (New York: Harper One, 1986), 12-15.

King, Martin Luther, Jr. "Preaching Ministry." In Carson et al. (eds.), *The Papers of Martin Luther King, Jr.*, Volume VI, 77-69. Available at: https://kinginstitute.stanford.edu/king-papers/documents/preaching-ministry.

King, Martin Luther, Jr. "Press Release from Dr. King (Inside Fulton County Jail)." In Carson et al. (eds.), *The Papers of Martin Luther King, Jr.*, Volume V, 527. Available at: https://kinginstitute.stanford.edu/king-papers/docume nts/press-release-dr-king-inside-fulton-county-jail.

King, Martin Luther, Jr. "Propagandizing Christianity." In Carson et al. (eds.), *The Papers of Martin Luther King, Jr.*, Volume VI, 184-187. Available at: https://kinginstitute.stanford.edu/king-papers/documents/propagandiz ing-christianity-sermon-dexter-avenue-baptist-church.

King, Martin Luther, Jr. "The Quest for Peace and Justice." Nobel Lecture, December 11, 1964.

King, Martin Luther, Jr. "Quotable Quotes from Rev. King." In Carson et al. (eds.), *The Papers of Martin Luther King, Jr.*, Volume III, 209-210. Available at: https://kinginstitute.stanford.edu/king-papers/documents/quotable-quotes-rev-king.

King, Martin Luther, Jr. "Read Martin Luther King Jr.'s 'I Have a Dream' Speech in Its Entirety.'" *Talk of the Nation*, National Public Radio, January 14, 2022. Available at: https://www.npr.org/2010/01/18/122701268/i-have-a-dream-speech-in-its-entirety.

King, Martin Luther, Jr. "A Realistic Look at the Question of Progress in the Area of Race Relations." In Carson et al. (eds.), *The Papers of Martin Luther King, Jr.*, Volume IV, 167-179. Available at: https://kinginstitute.stanford.

edu/king-papers/documents/realistic-look-question-progress-area-race-relations-address-delivered-st.

King, Martin Luther, Jr. "A Realistic Look at Race Relations," given at NAACP Legal Defense and Educational Fund banquet at New York's Waldorf-Astoria Hotel, May 1956, 6.

King, Martin Luther, Jr. "Remaining Awake Through a Great Revolution." In Carson et al. (eds.), *The Papers of Martin Luther King, Jr.*, Volume V, 219–226. Available at: https://kinginstitute.stanford.edu/king-papers/documents/remaining-awake-through-great-revolution-address-morehouse-college.

King, Martin Luther, Jr. "Remarks Delivered at Africa Freedom Dinner at Atlanta University." In Carson et al. (eds.), *The Papers of Martin Luther King, Jr.*, Volume V, 197–202. Available at: https://kinginstitute.stanford.edu/king-papers/documents/remarks-delivered-africa-freedom-dinner-atlanta-university.

King, Martin Luther, Jr. "Remarks in Acceptance of the Forty-Second Spingarn Medal at the Forty-Eighth Annual NAACP Convention." In Carson et al. (eds.), *The Papers of Martin Luther King, Jr.*, Volume IV, 228–233. Available at: https://kinginstitute.stanford.edu/king-papers/documents/remarks-acceptance-forty-second-spingarn-medal-forty-eighth-annual-naacp.

King, Martin Luther, Jr. "Revolt Without Violence—The Negroes' New Strategy." In Carson et al. (eds.), *The Papers of Martin Luther King, Jr.*, Volume V, 392–396. Available at: https://kinginstitute.stanford.edu/king-papers/documents/revolt-without-violence-negroes-new-strategy

King, Martin Luther, Jr. "The Rising Tide of Racial Consciousness." In Carson et al. (eds.), *The Papers of Martin Luther King, Jr.*, Volume V, 499–508. Available at: https://kinginstitute.stanford.edu/king-papers/documents/rising-tide-racial-consciousness-address-golden-anniversary-conference.

King, Martin Luther, Jr. "Six Talks Based on Beliefs That Matter by William Adams Brown." In Carson et al. (eds.), *The Papers of Martin Luther King, Jr.*, Volume I, 280–289. Available at: https://kinginstitute.stanford.edu/king-papers/documents/six-talks-based-beliefs-matter-william-adams-brown.

King, Martin Luther, Jr. "Sermon Notes and Outlines I." In Carson et al. (eds.), *The Papers of Martin Luther King, Jr.*, Volume VI, 561–566. Available at: https://kinginstitute.stanford.edu/king-papers/documents/sermon-notes-and-outlines-i.

King, Martin Luther, Jr. "Sermon Sketches." In Carson et al. (eds.), *The Papers of Martin Luther King, Jr.*, Volume VI, 81–83. Available at: https://kinginstitute.stanford.edu/king-papers/documents/sermon-sketches.

King, Martin Luther, Jr. "Showdown for Nonviolence." In James M. Washington (ed.), *A Testament of Hope* (New York: Harper Collins, 1986), 64–72.

King, Martin Luther, Jr. "Some Things We Must Do." In Carson et al. (eds.), *The Papers of Martin Luther King, Jr.*, Volume IV, 328–342. Available

at: https://kinginstitute.stanford.edu/king-papers/documents/some-thi ngs-we-must-do-address-delivered-second-annual-institute-nonviolence.
King, Martin Luther, Jr. "Speech at SMU." March 17, 1966, 1–8. Transcript available at: https://www.smu.edu/AboutSMU/MLK#transcript.
King, Martin Luther, Jr. "Statement on Ending the Bus Boycott." In Carson et al. (eds.), *The Papers of Martin Luther King, Jr.*, Volume III, 485–487. Available at: https://kinginstitute.stanford.edu/king-papers/documents/statement-ending-bus-boycott.
King, Martin Luther, Jr. "A Statement to the South and Nation." In Carson et al. (eds.), *The Papers of Martin Luther King, Jr.*, Volume IV, 103–106. Available at: https://kinginstitute.stanford.edu/king-papers/documents/statement-south-and-nation-issued-southern-negro-leaders-conference.
King, Martin Luther, Jr. "Statement to the Press at the Beginning of the Youth Leadership Conference." In Carson et al. (eds.), *The Papers of Martin Luther King, Jr.*, Volume IV, 426–427. Available at: https://kinginstitute.stanford.edu/king-papers/documents/statement-press-beginning-youth-leaders hip-conference#fn4.
King, Martin Luther, Jr. *Strength to Love* (Minneapolis: Fortress Press, 2010).
King, Martin Luther, Jr. *Stride Toward Freedom: The Montgomery Story* (Boston: Beacon Press, 1958).
King, Martin Luther, Jr. "Suffering and Faith." In Carson et al. (eds.), *The Papers of Martin Luther King, Jr.*, Volume V, 443–444. Available at: https://kinginstitute.stanford.edu/king-papers/documents/suffering-and-faith.
King, Martin Luther, Jr. "A Talk with Martin Luther King." In Carson et al. (eds.), *The Papers of Martin Luther King, Jr.*, Volume V, 569. Available at: https://kinginstitute.stanford.edu/king-papers/documents/talk-martin-luther-king.
King, Martin Luther, Jr. "The Three Dimensions of a Complete Life." In Carson et al. (eds.), *The Papers of Martin Luther King, Jr.*, Volume VI, 395–405. Available at: https://kinginstitute.stanford.edu/king-papers/documents/three-dimensions-complete-life-sermon-delivered-friendship-baptist-church.
King, Martin Luther, Jr. "The Three Dimensions of a Complete Life (Germantown)." In Carson et al. (eds.), *The Papers of Martin Luther King, Jr.*, Volume V, 571–579. Available at: https://kinginstitute.stanford.edu/king-papers/documents/three-dimensions-complete-life-sermon-delive red-unitarian-church-germantown
King, Martin Luther, Jr. "The Three Dimensions of a Complete Life [Unitarian]." In Carson et al. (eds.), *The Papers of Martin Luther King, Jr.*, Volume V, 571–579. Available at: https://kinginstitute.stanford.edu/king-papers/documents/three-dimensions-complete-life-sermon-delivered-unitarian-church-germantown.
King, Martin Luther, Jr. "A Testament of Hope." In James M. Washington (ed.), *A Testament of Hope* (New York: Harper Collins, 1986), 322–323.

King, Martin Luther, Jr. *The Trumpet of Conscience: Dr King's Final Testament on Racism, Poverty and War* (Boston, MA: Beacon, 1967).
King, Martin Luther, Jr. "Unfulfilled Hopes, Sermon." In Carson et al. (eds.), *The Papers of Martin Luther King, Jr.*, Volume VI, 357–367. Available at: https://kinginstitute.stanford.edu/king-papers/documents/unfulfilled-hopes-0.
King, Martin Luther, Jr. "When Your String Breaks." In Carson et al. (eds.), *The Papers of Martin Luther King, Jr.*, Volume VI, 354–355. Available at: https://kinginstitute.stanford.edu/kingpapers/when-your-string-breaks.
King, Martin Luther, Jr. *Why We Can't Wait* (New York: Signet, 1963).
King, Martin Luther, Jr, "Where Do We Go from Here," In Clayborne Carson and Kris Shepard (eds.), *A Call to Conscience: The Landmark Speeches of Martin Luther King, Jr.* (New York: IPM/Warner Books, 2001), 171–199. Available at: https://kinginstitute.stanford.edu/where-do-we-go-here.
King, Martin Luther, Jr. *Where Do We Go From Here: Chaos or Community* (Boston, MA: Beacon, 1968).
King, Martin Luther, Jr. "Who Speaks for the Negro." In *Martin Luther King, Jr.: The Last Interview and Other Conversations* (New York: Melville House, 2017), 43–84.
King, Martin Luther, Jr. "Worship." In Carson et al. (eds.), *The Papers of Martin Luther King, Jr.*, Volume VI, 222–225. Available at: https://kinginstitute.stanford.edu/king-papers/documents/worship-sermon-dexter-avenue-baptist-church.
King, Martin Luther, Jr. "Worship at Its Best." In Carson et al. (eds.), *The Papers of Martin Luther King, Jr.*, Volume VI, 350–351. Available at: https://kinginstitute.stanford.edu/king-papers/documents/worship-its-best-sermon-dexter-avenue-baptist-church.
Krishnamurthy, Meena. "From Shattered Dreams to Dreams in the Making: Martin Luther King Jr. on the Transformative Power of Democratic Disappointment" (work in progress).
Krishnamurthy, Meena. "Martin Luther King Jr., on Democratic Propaganda, Shame, and Moral Transformation." *Political Theory*, 50.2 (2022): 305–336.
Krishnamurthy, Meena. "(White) Tyranny and the Democratic Value of Distrust." *The Monist*, 98.4 (2015): 391–406.
"Letter from Birmingham Jail." In Clayborne Carson, Tenisha Armstrong, Susan Carson, Erin Cook, Susan Englander (eds.), *Martin Luther King, Jr. Encyclopedia* (Westport, CT: Green Wood, 2008). Available at: https://kinginstitute.stanford.edu/encyclopedia/letter-birmingham-jail.
Lischer, Richard. *The Preacher King: Martin Luther King, Jr. and the Word That Moved America* (New York: Oxford University Press, 1995).
Livingston, Alexander. "'Tough Love': The Political Theology of Civil Disobedience." *Perspectives on Politics*, 18.3 (2020): 851–866.
Lomax, Louis E. "A Summing Up: Louis Lomax Interviews Malcolm X." *When the Word Is Given: A Report on Elijah Muhammad, Malcolm X, and the*

Black Muslim World. Available at: https://teachingamericanhistory.org/document/a-summing-up-louis-lomax-interviews-malcolm-x/.
Lorde, Audre. *A Burst of Light* (Ithaca, NY: Firebrand Books, 1988).
Lorde, Audre. *Sister Outsider* (Berkeley, CA: Crossing Press, 2007).
Lorde, Audre. "The Uses of Anger." In Lorde, *Sister Outsider* (Berkeley, CA: Crossing Press, 2007), 124–134.
"Malcolm X." In Clayborne Carson, Tenisha Armstrong, Susan Carson, Erin Cook, Susan Englander (eds.), *The Martin Luther King, Jr., Encyclopedia* (Westport, CT: Green Wood, 2008). Available at: https://kinginstitute.stanford.edu/encyclopedia/malcolm-x.
Mantena, Karuna. "Showdown for Nonviolence." In Tommie Shelby and Brandon M. Terry (eds.), *To Shape a New World* (Cambridge, MA: Harvard University Press, 2018), 78–101.
Martin, Adrienne. *How We Hope: A Moral Psychology* (Princeton, NJ: Princeton University Press, 2013).
"Memphis Sanitation Workers' Strike." In Clayborne Carson et al. (ed.), *The Martin Luther King, Jr., Encyclopedia* (Westport, CT: Greenwood, 2008). Available at: https://kinginstitute.stanford.edu/memphis-sanitation-workers-strike.
Miller, Keith D. *Voice of Deliverance* (Athens: University of Georgie Press, 2008).
Moody-Adams, Michele. "Race, Class and the Social Construction of Self-Respect." *The Philosophical Forum*, 24.1–3 (1992–1993): 251–266.
Mott, Wesley T. "The Rhetoric of Martin Luther King, Jr.: Letter from Birmingham Jail." *Phylon*, 36.4 (1975): 411–421.
"Negro Minister Questions Plan for All-White Buses." *Montgomery Advertiser*, January 16, 1957.
Nicol, D. J., and J. A. Yee. "Reclaiming Our Time: Women of Color Faculty and Radical Self-Care in the Academy." *Feminist Teacher*, 27.2–3 (2017): 133–156.
Niebuhr, Reinhold. *Moral Man and Immoral Society: A Study in Ethics and Politics* (Louisville, KY: Westminster John Knox Press, 2013).
Nussbaum, Martha. *Anger and Forgiveness: Resentment, Generosity, Justice* (New York: Oxford University Press, 2016).
Nussbaum, Martha. "From Anger to Love: Self-Purification and Political Resistance." In Brandon M. Terry and Tommie Shelby (eds.), *To Shape a New World* (Cambridge, MA: Harvard University Press, 2018), 105–126.
Parini, Jay, "There's More to Tolstoy than War and Peace." *The Guardian*, January 6, 2010. Available at: https://www.theguardian.com/books/booksblog/2010/jan/06/more-to-tolstoy-war-peace.
Pineda, Erin. *Seeing Like an Activist* (Oxford: Oxford University Press, 2021).
"Poorly Timed Protest." *Time Magazine*, April 19, 1963.
Rawls, John. *Political Liberalism, Expanded Edition* (New York: Columbia University Press, 2005).

Rawls, John. *A Theory of Justice* (Cambridge, MA: Harvard University Press, 1999).
Rieder, Jonathan. *Gospel of Freedom* (New York: Bloomsbury, 2013).
Rieder, Jonathan. *The Word of the Lord Is Upon Me: The Righteous Performance of Martin Luther King, Jr.* (Cambridge, MA: Belknap, 2008).
Robins, Corey. *Fear: The History of a Political Idea* (Oxford: Oxford University Press, 2004).
Robinson, Cedric J. *Black Movements in America* (New York: Routledge, 1997).
Rogers, Melvin Lee. "The People, Rhetoric, and Affect: On the Political Force of Du Bois's The Souls of Black Folk." *American Political Science Review*, 106.1 (2012): 188–203.
Rose, Justin. *The Drum Major Instinct: Martin Luther King Jr's Theory of Political Service* (Atlanta: University of Georgia Press, 2019).
Scarantino, Andrea, and Ronald de Sousa. "Emotion." In *The Stanford Encyclopedia of Philosophy* (Summer 2021 Edition), Edward N. Zalta (ed.). Available at: https://plato.stanford.edu/archives/sum2021/entries/emotion/.
Scott King, Coretta. *My Life with Martin Luther King, Jr.* (New York: Henry Holt & Co, 2017).
Shelby, Tommie, and Brandon Terry (eds.). *To Shape a New World: Essays on the Political Philosophy of Martin Luther King Jr.* (Cambridge, MA: Harvard University Press, 2018).
Shelton, Robert. "Songs a Weapon in Rights Battle." *New York Times*, August 20, 1962, p. 1.
Shridharani, Krishnalal. *My India My America* (New York: Duell, Sloan, and Pearce, 1941).
Shridharani, Krishnalal. *War Without Violence* (New York: Harcourt and Brace, 1939).
"Sit Ins." In Clayborne Carson (ed.), *The Martin Luther King, Jr., Encyclopedia* (Westport, CT: Greenwood, 2008). Available at: https://kinginstitute.stanford.edu/encyclopedia/sit-ins.
Sitton, Claude. "Negro Criticizes N.A.A.C.P. Tactics." *New York Times*, April 17, 1960. Available at: https://timesmachine.nytimes.com/timesmachine/1960/04/17/99732190.html?pageNumber=32.
Snow, Malinda. "Martin Luther King's 'Letter from Birmingham Jail' as Pauline Epistle." *Quarterly Journal of Speech*, 71 (1985): 318–334.
Spillers, Hortense. "Martin Luther King Jr and the Style of the Black Sermon." *The Black Scholar*, 3.1 (1971): 14–27.
Sreenivasan, Amia. "The Aptness of Anger." *Journal of Political Philosophy*, 26.2 (2018): 123–144.
Sreenivasan, Amia. "In Defense of Anger." BBC Radio 4, *Four Thought*, August 27, 2014.
Stanley, Jason. *How Propaganda Works* (Princeton, NJ: Princeton University Press, 2015).

Terry, Brandon M. "Requiem for a Dream: The Problem-Space of Black Power." In Tommie Shelby and Brandon M. Terry (eds.), *To Shape a New World* (Cambridge, MA: Harvard University Press, 2018), 290–324.

Threadcraft, Shatema, and Brandon M. Terry. "Gender Trouble: Manhood, Inclusion, and Justice." In Tommie Shelby and Brandon M. Terry (eds.), *To Shape a New World* (Cambridge, MA: Harvard University Press, 2018), 137–204.

Thurman, Howard. *Jesus and the Disinherited* (Boston, MA: Beacon Press, 1996).

Tolstoy, Leo. *What Is Art?* (New York: Thomas Crowell & Co. Publishers, 1899).

Tuttle, Sheryl Ross. "Understanding Propaganda: The Epistemic Merit Model and Its Application to Art." *Journal of Aesthetic Education*, 36.1 (2002): 16–30.

"White Clergymen Urge Local Negroes to Withdraw from Demonstrations." *The Birmingham News*, April 13, 1963, p. 2.

Wallace, Maurice O. *King's Vibrato: Modernism, Blackness, and the Sonic Life of Martin Luther King, Jr.* (Durham, NC: Duke University Press, 2022).

Walker, Wyatt T. "Introduction." In Birmingham, Alabama, 1963, Mass Meeting, Album no. FD5487, Folkway Records, Broadway, New York. Available at: https://www.crmvet.org/crmpics/albums/63_bham_liner.pdf.

Wells-Barnett, Ida B. *Red Record: Tabulated Statistics and Alleged Causes of Lynching in the United States, 1892–1893–1894* (Chicago: Donohue & Henneberry, 1895).

Wells-Barnett, Ida B. *Southern Horrors: Lynch Law in All Its Phases* (1892). In Ida B. Wells-Barnett, *The Light of Truth: Writings of an Anti-Lynching Crusader* (New York: Penguin, 2014), 57–82.

Woodward, C. Vann. *The Strange Career of Jim Crow* (Oxford: Oxford University Press, 1955).

Wright, Richard. *Black Boy: A Record of Childhood and Youth* (New York: Harper & Row, 1966).

X, Malcolm. "Malcolm X at the Audubon." In George Breitman (ed.), *Malcolm X Speaks: Selected Speeches and Statements* (New York: Grove Press, 1965). Available at: https://teachingamericanhistory.org/document/at-the-audubon/.

X, Malcolm. "Malcolm X at Open Mind Roundtable," October 15, 1961. Available at: https://www.icit-digital.org/articles/malcolm-x-at-open-mind-roundtable-october-15-1961.

X, Malcolm. "From Malcolm X." In Carson et al. (eds.), *The Papers of Martin Luther King, Jr.*, Volume V, 491. Available at: https://kinginstitute.stanford.edu/king-papers/documents/malcolm-x-0.

Index

For the benefit of digital users, indexed terms that span two pages (e.g., 52–53) may, on occasion, appear on only one of those pages.

Abernathy, Ralph, 4, 5, 6–7, 8–10, 21–22, 63, 86–87, 178, 180–82
Adler, Alfred, 43
Alabama Christian Movement for Human Rights (ACMHR), 1–2, 3–4, 181–82
Allen, Danielle, 222
altruism, 167–70
American Friends Service Committee, 12–13
Angelou, Maya, 203–4
anger
    as an appropriate response, 143–45
    love and, 145–47
    motivational effects of, 142–43
    narcissistic anger, 144–45
    as a political action barrier, 212
    retribution and, 147–49
    righteous indignation and, 141–43, 144–45, 147
    skills to channel, 148–49
    violence and, 145, 147
Anger and Forgiveness (Nussbaum), 143
Anzaldua, Gloria, 200
Apostle Paul, 13–14
Aristotle, 147
Augustine, Saint, 13–14
Autobiography (King), 177

Baldwin, James, 201
Balfour, Lawrie, 81–82
Ballou, Maude, 234–35
Belafonte, Harry, 142–43
Bevel, Dianne Nash, 178–79
Bevel, James, 86–87, 178–79, 182–83
Billups, Charles, 1–2
Birmingham
    Black elites in, 19–21
    campaign in, 177–85
    collective social movement in, 224
    lack of support from Black community in, 6–7
    segregation of, 1–4
    violence within, 1–2
    white moderates in, 46–56, 47n.4
Birmingham News, 10–11
Black Muslim movement, 186
Black Nationalist movement, 232–34
Black Power movement, 191, 232–33
Boggs, Grace Lee, 67–68
Boston University Divinity School, 83–84, 88, 188
Boutwell, Albert, 4–6, 15, 180–81
Brightman, Edgard S., 188
Bromell, Nick, 131–32, 132n.43
Brown v. Board of Education, 1–2, 30, 44, 123–24, 186
Buber, Martin, 34, 87, 152
Buddhism, 71–72n.14
Burrows, Rufus, 136

"A Call for Unity," 10n.37, 10–12, 13–14, 46–47, 138–39, 142, 158–59
Carmichael, Stokely, 189–90, 232–33

Chalmers, Allen Knight, 188
Cherry, Myisha, 141, 201, 202
Children's Crusade, 183–84, 195
civil disobedience, 13, 22–23, 215
Civil Rights Act, 12–13, 62, 184–85, 225
Civil Rights Movement
   Connor and, 2–3
   history of, 29–30
   influence of other anti-colonial movements on, 123–24
   nonviolence resistance as the basis for, 188
   political motivation and, 232–33
   role of Birmingham in, 177
   role of the Black church in the, 188–89
   "We Shall Overcome" and, 115
Civil War, 34–35, 162, 228–29
Clark, Kenneth B, 235–36
Cold War, 96
Collacut, James, 190–91
Collins, Patricia Hill, 200
Congress on Racial Equality (CORE), 79
Connor, Bull
   banning of demonstrations by, 7–8, 9, 10, 180–82
   mayoral election of, 4–6
   morality of, 50n.15
   as a segregationist, 2–4
   violence used by, 14–15, 49–50, 60, 149, 183–84
Cotton, Andrew, 178–79
Cotton, Dorothy, 86–87, 178–79, 182–83
Covey, Edward, 130–32
Covey, William, 189–90
Crane, H.H., 83–84, 87
Crozier Theological Seminary, 83–84, 88, 188

Darby, Derrick, 126–27, 130, 149
Darkwater (Tolstoy), 81–82

Davis, Angela, 203–4
Declaration of Independence, 77, 126, 168–69
desegregation, 30–32, 31n.15, 32n.17, 39, 40–41, 43–45, 77
DeWolf, L. Harold, 188
dignity
   action and, 127, 129–32, 133, 149
   discipline and, 199
   equality and, 126
   fear and, 99–100, 125, 131–32
   freedom and, 126–28
   historical processes and, 122–24
   King's definition of, 125n.15, 125
   King's personal experiences with, 133–38
   love and, 151–52
   nonviolence and, 132–33, 198–200, 215n.40
   righteous indignation and, 133–34, 138
   segregation and, 32–34, 37
   self-assertion and, 128–29, 132–33
   self-defense and, 201–2
Douglas, Andrew, 207
Douglass, Frederick, 22, 56n.35, 130–32, 189–90, 201–2, 228n.3, 229–30, 239–40
Du Bois, W.E.B, 36, 80–82, 130–31, 142–43, 185–86, 230–32, 239–40

Eastland, James O., 154–55
Ebenezer Baptist Church, 84–85
economic injustice (against Black Americans), 2, 36, 94–95
Emancipation Proclamation, 29–30
emasculation (of Black men), 192, 193n.52
emotion, 75–76, 227. *See also* nonviolent resistance; political action; propaganda; tactics (utilized by King)

emotionalism. *See* political action; tactics (utilized by King)
Estes, Steve, 192

faith. *See also* fear; religion
  in God, 112–14, 118–19
  hope/optimism and, 115–16
  in humanity, 114–15, 117
  nonviolence and, 197–98
  overcoming fear with, 110–11
  political action and, 111–12, 114–16
  unfulfilled, 118–19
Farmer, James, 79
Faulkner, William, 46n.1, 46–47
fear. *See also* faith
  anger and, 102–3
  Black fear, 98–99, 101–2, 103
  death and, 131–32
  dignity and, 99–100, 125
  existential, 95–96
  fearlessness, 108–11, 132, 198–99
  harnessing of, 104–5, 107–8, 121–22
  humiliation and, 97–98
  King's views on, 93n.4, 93, 100n.27, 103–4
  motivation and, 103–4
  normal/abnormal, 100–2
  personal anxiety and, 100n.26, 101n.34
  personal fear/inferiority, 93–94, 110
  as a political action barrier, 212
  righteous indignation and, 104
  segregation and, 96–97
  selfishness and, 102
  social fears, 94–95
  violence and, 97, 191
  white backlash and, 97, 100
Fellowship of the Concerned of the Southern Regional Council, 115

"Fill up the Jails" (Gandhian principle), 183
Fosdick, Henry, 83–84, 87, 103–4, 118–19
Fourth of July Speech (Douglass), 229
freedom, 37–39
Freedom Budget, 62
Freedom Riders, 2–3
Freud, Sigmund, 43, 240–41

Gaines, Kevin, 19–20
Gandhi, Mahatma, 59n.46, 78–80, 114–15, 183, 188, 191n.46, 211–12
Garvey, Marcus, 186
Gaston, A.G., 7
Gooding-Williams, Robert, 81–82, 127, 130–32
Gregg, Richard, 211–13, 218–20
Griffin, Marvin, 154–55

Haley, Alex, 39–40
Hamer, Fannie Lou, 237–40
Heffner, Richard D., 121–22
Henry, Aaron, 239
Hind Swaraj (Gandhi), 79–80
hooks, bell, 173–74, 193n.52, 199–200, 201–2, 203–4
hope, 47n.3
Horney, Karen, 94–95
Howard University, 233

Indian Opinion, 79–80
indignation
  anger and, 141–43, 144–45, 147
  dignity and, 133–34, 138
  fear and, 104
  within the Letter, 87–88
  morality and, 184–85
  political action and, 141–43, 229–30
  segregation and, 137–43
  toward white moderates, 65–67

inferiority, 34–36, 53n.27, 53, 93–94, 110
integration, 30n.7, 30–32, 31n.15, 39–42, 40n.50, 42n.60, 43–44, 77
intellectualism. *See* political action; tactics (utilized by King)

Jackson, Mahalia, 84–85
James, Roy, 197
Jesus Disinherited (Howard), 97
Jim Crow laws, 17–18, 34–35, 51, 57, 97–99, 108–10, 136, 172–73. *See also* laws
Johnson, Lyndon, 184–85
Johnson, Mordecai, 188
Jung, Carl, 43, 240–41

Kant, Immanuel, 126–27, 152
Kelsey, George, 83–84, 87
Kennedy, John F, 184–85
King, Coretta Scott, 85–86
King, Tom, 4–6

laws, 13–14, 44–45. *See also* Jim Crow laws
"The Letter from Birmingham Jail" (King)
 audience of, 16–19, 23–24, 46–47, 68
 emotions of nonviolence and, 225
 faith within, 117–18
 fear and, 93
 as a form of propaganda, 77–78
 as a fundraiser, 12–13
 musicality and, 87–89
 response to "A Call for Unity," 13–14
 segregation and, 39–40
 significance of, 22–23, 24–25
 white moderates and, 65–68
 writing of, 11–12, 18n.64

Lincoln, Abraham, 29, 56–57, 162
Lischer, Richard, 88
Livingston, Alexander, 52, 198, 199–200
Locke, Alain, 122–23
Loggins, Jared A, 207
Lomax, Louis, 201–2
Lorde, Audre, 141, 200
Lordean rage, 141
love
 agape, 155–58, 161–62, 165, 168–71, 194–95, 201, 202–4
 anger and, 145–47
 collective, 203–4
 compassion as, 168–69
 of enemies, 159–62, 163–65
 of God, 158–59
 Gregg's view of, 212–13
 humanitarian love, 155
 King's definition of, 150–51, 196–97
 motherly love, 153
 music and, 214n.35
 nonviolence resistance and, 193–95, 215n.40
 philio, 153–55
 as the reigning ideal for change, 171–72
 romantic love, 153
 self-care as, 199–201
 self-love, 151–52, 173–74, 198, 199–204
 self-sacrifice and, 165–67, 172–74, 199–204
 utilitarian love, 152
Lucretius, 102–3
Lucy, Autherine, 118
lynching, 228–29

Malcolm X, 59n.46, 143, 189–90, 199–200, 201–2, 233–38
Mantena, Karuna, 199

INDEX 265

March Against Fear (1966), 117–18
media, 6, 46–47
Meredith, James, 87, 117–18
Miller, Keith D., 83–84
Modern Man in Search of a Soul (Jung), 240–41
modus vivendi, 221
Montgomery
   Black student movement in, 115
   campaign in, 128–29, 171–72
   Montgomery bus boycott, 17–18, 64–65, 104, 220–21
   nonviolent resistance in, 188, 215
   resistance in, 130–31, 132–33
   training sessions in, 178–79
   use of prayer in, 210
Montgomery Improvement Association (MIA), 210
Moody-Adams, Michele, 93–94, 130
Moore, Jamie, 181–82
morality
   collective action and, 59–60
   Douglass and, 229–30
   indignant disappointment and, 65–67
   Kings views on, 13–14, 67–68, 84, 112–14
   as motivation to end segregation, 57–58n.36, 57–58, 77
   racism and, 50n.15, 50–51
Morehouse University, 83–84, 188
Mott, Wesley T., 87
Muelder, Dean Walter, 188
Muhammad, Elijah, 233–34
music
   Black Freedom songs, 85–86
   within King's works, 87–89
   love and, 214n.35
   mass meetings and, 85–87, 178
   religious music, 84–85
Muste, A.J., 188
My Song (Belafonte), 142–43

Narrative of the Life of Frederick Douglass an American Slave (Douglass), 230
National Association for the Advancement of Colored People (NAACP), 1–2, 186
negative peace, 122
"New Negro," 121–23, 128
New York Times, 86–87
Niebuhr, Reinhold, 87, 188
nonviolent resistance. *See also* political action; tactics (utilized by King)
   appeal to Black masses for, 188–89
   collective social movements and, 222–24
   commitment cards for, 179–80
   dignity and, 132–33, 198–200, 215n.40
   effects on oppressor, 216–21
   emotions of, 224–26, 227
   faith and, 197–98
   fearlessness and, 198–99
   King's definition of, 193–96
   love and, 174, 194–95, 196–97, 199–204, 215n.40
   masculinity and, 189–93, 193n.52
   in Montgomery, 188, 215
   psychological impact of, 214–16
   shame and, 217–21
   sit-in campaigns, 109
   theory behind, 60–61, 185–88
   training workshops for, 178–79
   transformation and, 205, 211–12, 213–15, 224–25
Nussbaum, Martha, 102–3, 143–47

Ovid, 163–64

Parks, Rosa, 129–30, 188–89
"Pilgrimage to Nonviolence," 188
Pineda, Erin, 52n.19, 52

Plato, 153
Playboy magazine, 39–40, 54–55
Plessy v. Ferguson, 29–30
political action. *See also* nonviolent resistance; tactics (utilized by King)
　barriers to, 69–71
　Carmichael and, 232–33
　church and, 227, 240–41
　collective action, 232–33, 237
　conformity and, 105–8
　Douglass and, 229–30
　Du Bois and, 230–32
　emotion and, 227, 229–32, 235, 237–39, 240–42
　Hamer and, 237–39
　King's views on, 227–29, 239–42
　knowledge/facts and, 228–29, 231, 233, 236–37
　Malcolm X and, 233–38
　propaganda and, 231–32
　respectability politics, 69n.1
　righteous indignation and, 229–30
　Wells and, 228–29, 231
Poor People's Campaign, 63, 64–65
Preston-Roedder, Ryan, 114, 115–16
"Project C," 4, 5–7, 12–13
propaganda. *See also* tactics (utilized by King)
　appeal to emotions as, 75, 76–77
　Du Bois and, 80–82, 231–32
　Gandhi and, 78–80
　political action and, 231–32
　sermonizing as, 73–75, 74n.23, 83–84
　Tolstoy and, 82–83
"Propagandizing Christianity" (King), 74–75

race relations (in the United States), 29–30
racial uplift ideology, 19–21, 36–37
racism, 122. *See also* segregation
Radhakrishnan, S., 71–72n.14
Rawls, John, 13, 126–27, 221
Ray, James Earl, 64–65
Reconstruction era, 35
Reider, Jonathan, 23–24, 48, 65–66, 87–88
religion. *See also* faith
　black masses and, 21
　King's concept of "sensible sermon," 73–74, 77–78
　political action and, 227–29, 240–41
　self-worth and, 124n.10
　social gospel/King's ministry, 20–21
　transformation and, 208–11
resistance (to supporting Black right causes), 6–8, 10–11, 14–15
Robins, Corey, 98–99
Robinson, Cedrick, 21
Rogers, Melvin, 231–32
Rose, Justin, 13–14, 59–60, 96, 157–58, 170–71
Rustin, Bayard, 79, 188
Ryan, William Fitts, 12–13

Screenivasan, Amia, 143
segregation
　of buses, 2–3
　economic system and, 36
　fear and, 96–97
　history of, 34–35
　indignation and, 137–43
　King's personal experiences with, 134–37, 137n.59
　moral arguments against, 32–34, 36–39, 50–51
　psychological impact of, 38–39, 122
　of schools, 1–2
　suffering and, 140
segregationists, 53–55

self-acceptance, 109–10, 151–52. See also love
self-care, 199–201
self-centeredness, 43–44n.69, 43–44
self-interest, 221–22
Shabazz, Betty, 234–35
shame, 217–21
Shaw University, 17
Shelton, Robert, 86–87
Shridharani, Krishnalal, 79
Shuttlesworth, Frederick Lee, 3–4, 86–87, 178
slavery, 29–30, 34, 35–36, 43, 52–53, 77
Souls of Black Folk, 81–82
Southern Christian Leadership Conference (SCLC), 3–4, 12–13, 181–82, 224
Spillers, Hortense, 21, 84–85
Stanton, Edwin M., 162
The Strange Career of Jim Crow (Woodward), 34–35
Stride Toward Freedom, 147–48
Student Nonviolent Coordinating Committee (SNCC), 109, 237–38
Swaraj (self-government), 79–80

tactics (utilized by King). *See also* nonviolent resistance; political action; propaganda
appeals to Black masses, 21–22
civil disobedience, 13
constructive coercion, 58n.42, 58, 63
direct action, 48n.9, 48
economic boycotts, 17–18, 64–65, 104, 181–82, 188–89, 220–21
economic equality, 62
emotionalism, 71–74, 72n.16
intellectualism, 71–74
jailing, 9–11, 180–82
mass meetings, 8–9, 178, 182, 210

music, 84–89, 178
political campaigns, 60
sit-ins, 177–78
sympathy, 63–64
violence against children, 61, 182–85
Terry, Brandon, 190–91, 193n.52, 206–7
Thoreau, Henry David, 188
Threadcraft, Shatema, 190–91, 193n.52, 206–7
Thurman, Howard, 83–84, 97–98, 99–100
Thurmond, Strom, 2–3
Till, Emmett, 44–45, 118
Tillich, Paul, 87
Tolstoy, Leo, 82–83
transformation
  in Black Americans, 214–17
  community and, 208
  of fear and anger, 213–14
  individual transformation, 59–60, 207–8
  King's definition of, 205–6
  of the oppressor, 216–21
  prayer and, 208–11
  reconstructing society through, 207
  shame as a way to, 217–21, 222
  sublimation, 206–7
  as way for racial progress, 205, 224–25
Truett, George, 207–8

Uplifting the Race (Gaines), 19–20

violence (against Black Americans), 1–2, 44–45, 61, 62, 97
Voting Rights Act, 62

Walker, Wyatt Tee, 4, 5, 11–13, 60–61, 84–85, 86, 138–39, 178, 182–83

Wallace, Maurice O., 88–89
Ware, J.L., 6–7
War without Violence (Shridharani), 79
Washington, Booker T., 122–23, 130–31, 185–86
Wells, Ida B., 228n.3, 228–29, 231, 239–40
"We Shall Overcome," 9n.34, 9, 115
Where Do We Go From Here? (King), 51
White Citizens Council (WCC), 44
white ignorance, 52n.19, 52–53

white supremacy, 15, 55–57, 58–59, 60, 191, 201
Why We Can't Wait (King), 12–13, 188–89, 191n.46, 196, 239–40
Williams, Alberta, 85–86
Williams, Hosea, 192
Wofford, Harris, 83–84, 87
"Woke Up This Morning with My Mind Stayed on Freedom," 85
Woodward, C. Vann, 34–35

Young, Andrew, 16, 83, 86–87, 182–83